This is the first book to provide a critical history of one of American theatre's most famous plays, *Death of a Salesman*. Brenda Murphy offers a detailed account of the most significant *Salesman* productions throughout the world, on the stage as well as on film, radio, and television. The *Death of a Salesman* first realized on stage was the culmination of the creative collaboration of playwright Arthur Miller, director Elia Kazan, and actor Lee J. Cobb, and was the starting point for hundreds of productions in many languages and styles. The play has also provided a number of memorable interpretations by actors such as Dustin Hoffman, George C. Scott, Fredric March, and Mel Gibson.

Drawing on valuable archival resources, including notebooks, drafts of the script, and director's notes, Murphy explores in detail the genesis of the first production and the role of subsequent performances in the development of American theatre. Important foreign language productions are also examined, especially as they reflect their social and cultural environment.

The volume includes a chronology, bibliography, discography, videography, and photographs from key productions.

D1313149

PLAYS IN PRODUCTION

Series Editor: Michael Robinson

MILLER

DEATH OF A SALESMAN

BRENDA MURPHY

University of Connecticut

CAMBRIDGE
UNIVERSITY PRESS

PUBLISHED BY THE PRESS SYNDICATE OF THE UNIVERSITY OF CAMBRIDGE
The Pitt Building, Trumpington Street, Cambridge, United Kingdom
CAMBRIDGE UNIVERSITY PRESS
The Edinburgh Building, Cambridge CB2 2RU, UK   http://www.cup.cam.ac.uk
40 West 20th Street, New York, NY 10011–4211, USA   http://www.cup.org
10 Stamford Road, Oakleigh, Melbourne 3166, Australia
Ruiz de Alarcón 13, 28014 Madrid, Spain

© Cambridge University Press 1995

First published 1995
Reprinted 2000

Printed in the United Kingdom at the University Press, Cambridge

A catalogue record for this book is available from the British Library

Library of Congress Cataloguing in Publication data
Murphy, Brenda.
Death of a salesman / Brenda Murphy.
    p. cm.
Includes bibliographical references (p.) and index.
ISBN 0 521 43451 3. – ISBN 0 521 47865 0 (pbk.)
1. Miller, Arthur, 1915– Death of a salesman.   2. Miller, Arthur,
1915– – Stage history.   3. Miller, Arthur, 1915– – Audio adaptations.
4. Miller, Arthur, 1915– – Film and video adaptations.   I. Title.
PS3525.I5156D4357   1995
812'.52–dc20
94-14923   CIP

ISBN 0 521 43451 3 hardback
ISBN 0 521 47865 0 paperback

For my father, Philip D. Murphy

CONTENTS

ILLUSTRATIONS

GENERAL PREFACE

Volumes in the series, Plays in Production, will take major dramatic texts and examine their transposition, firstly onto the stage and secondly, where appropriate, into other media. Each book will include concise but informed studies of individual dramatic texts, focusing on the original theatrical and historical context of a play in relation to its initial performance and reception followed by subsequent major interpretations on stage, both under the impact of changing social, political, and cultural values, and in response to developments in the theatre generally.

Many of the plays will also have been transposed into other media – film, opera, television, ballet – which may well be the form in which they are first encountered by a contemporary audience. Thus, a substantial study of the play text and the issues it raises for theatrical realization will be supplemented by an assessment of such adaptations as well as the production history, where the emphasis will be on the development of a performance tradition for each work, including staging and acting styles, rather than archaeological reconstruction of past performances.

Plays included in the series are all likely to receive regular performance and individual volumes will be of interest to the informed reader as well as to students of theatre history and literature. Each book also contains an annotated production chronology as well as numerous photographs from key performances.

Michael Robinson
University of East Anglia

PREFACE

This volume is a critical history of *Death of a Salesman* in production. It gives as detailed an account as is feasible of *Salesman* productions throughout the world, on the stage and in the media of film, radio, and television, which have contributed significantly to the play's life as an immediate theatrical experience for an audience, and which, in several cases, are themselves significant events in twentieth-century theatre history.

The account of the original New York production – its writing, direction, and design – takes up about a third of the volume, an emphasis commensurate with its importance to the creation of the play. The *Death of a Salesman* that was realized on stage as the culmination of the creative collaboration among writer Arthur Miller, director Elia Kazan, designer Jo Mielziner, producer Kermit Bloomgarden, the actors, and the other artists and craftsmen who worked on the production is the *Death of a Salesman* that was recorded in the published texts, since read by millions of readers and used as starting points for hundreds of productions. It is the primary production text. To arrive at as accurate an account as possible of its creation, primary sources have been used wherever they are available. These include the notebooks and various drafts of the script written by Arthur Miller both before and during the rehearsal process; the director's notes written by Elia Kazan, and notes on movement, props, gestures, etc. recorded by the stage manager at various stages of the production; sketches, drawings, and paintings of the set and props by designer Jo Mielziner, as well as prop, costume, and lighting charts. Secondary sources such as letters, interviews, and memoirs have been used to supply context and depth to the narrative, but always with the caveat that they are subjective sources whose reliability is limited by the subject's personal point of view and ever-less-reliable memory. Where versions conflict, the inconsistencies have been noted.

Subsequent chapters offer necessarily less detailed accounts of productions. The guiding principle in the narrative of later productions has been to focus on the elements of a production that make it particularly significant in *Salesman*'s stage history. Where possible, scripts, videotapes, recordings or films of the productions have been examined. Where these are not available, it has been necessary to rely on secondary evidence such as interviews, memoirs, reviews, and criticism to construct an account of the production. In every case, the aim has been to give as accurate an account as possible, and also to reflect the audience's view of the historical and cultural significance of the production and its aesthetic quality. The Production Chronology lists approximately fifty productions that have been significant in the stage life of *Death of a Salesman*. The Bibliography, Discography, and Videography are arranged to provide readers with quick access to information on particular productions as well as a general survey of criticism. The guiding principle in arranging the scholarly apparatus has been the hope that this volume will serve as a starting point for future research into the stage life of *Death of a Salesman*.

ACKNOWLEDGMENTS

This book has accumulated an enormous debt for its author. The first is to my parents, Phil and Priscilla Murphy, who have contributed more than they may know to my understanding of the Loman family and of the America that Arthur Miller depicts in *Death of a Salesman.*

Primary thanks are also due to Susan Abbotson for her invaluable research assistance, to Michael Robinson for his editorial advice and support, and to Arthur Miller, George Monteiro, and Richard Murphy for their constructive criticism at crucial times in the manuscript's development. I am indebted to Elaine Rusinko and George Monteiro for their expert translations.

The next acknowledgment must go to libraries and their staffs, without whom this book could not have been written: to Ken Craven, Cathy Henderson, Melissa Miller, Patrice Fox, and the rest of the staff of the Harry Ransom Humanities Research Center; to Dorothy L. Swerdlove and her staff at the Billy Rose Theatre Collection, New York Public Library for the Performing Arts; to Jeanne T. Newlin and her staff at the Harvard Theatre Collection, Harvard College Library; to Geraldine Duclow and her staff at the Theatre Collection, Philadelphia Free Library; to Andrew Kirk of the National Museum of the Performing Arts in London; and to the staffs of the Lilly Library at Indiana University, the Museum of Modern Art, the Museum of Television and Radio, and the University of Connecticut Libraries I owe my thanks for their expertise and help.

I am grateful for the financial support and the time for research and writing provided to me by the National Endowment for the Humanities, the University of Connecticut Research Foundation, and the Provost's Research Fellowship, University of Connecticut.

Arthur Miller has kindly allowed me to quote from his unpublished manuscripts.

Thanks are due to the following people for their help in securing permission to reproduce drawings and photographs: Bud H. Gibbs for the Estate of Jo Mielziner, Lynda Barnett for the Canadian Broadcasting Company, Richard M. Buck and Betty Travensky for the New York Public Library for the Performing Arts, Melissa Miller for the Harry Ransom Humanities Research Center, Jeanne T. Newlin for the Harvard Theatre Collection, Amy Forton for the Guthrie Theater, and James Magruder for Center Stage of Baltimore.

ABBREVIATIONS

The following abbreviations are employed in the Notes and Bibliography:

HRHRC: Harry Ransom Humanities Research Center, University of Texas at Austin

HTC: Harvard Theatre Collection, Harvard College Library

NYPL: Billy Rose Theatre Collection, New York Public Library for the Performing Arts

NYTC: *New York Theatre Critics' Reviews*

PFL: Theatre Collection, Philadelphia Free Library

CHAPTER 1

THE BROADWAY PRODUCTION

As Arthur Miller tells it, the writing of *Death of a Salesman* began in the winter of 1946/47 with a chance meeting between Miller and his uncle Manny Newman outside the Colonial Theatre in Boston, where Miller's *All My Sons* was having its pre-Broadway preview:

> I could see his grim hotel room behind him, the long trip up from New York in his little car, the hopeless hope of the day's business. Without so much as acknowledging my greeting, he said, "Buddy is doing very well."[1]

Newman, Miller has written, "was a competitor, at all times, in all things, and at every moment" (*T* 122). He saw Miller and his older brother Kermit "running neck and neck" with his sons Buddy and Abby "in some race that never stopped in his mind" (*T* 122). Although Miller had not spent more than a few hours in Newman's company, he had been fascinated by his traveling salesman uncle since his childhood. "He was so absurd," Miller remembers, "so completely isolated from the ordinary laws of gravity, so elaborate in his fantastic inventions, and despite his ugliness so lyrically in love with fame and fortune and their inevitable descent on his family, that he possessed my imagination until I knew more or less precisely how he would react to any sign or word or idea" (*T* 123).

Deeply involved in the production of *All My Sons*, Miller gave no more than a passing thought to the meeting with his uncle at the time, but the moment and its suggestiveness remained in his imagination. The sudden appearance of Manny Newman had "cut through time like a knife through a layer cake" (*T* 131), turning the promising young playwright into an uncertain nephew who felt that his success was something to apologize for. Miller has identified the incident as the spark that brought him back to an idea for a play about a salesman that he had had ten years earlier. Now he had a new focus of interest in the simultaneity of past and present that had occurred in that meeting. Miller had known that he and his cousins were as alive to Manny Newman at that moment as adolescent competitors as they were as men in their thirties. He thought that it would be wonderful "to do a play without any transitions at all, dialogue that would simply leap from bone to bone of a skeleton that would not for an instant cease being added to, an organism as strictly economic as a leaf, as trim as an ant" (*T* 131).

Manny Newman and his sons were not the sole origin of the Lomans, of course. Miller has acknowledged at various times that his own relationship with his father informs the play, and that one salesman in particular besides Manny had contributed to his conception of Willy.[2] But it was Manny who lodged himself in Miller's imagination and created a dramatic problem that he felt compelled to solve. The plot of the play might have come from Miller's questions about Manny's death, not long after the *All My Sons* meeting. Miller wrote that he had known three suicides up to that point, two of them salesmen, and that "Manny had died with none of the ordinary reasons given" (*T* 129). He sought a meeting with his cousin Abby, the younger of Manny's sons, in order to ask him what had been the one thing Manny had wanted most. Miller's suspicion about Manny's death provided *Salesman*'s minimal plot; Abby's answer to his question supplied its motive: "He wanted a business for us. So we could all work together . . . A business for the boys" (*T* 130). Miller remembers, "I suddenly understood him with my very blood" (*T* 130):

> Manny was transformed into a man with purpose: he had been
> trying to make a gift that would crown all those striving years;
> all those lies he told, all his imaginings and crazy exaggerations,

even the almost military discipline he had laid on his boys,
were in this instant given form and point. To be sure, a business
expressed his own egotism, but love, too. That homely, ridiculous
little man had after all never ceased to struggle for a certain victory,
the only kind open to him in this society – selling to achieve his
lost self as a man with his name and his sons' names on a business
of his own.   *(T 130)*

The intense sexuality that drives the Lomans also came from the
Newmans' home, a house that seemed to the adolescent Miller
"dank with sexuality" (*T* 124). His aunt and uncle were "obviously
bound to each other sexually" (*T* 123), even in middle age. One of
Manny's attractions for the adolescent Miller, as no doubt for some
of his customers, was the possession of a vast collection of porno-
graphic postcards. His sons remained bachelors well into their
thirties, boasting of their sexual conquests, which they saw as confirming their lifelong superiority to their cousin. In fact, Miller has
described himself as a model for the young Bernard:

> As fanatic as I was about sports, my ability was not to be compared
> to [Manny's] sons', and since I was gangling and unhandsome into
> the bargain I lacked their promise, so that when I stopped by I
> always had to expect some kind of insinuation of my entire life's
> probable failure, even before I was sixteen.   *(T 124)*

Miller has also suggested that his relationship with his father was
similar to that of Bernard and Charley:

> My father was a very ordinary kind of businessman really and his
> attitude was very tolerant. Whatever you wanted to do, you did. If
> not he was uninterested, basically. He just assumed you would come
> out all right . . . he never leaned on his son. He never insisted that he
> become something that he might not want to be.   *(CB 12)*

As the pieces of the play took shape in his imagination, Miller made
notes in his Brooklyn Heights home, bought with the

royalties from *All My Sons*. But the time came when he felt the need
to write the play out "in a single sitting, in a night or a day" (*T* 182),
and in a space of his own making. In April of 1948, he drove up to
the Connecticut farm he had bought the previous summer, and
built himself a ten- by twelve-foot studio to work in. As he sat down
to write, he remembers, "all I had was the first two lines and a death"
(*T* 183), although the play's plot, originally in three acts, had been
worked out fairly carefully in his notes.[3] What he needed was a form
that would allow for the simultaneity of past and present and for the
tragic trajectory of events to proceed from the fragmented logic of
Willy's subjective experience. When he finally sat down to write, he
worked all day and most of the night, skipping the parts that he
knew would be easy to write. In one sitting he drafted the whole first
act of the now two-act play. In six weeks he had a draft of the play.

Miller has spoken often of the initial image of the play that was
called at one early point in its development *The Inside of His Head*.
The image "was of an enormous face the height of the proscenium
arch which would appear and then open up, and we would see the
inside of a man's head . . . it was conceived half in laughter, for the
inside of his head was a mass of contradictions."[4] The image is a
clear visual representation of expressionism, the dramatization of
subjective reality, in direct opposition to the realism in which Miller
had composed *All My Sons*. Miller did not want, however, to represent Willy's experience as a subjective nightmare, detached from the
reality around him, which is the usual method of expressionism.
Miller said in an interview that, while he had been moved by expressionist plays, he found the traditional expressionist aesthetic perverse: "there are no people in it any more . . . it's the bitter end of the
world where man is a voice of his class function, and that's it."[5]

In *Salesman*, Miller was after a more complex representation. He
wanted the audience to see reality as Willy saw it, but also to recognize it as objectively real. Onstage there would be three epistemological levels: Willy's fantasies of the past, Willy's perception of the
present, and the audience's perception of present stage-reality.

Miller needed a dramatic form that would combine the subjectivity of expressionism with the illusion of objectivity afforded by realism.

One important step in the development of his form was going with director Elia Kazan to see Tennessee Williams's *A Streetcar Named Desire* during its New Haven preview in November of 1947. Miller has written that *Streetcar* "opened one specific door for me . . . the words and their liberation, the joy of the writer in writing them, the radiant eloquence of its composition" (*T* 182). This new freedom in the use of language was clearly important to the poetry of the mundane that infuses *Salesman*, but Kazan has suggested an even more important contribution. After seeing the performance, he wrote, Miller "appeared to be full of wonder at the theatre's expressive possibilities. He told me he was amazed at how simply and successfully the non-realistic elements in the play – '*Flores! Flores para los muertos!*' – blended with the realistic ones."[6] *Streetcar*'s style of subjective realism, which Kazan and Williams had created with designer Jo Mielziner, went a long way toward solving Miller's dramatic and theatrical problems.

Subjective realism provides an anchor in reality – a series of events that are accepted by the audience as the objective reality of the play – but presents them through the mediating consciousness of a single character, a Blanche DuBois or a Willy Loman, whose mind is often in the process of breaking down. While the audience can share the nightmare experience of the protagonist, it never quite loses touch with the "real" events that the character is interpreting in what is perceived to be a distorted way. As Miller puts it, Willy "is literally at that terrible moment when the voice of the past is no longer distant but quite as loud as the voice of the present . . . the form, therefore, *is* this process, instead of being a once-removed summation or indication of it" (*TE* 138). From this dual perspective, the audience can both empathize with the character's ordeal and judge it objectively. This mode of drama combines the strengths of expressionism with those of realism. Miller has explained, "*Death of a Salesman* was conceived literally on two dimensions at the same time. On one level there are autonomous characters while on another there are characters who exist as symbols for Willy Loman" (CB 59).

In writing *Salesman*, Miller had to deal with the exciting but complex problems of his formal experiment simultaneously with the more workmanlike problems of the plot on which it was hung. His early notes indicate that he had a clear tragic trajectory in mind, leading to Willy's suicide, but he had trouble linking it up with Biff's story. At one point, he reminded himself that he would have to find a way to make Biff responsible for Willy's life through the events of the play, wondering whether the incident with the Woman would be retrievable dramatically. He also noted that he had to find a link between Biff's attitude toward work and his feelings against Willy (NB). At this early stage, Miller planned that the climax would arise from Biff's conflict between his desire for success in New York and his hatred of Willy. His climactic action would be his refusal to return the pen he has stolen from Bill Oliver, thus ending his chances for business success.

In the play's earlier versions, including the preproduction script that was distributed to the production team in September, 1948, Biff's two confrontations with Willy, in the restaurant and later, when Biff tells Willy that he is leaving for good, were considerably different from the same scenes in the published texts. In the earlier versions, Biff does not come into the restaurant with the intention of revealing his disastrous meeting with Oliver and forcing his father and brother to face the truth about the family myths. Instead, he tells both Hap and Willy a lie about having a lunch meeting with Oliver, covering it with the story of taking the pen. His revelation in the final, climactic scene is not about the rubber tubing with which Willy plans to kill himself and his own past convictions for stealing, but that he has lied about the appointment with Oliver. In the earlier versions, the reasons for the opposition between Biff and Willy were less clearly defined than they were to be after the production process, but the functions of Willy as motivating force and of Biff as both object of and obstacle to his desire were clear. The play's trajectory was to be an inevitable and relentless march toward Willy's death with only the simplest of plots to propel it.

Miller put his effort into the play's narrative, the telling of the tale, the juxtaposition of incidents from Willy's internal and external experience that would bring the audience to a sympathetic understanding of his inevitable fate. He has written that "the structure of events and the nature of its form are also the direct reflection of Willy Loman's way of thinking at this moment of his life . . . The way of telling the tale, in this sense, is as mad as Willy and as abrupt and as suddenly lyrical" (*TE* 138). In order to represent reality as Willy experienced it, Miller juxtaposed the scenes of the play's present with what he called from the beginning not "flashbacks," but "daydreams," reminding himself in his notebook that daydreams black out when they become threatening. Miller has explained several times that "there are no flashbacks in this play but only a mobile concurrency of past and present . . . because in his desperation to justify his life Willy Loman has destroyed the boundaries between now and then" (*TE* 138–39). In the early versions, the line between past and present was much clearer than it was to become. The daydreams were more sharply defined against the scenes in the present, but the line of the narrative was clear from the beginning. The events of the play are the events of twenty-four hours in Willy's life as Willy experiences them.

In creating his characters, Miller naturally went back to their images in life, building on the characteristics that had impressed him as central to their meaning for him. In life, "Manny Newman was cute and ugly, a Pan risen out of the earth, a bantam with a lisp, sunken brown eyes, a lumpy, pendulous nose, dark brown skin, and gnarled arms" (*T* 122). In the preproduction script, Willy Loman is described as "a very small man. His several auto accidents have marred his face, but not in a repulsive way. His nose is bent and a little flattened. A healed scar makes his right jaw different from his left. He wears little shoes and little suits. He is a little man, and not handsome either. His emotions, in a word, are mercurial."[7] The small size and the physical distortions that Miller saw in his uncle were central to his first conception of Willy, as were Manny's need for success and his need to pass that success on to his boys. Central to Willy's motivation was his guilt in regard to both Biff and Linda. Over and over in his notebook, Miller reminded himself that Willy's guilt must be clear, both as a cause of his current state and as a motivation for Biff's revenge. As for Linda, Miller noted that Willy resents Linda's patient and consistent forgiveness because he knows that there must be great hatred for him hidden in her heart.

The early versions of Linda physically resemble Miller's Aunt Annie Newman as much as the early Willy resembles Manny. Annie Newman was "big and broad-chested," and overweight, "with her gale of a laugh, her pink, pockmarked face often reddening with the hypertension that would kill her at sixty" (*T* 123). The Linda of the early scripts is "taller, and much larger than Willy" (R 1:1), and she has a heart condition. As in the published script, "most often jovial, she has developed an iron repression of her objections to him. Her struggle is to spiritually support him while trying to insinuate guidance and her superior and calmer intelligence."[8] Linda's physical size and power, in contrast to Willy's small stature, were important to Miller's original conception of the character, as was her repressed resentment. Miller has noted in an interview that the women characters in his plays are very complex:

> They've been played somewhat sentimentally, but that isn't the way they were intended. There is a more sinister side to the women characters in my plays. These women are of necessity auxiliaries to the action, which is carried by the male characters. But they both receive the benefits of the male's mistakes and protect his mistakes in crazy ways. They are forced to do that. So the females are victims as well.[9]

While the characters of Willy and Linda seem to have been clear in his mind from the start, Miller had as much trouble in conceptualizing Biff's character as he did in conceiving the motivation for his necessary function in the plot. As mentioned earlier, Miller at first saw Biff's central conflict as being between hatred for Willy and his own desire for success, but Miller had trouble developing a motivation for Biff's hatred. He also wrote in his notebook that Biff was not really bright enough to make a businessman and that he wanted everything too fast.

As Miller first wrote the climactic confrontation between father and son, Biff's conflict in the scene was based on his feeling that "to tell the truth [about not having an appointment] would be to diminish himself in his own eye. To admit his fault" (NB). Miller specifically noted that Biff's actions in this scene were not directed toward Willy's elucidation or salvation, but "toward a surgical break which [Biff] knows in his heart Willy could never accept" (NB). His motive, then, was to "destroy Willy, free himself" (NB). Biff's guilt came about because, although his vengeance on Willy was justified in some sense by Willy's having built up his ego and then betrayed him, Biff knew at some level that he was incompetent, and could never have had the success that he desired. Over the course of the production, both Biff's character and the play's plot were to undergo some significant changes, but traces of Miller's original lack of clarity about Biff remain in the published script.

The character who was to undergo the most substantial change during the production process was Uncle Ben. Appearing solely in Willy's daydreams, Ben is the most expressionistic character in the play. Miller has said that he "purposefully would not give Ben any character, because for Willy he *has* no character – which is, psychologically, expressionist because so many memories come back with a simple tag on them: somebody represents a threat to you, or a promise."[10]

In his notebook, Miller described Ben as "a heavy-set man. Pompous, the father." And it is as a representation of the father that he figured most prominently in the early versions of the play. Ben's function as a symbol of success was secondary to his function as a representative of the absent father, whom Willy kept asking Ben to go and find. In the early drafts, Miller emphasized the link between Willy's loss of his father and his failure in bringing up his sons, noting that the point of the scenes with Ben was to establish, first, that Willy has "an unusual, superior family" and, second, that "something great is in store for him too" (NB).

Miller's vision of the set for *Salesman* was far less detailed than his vision of the characters. He has mentioned that his first notion of the set, in keeping with his idea for the play as *The Inside of His Head*, was "the inside of Willy's skull in which he would be crawling around, playing these scenes inside of himself," a purely expression-istic notion.[11] As the play took shape, however, he dropped this notion in favor of a minimal set, which he has variously described as "without any setting at all,"[12] "three unadorned black platforms" (*T* 195), and "three bare platforms and only the minimum necessary furniture for a kitchen and two bedrooms, with the Boston hotel room as well as Howard's office to be played in open space" (*T* 188).

Elia Kazan has described *Salesman's* preproduction script as "a play waiting for a directorial solution" (*K* 361). As Kazan has noted, the script the production team received had a minimal description of the scene: "A pinpoint traveling spotlight hits a small area on stage left. The Salesman is revealed. He takes out his keys and opens an invisible door" (*K* 361). Jo Mielziner, who was to conceive and develop the design for the set that is described in the published scripts, commented in his memoir that, in the script he was first given: "At the end of his forty-odd scenes Miller says, 'The scenic solution to this production will have to be an imaginative and simple one. I don't know the answer, but the designer must work out something which makes the script flow easily.'"[13] Based on Mielziner's design concept, Kazan and Miller were to find a key to the play's realization on stage, but the playwright's vision while writing was of his characters enacting his play on a bare stage.

ASSEMBLING THE PRODUCTION TEAM

Many people have reported weeping when they first read *Death of a Salesman*. Perhaps the first was Elia Kazan, who had become a close friend of Miller's after directing *All My Sons*. Miller remembers that he "did not move far from the phone for two days after sending the script to Kazan" in July of 1948 (*T* 185). Kazan reports that after reading it, "I didn't wait for the next morning to see if I'd have a more 'balanced' judgment, didn't delay as I generally did in those years . . . but called Art as I turned the back cover and told him his play had 'killed' me" (*K* 356). To Miller, Kazan's tone sounded "alarmingly somber" (*T* 185):

> "I've read your play." He sounded at a loss as to how to give me
> the bad news. "My God, it's so sad."
>   "It's supposed to be."
>   "I just put it down. I don't know what to say. My father . . ." *(T 185)*

Kazan was the first of a great many people to tell the playwright that in Willy Loman he had written a portrait of his father. His response was immediate and definite; he wanted to direct the play that season.

Finding a producer with the same enthusiastic response did not prove easy. Kazan first suggested Cheryl Crawford, his old friend and colleague from the Group Theatre and co-founder of the Actors Studio, who was producing the musical *Love Life* that Kazan was then directing toward a New York premiere on 6 October. According to Crawford, Kazan handed her the *Salesman* manuscript at the end of a rehearsal and told her she must decide overnight whether she wanted to produce it. Her reaction was not enthusiastic:

> I didn't care much for the title, *Death of a Salesman*, but what really
> bothered me was the flashbacks – I couldn't see how they would

work out. And the main character struck me as pathetic rather than tragic. Who would want to see a play about an unhappy traveling salesman? Too depressing.[14]

As Kazan remembers it, "She hesitated; the time allowed for hesitation in the theatre is brief. Cheryl seemed especially dubious about the play's commercial potential. She'd given it to friends to read; they hadn't been sure either" (*K* 360). By mutual consent, the play was withdrawn.

Miller remembers that he and Kazan decided on the spur of the moment, while walking down Broadway, to stop at the office of Kermit Bloomgarden, another old Group Theatre friend of Kazan's who was now working as a producer. After some discussion, Miller decided to give the play to him and his associate Walter Fried despite the fact that "they were not sure of its box office strength" (*K* 360), and the New York *Sun* of 3 September carried an announcement that Kermit Bloomgarden was "elated over the acquisition of Arthur Miller's new play."[15]

Bloomgarden's chief box-office worry was the play's title. He told Kazan that everyone in the theatre business had cautioned him that the word "death" in a title was death to the box office (*K* 360). Robert Dowling, the owner of the Morosco Theatre where the play was to be produced, wanted to keep the title from appearing on the front of the theatre if the word "death" was to appear in it.[16] According to Kazan, Bloomgarden suggested that the title be changed to *Free and Clear*, a phrase from Linda's speech in the Requiem (*K* 360). Both Miller and Kazan were adamant about the title, and *Variety* reported finally on 29 December that the "'Death of a Salesman' title for the new Arthur Miller play is being retained at the author's insistence." Noting that the producers disliked the title, "figuring it has a sombre connotation that may tend to repel prospective playgoers, besides being a story tipoff," the article concluded that "Miller has been adamant and under Dramatists Guild rules has final say."[17]

The question of the title sparked a controversy that the critics were well aware of before the play had opened. The advance publicity no doubt counteracted any negative effect the title might have had on ticket sales. As for the cast, Alan Hewitt, who played Howard, has written that none of the actors in the company had any doubt about the power of the play, or its prospects for success. The title did not disturb them at all.[18]

At first the producers had trouble attracting investors to the play. Like Crawford, several very acute theatre people, such as director Joshua Logan and agent Leland Hayward, were reluctant to invest because they did not see how the play could work theatrically.[19] Despite the difficulties, Bloomgarden proved to be a very capable producer. Although he had raised $100,000 to capitalize the show, he managed to produce it for $50,000, an unusual circumstance in the New York theatre, to say the least (JM 61). The advance sales were just as unusual. On 7 February, three days before the New York opening, the advance sales stood at $250,000.[20] And this was when an orchestra seat ticket cost less than $4.00. Three months after the play had opened, it was reported to be sold out for twenty-three weeks in advance.[21] Serendipitous as the choice of Bloomgarden may have been, it proved a fortunate one for *Death of a Salesman*.

Since they had first come together for the production of *All My Sons*, Arthur Miller and Elia Kazan had recognized their close artistic and personal affinity. As Kazan has put it:

> We were immediately compatible in the sense that his background
> was very much like my own. His father was a salesman like mine, he
> came out of the lower middle-class like me, he was also from New
> York. We understood each other immediately. I was for a time
> the perfect director for him and this showed most in *Death of a
> Salesman*, which is a play that dealt with experiences I knew well
> in my own life.[22]

As *All My Sons* passed its two-hundredth performance in the spring of 1948, Arthur Miller was at work on two scripts. "Death of a

Salesman" was one, but further along was a play he and Kazan had been tinkering with throughout the winter, a comedy called "Plenty Good Times," about an Italian–American worker, "his wife and his girl," which took place on Manhattan's lower East Side in the twenties. Kazan was quoted as saying "it's a light play and has no specific social theme."[23] *Salesman* quickly displaced all thoughts of "Plenty Good Times" when Kazan read it in the summer of 1948.

As the son of an Anatolian Greek carpet dealer who had expected him to go into the business, Kazan understood Miller's play from within, a strong asset for the Method director that he was. Kazan had been educated at Williams College and the Yale School of Drama, and had spent his twenties in the Group Theatre, working as stage manager, actor, and finally director, and studying the principles of Stanislavsky, Vakhtangov, and Meyerhold as interpreted by Harold Clurman and Lee Strasberg. After ten years of directing plays and films on his own, in 1948 Kazan was one of Broadway's most sought-after directors, having directed both the Oscar-winning *Gentleman's Agreement* and the Pulitzer and Drama Critics Circle Award-winning *All My Sons* in the previous year. *Death of a Salesman* proved to be the perfect play for Miller and Kazan to collaborate on at this time in their lives and careers.

Once the problem of securing a producer was out of the way, the first artistic function for Kazan was casting. For a Method director like Kazan, choosing the cast was perhaps the most important decision he would make. He once told Miller that "casting is ninety-five percent of" directing (*T* 272). As he described it:

> The problem is that the basic channel of the role must flow through the actor. He has to have the role in him somewhere. He must have experienced it to some extent. That's why I don't cast by reading. I take the actor for a walk or I take him to dinner or I watch him when he doesn't notice it and I try to find what is inside him. I am known for casting "on instinct," which is not the correct word because I

have studied the actor carefully, even if quickly. Sometimes I make very rapid decisions but I never cast by looks because looks are false.[24]

In his typical fashion, Kazan cast many of the parts in *Salesman* with actors he had worked with before, so that he felt he knew the roles were in them. Arthur Kennedy, who played Biff, had played the son, Chris, in *All My Sons*, a character who differed a great deal on the surface from Biff, but in whom were many of the same motives and desires. Thomas Chalmers, who played Ben, and Hope Cameron, who played Letta, had also been in the *All My Sons* cast. Don Keefer, who played Bernard, was a member of Kazan's newly formed Actors Studio and had been in his production of *Harriet*.

The most important casting, of course, was for the roles of Willy and Linda. Since his conception of Willy was deeply tied to the character's small size, Miller at first thought it vital to have a small actor, certainly not, as Kazan has put it, "great lumbering Leo Jacob Cobb" (*K* 356). Miller remembers that they auditioned actors who fitted his image of Willy, but that "Roman Bohnen and Ernest Truex and a few other very good actors seemed to lack the size of the character even if they fit the body" (*T* 186). Miller had seen Lee J. Cobb only as "a mountainous hulk covered with a towel in a Turkish bath in an Irwin Shaw play, with the hilarious *oy vey* delivery of a forever persecuted businessman" (*T* 186). He had his doubts as the big, thirty-seven-year-old Cobb announced to him, "This is my part. Nobody else can play this part. I know this man" (*T* 186). But Miller's doubts were eased as he watched Cobb over the next few days, smiling winsomely at a young waitress in a coffee shop "as though he had to win her loving embrace before she could be seduced into bringing him his turkey sandwich and coffee" (*T* 186), and laughing at something Miller's young son had said: "The sorrow in his laughter flew out at me, touched me; it was deeply depressed and at the same time joyous, all flowing through a baritone voice that was gorgeously reedy. So large and handsome a man pretending to be thoroughly at ease in a world where he obviously did not fit could be moving" (*T* 187).

Kazan knew Cobb well. They had been in the Group Theatre together and on a road tour of Odets's *Golden Boy*. They had been close friends as young men. Cobb had recently been in Kazan's film *Boomerang*. Kazan reports:

> I knew him for a mass of contradictions: loving and hateful, anxious yet still supremely pleased with himself, smug but full of doubt, guilty and arrogant, fiercely competitive but very withdrawn, publicly private, suspicious but always reaching for trust, boastful with a modest air, begging for total acceptance no matter what he did to others. In other words, the part was him; I knew that Willy was in Cobb, there to be pulled out. *(K 362)*

Despite his size and the fact that he was more than twenty-five years younger than Willy, Cobb was cast.

Linda's size was nearly as important in Miller's script as Willy's. Willy was small and battered; Linda was large and protective. The contrast was significant. Mildred Dunnock, a diminutive and cultivated woman who had taught speech in a women's college, was chiefly known for her portrayal of delicate, fluttery characters such as Lavinia Hubbard in Hellman's *Another Part of the Forest* and a spinster school teacher in *The Corn Is Green*. She looked like anything but Miller's image of Linda: "A woman who looked as though she had lived in a house dress all her life, even somewhat coarse and certainly less than brilliant."[25] But Dunnock was convinced she could play the part. After being told at her audition that she simply was not right for Linda, she returned the next day to audition again, padded from neck to hemline. Her appearance was so altered that the production team did not recognize her until she read her first line. Everyone agreed that her reading was a fine one, but still thought she was not the right person to play Linda. Dunnock returned again and again, altering her appear-ance and giving a new reading each time until she convinced the production team that Linda was indeed within her. Kazan was so impressed with her work that he eventually cast her again "against type" as Big Mama in *Cat on a Hot Tin Roof* and as Aunt Rose Comfort in the film *Baby Doll*.

THE DESIGN PROCESS

While the casting proceeded, the biggest unanswered question about the script, the design concept, was being addressed. On 24 September, Jo Mielziner received a call from Kermit Bloomgarden asking whether he could come straight over and talk to him about "something very interesting" (JM 24). After learning that Kazan hoped to begin rehearsal of the play in two weeks, Mielziner left the meeting with the *Salesman* script to read. During that afternoon and evening, Mielziner began to understand the difficulty of the job he was faced with: "It was not only that there were so many different scenic locations but that the action demanded instantaneous time changes from the present to the past and back again. Actors playing a contemporaneous scene suddenly went back fifteen years in exactly the same setting – the Salesman's house" (JM 25).

As he looked for a design solution to the many changes in scene and time demanded by the script, Mielziner hit on the concept that was to become the key to the production:

> The most important visual symbol in the play – the real background of the story – was the Salesman's house. Therefore, why should that house not be the main set, with all the other scenes – the corner of a graveyard, a hotel room in Boston, the corner of a business office, a lawyer's consultation room, and so on – played on a forestage? If I designed these little scenes in segments and fragments, with easily moved props and fluid lighting effects, I might be able, without ever lowering the curtain, to achieve the easy flow that the author clearly wanted. *(JM 25–26)*

The problem was that developing this design scheme would require more than the two weeks that remained before rehearsals were scheduled to begin. Miller would have to make substantial revisions in the script to change blackouts at the end of each scene to instantaneous scene changes, and Kazan would have to reconceive the whole production. What's more, if the play's opening was delayed, the pre-Broadway theatre bookings and the New York opening would have to be canceled and rescheduled. Mielziner asked for a meeting with Bloomgarden, Miller, and Kazan for that afternoon.

A long discussion followed Mielziner's presentation of his ideas on 25 September. In the end, the aesthetic advantages of the single-set design scheme built around the material symbol of the house were determined to far outweigh the difficulties:

> To Arthur Miller, a design scheme allowing him as author to blend scenes at will without even the shortest break for physical changes was a significant decision. To Kazan, with his strong sense of movement, stimulated by his already proven genius as a film director, the scheme would permit use of some of the best cinematic techniques. *(JM 26)*

In the end, it was decided to postpone the start of rehearsals until the end of December and the New York opening until 10 February, allowing enough time for Miller's revisions and Kazan's rethinking of the direction as well as for the development of the design. Kazan was to consider Mielziner's "concept of a house standing like a specter behind all the scenes of the play, always present as it might be always present in Willy's mind, wherever his travels take him, even behind the office he visits, even behind the Boston hotel room and above his grave plot," the "single most critically important contribution and the key to the way [he] directed the play" (*K* 361). Eloquently described by Miller on the opening pages of the published play, it has served the same purpose for millions of readers who have never seen a production of *Death of a Salesman*.

Mielziner set to work immediately to realize his ideas scenically. He made a number of rough sketches over the next few days, along with a ground plan of the stage, and worked on a breakdown of the script, which gave a page reference for each key scene and a notation of the needed lighting, scenery, props, and elevations. On 28 September, he flew to Boston, where Kazan was rehearsing the pre-Broadway previews for *Love Life*, and went over his ideas at a breakfast meeting, leaving his director "after a brief hour with about ninety-percent approval" (JM 30). During the next week, Mielziner made about twenty black and white sketches representing the scenic design of the whole production and set his assistants to work on translating his sketches into an accurate floor plan and building a scale model of the set. When he met on 4 October with Bloomgarden, Kazan, and Miller, the designer had "a group of ground plans and sketches that . . . solved the major puzzles and were at least indications of the right style" (JM 32) for the production.

Mielziner's set was the culmination of a style of design he had been developing in his productions of Tennessee Williams's plays. In *The Glass Menagerie*, *A Streetcar Named Desire*, and *Summer and Smoke*, he had combined translucent scenery, expert lighting effects, and sets that went, as the eye traveled upward, from drab realistic interiors to light, delicate frameworks that were mere suggestions of buildings. The result was a style that was beginning to be recognized as his signature, and that signaled to audiences a subjective realism in the play that juxtaposed ostensibly objective reality with a character's fantasy as easily as the scenery juxtaposed realism with symbolic abstraction.

Mielziner's *Salesman* set developed from his careful reading of the dialogue and the brief descriptive note that Miller had given him. Miller's note read: "[The house] had once been surrounded by open country, but it was now hemmed in with apartment houses. Trees that used to shade the house against the open sky and hot summer sun now were for the most part dead or dying" (JM 25). In the

1. Early sketch for the design of *Death of a Salesman* by Jo Mielziner

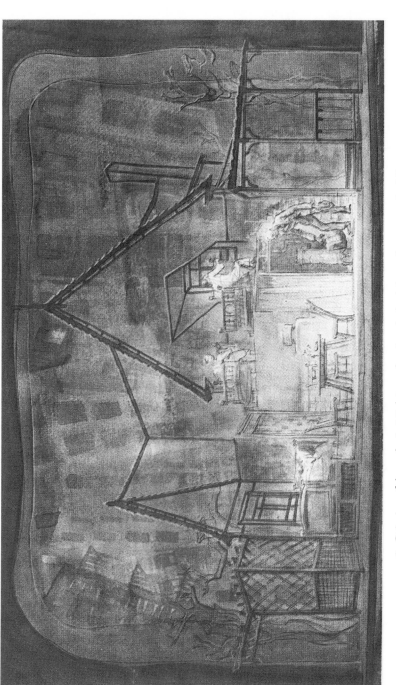

2. Painting of the set by Jo Mielziner, showing the backdrop of apartment buildings

dialogue, Mielziner had underlined the lines "Boxed us in here"; "Bricks and windows, windows and bricks"; and "beautiful elm trees out there."[26] From these visual suggestions, he conceived a tri-level set for the house, with Willy and Linda's bedroom on the lower floor, at stage right, one step up from the kitchen, which, at center stage, formed the largest playing space. On the far left of the kitchen were steps leading up to the boys' bedroom, above and behind the kitchen. All three rooms could be seen simultaneously. Although there was no wall between the parents' bedroom and the kitchen, the rear wall of each room was hung with translucent backdrops stenciled with "wallpaper" patterns. The lower floor also contained a bed, several chairs, a table, a telephone stand, and a refrigerator. Mielziner's original sketches also showed the hot water heater in the kitchen, but it was eventually hidden behind a curtain because it had become intrusive (*T* 188).

Rising above the lower floor there were only the skeletal rafters representing the gabled roof line and a platform holding the boys' beds and a chest. Behind the house was a translucent backdrop with two trees, the outline of the roof, and the boys' dormer window painted on the facing side. On the back were painted the outlines of bare, rectangular buildings with rectangular windows. When lit from the front with a soft golden light, the backdrop showed the Lomans' house as it used to be, a small but brave structure rising with hope and light to the sky. When lit from the back with a threatening reddish glow, it showed the house in the play's present, its fragile skeleton threatened by the huge, glowering apartment buildings.

On 4 October, the main design problems that remained were lack of room for movement on the stage and transitions in time. The lack of room was solved only on 8 December, when Kazan convinced Bloomgarden to take eleven seats out of the first row (at a cost of $323.40 per week in receipts) in order to extend the forestage (JM 43). One of the biggest transition problems was getting Biff and Hap from the scene in their bedroom dressed in

3. Mildred Dunnock, Lee J. Cobb, Arthur Kennedy, and Cameron Mitchell on the original set of *Death of a Salesman*

pajamas to the immediately following scene in which they appear to Willy in the kitchen as they were in the past, dressed in football uniforms. To manage this without closing the curtain or blacking the stage out, Mielziner had elevators built into the boys' beds so the actors could be moved unnoticed from one scene to the other. In order to give them time for a costume change, Miller expanded Willy's monologue about polishing the car by several minutes.

As the autumn progressed, Mielziner confronted the questions of lighting and props. Arthur Miller remembers that Mielziner and lighting expert Eddie Kook together "once worked an entire afternoon lighting a chair" (*T* 190). The chair was the one that Willy addresses as if it were his old boss Frank Wagner in Howard's office, reminding him of the promises he had made. As Willy speaks to it, "the chair must become alive, quite as though his old boss were in it as he addresses him" (*T* 190). Miller marveled that, "rather than being lit, the chair subtly seemed to begin emanating light" (*T* 190) in the production. To achieve this effect, all of the surrounding lights on the stage had to be dimmed imperceptibly, rather than bringing up the spotlight on the chair, which would produce an effect too obvious to the audience.

This effect, and the attention that Mielziner and Kook gave to it, provide a good illustration of the designer's attitude toward the lighting of *Death of a Salesman*. Always a designer who made full artistic use of the scenic expression of lighting, Mielziner had decided that lighting was the key to *Salesman's* time shifts. He decided to signify the passage of time on stage by creating two environments for the house through the lighting. When the set was first revealed, the audience saw the muslin backdrop lit from behind to show the oppressive apartment houses towering over the fragile house. When the scene shifted to the past, the lights behind the backdrop were dimmed out, and the buildings faded out as soft amber light and images of green leaves were projected onto the backdrop from a number of projection units that were carefully placed backstage, throughout the auditorium, and on the balcony. Mielziner felt that this visual symbol of

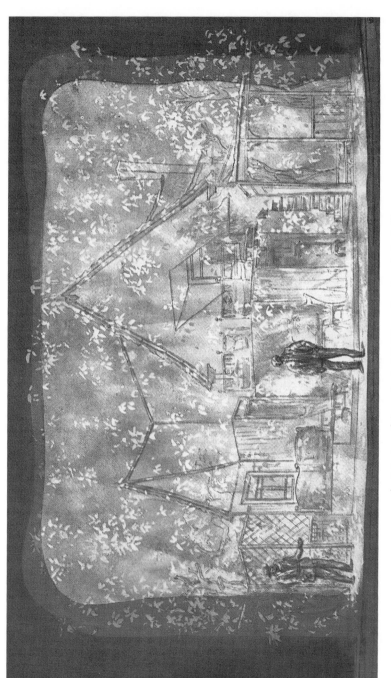

4. Painting of the set by Jo Mielziner, showing the leaf effect

the spring leaves, "liberating the house from the oppression of the surrounding structures and giving the stage a feeling of the free outdoors," was an "integral part of the Salesman's life story and had to be an easily recognized symbol of the springtime of that life" (JM 35). Combined with the music provided by Alex North, this lighting change would bring the audience effectively into the past along with Willy as each daydream began.[27]

The painstaking work involved in the lighting of the original *Death of a Salesman* is almost inconceivable in these days of computerized stage lighting. Each of the 141 lighting units on the eight pipe battens above the stage had to be carefully hung and angled, and each light cue individually adjusted and marked up so that it could be recreated manually during each performance. It took three days for the hanging and angling, and another twenty-hour-day to set the approximately 150 light cues when the production was moved into the theatre.[28] In addition to the projection units, Mielziner had also persuaded Bloomgarden of the necessity of two special follow-spots, which could be manipulated to produce particular effects. Because their fine adjustments needed careful attention, each of these lights required a trained technician for its operation throughout the performance, a significant expense. Mielziner used the projection units to address spatial as well as temporal difficulties. He and Kazan had agreed early on that the most minimal of visual suggestions would suffice in creating the sets for the scenes to be played on the forestage – the Boston hotel room, the restaurant, and Howard's and Charley's offices. He created the hotel room by projecting a seedy wallpaper design from the theatre balcony onto a section of the trellis at the side of the house. With the rest of the stage dimmed, this was enough to evoke the environment where Biff is disillusioned when he surprises Willy with The Woman.

This suggestiveness went along with the minimalism that Mielziner and Kazan had agreed on in the props. A few objects, such as the beds, the chairs, and the table, were required by the action on the stage. Most of the props, such as the refrigerator, the hot water heater, Willy's sample cases, the silk stockings, the rubber tubing, the hoe and seeds, and the gold fountain pen, served a necessary function, but also took on a symbolic resonance. Kazan and Mielziner also agreed on several props which served primarily as material signifiers for the audience of some theme in the play, such as Biff's football trophy on a shelf over Willy's bed and a deflated football in the boys' room. The fact that props were kept to a minimum, with no attempt at realism, helped to foreground the few objects that did appear, encouraging the audience to perceive their symbolic significance.

Throughout the production process, the impulse was toward greater abstraction and symbolism, less realism. A good example is the Requiem scene, in which the original plan was to have a gravestone rise from a trick trapdoor in the forestage. Mielziner persuaded Kazan to use a simple bouquet of flowers to signify the grave instead, using a projection of autumn leaves to complete the symbolic statement of death in opposition to the life and hope suggested by the spring leaves in the daydream scenes. What made the production's style unique, however, was the juxtaposition of the abstract and poetic with the real and prosaic. The props that were introduced into the abstract suggestiveness of the set were authentic, battered objects that the Lomans might very well have owned. The kitchen table was covered with a cloth painted with an "oilcloth" design. The refrigerator was a careful reproduction of a typical model from the 1929 Sears Roebuck catalogue. It was vital to the production's aesthetic that these objects signify a specific time, place, class, and way of life in juxtaposition with the insistent visions in Willy's mind, and that they resonate with symbolic significance in the context of the play as a total experience.

THE MUSIC

Music played an important part in Miller's earliest versions of *Salesman.* The September 1948 preproduction script indicates that, as Willy appears on stage, "a flute is heard in the distance, soft, beguiling, memorable. He hears it, but is not aware of it. It plays a tiny melody of grass and trees and the horizon" (R 1:1). In this version, the flute is an aural evocation of Willy's father, the wild and free adventurer who went where the road took him, making and selling flutes along the way. This is the hint that Alex North had to go on as he composed the score for the twenty-two-and-a-half minutes of music that eventually accompanied *Death of a Salesman.*

The script's requirement of flute music and the fact that the Morosco Theatre had no orchestra pit severely limited North's choices for the score. The music for each performance had to be played in an upstairs dressing room of the theatre and piped into the auditorium through the public address system, with an assistant stage manager giving the cues as he watched the production from the wings (JM 45, 55). There was no question of using a full orchestra. North settled on a quartet: the all-important flutist who played the alto flute, doubling with the C flute, a clarinetist who doubled with the bass clarinet, a trumpeter, and a cellist.[29]

The score was based on four major leitmotifs. The first, played most often by the alto flute alone, was Willy's theme, the haunting melody that opened the play. The second was the energetic "Ben" theme, played most often on the trumpet, which signaled Ben's appearance and Willy's attempt to recapture the hopeful dream he represented. The third was the lullaby with which Linda sang Willy to sleep at the end of Act I. In a distorted jazz version, it was also played on the trumpet to introduce The Woman. The fourth motif was the boys' music, light and gay, and played on all four instruments. Along with the leaf projections, it signaled to the audience that Willy had entered the world of his memories.[30] There were also several incidental themes, such as a "Grand Pop" theme when Ben told Willy about their father; a "Honky Tonk" theme as Hap and the waiter Stanley entered the restaurant; "Think" music as Willy made his final decision to commit suicide; and a "Crash" theme, fading into a dirge as the sound of the screeching car faded into the preparations for the funeral.[31] Like a film score, the music emphasized Willy's subjective experience, drawing the audience more closely into his perception of the events of his reality, both external and internal.

THE DIRECTING

In his work on the Broadway stage throughout the forties and fifties, Elia Kazan was a Method director, perhaps *the* Method director. He firmly believed in the organic form of a play's action, which he described as a tree with the branches coming from it.[32] He believed that an actor must know what he is on stage to do at every moment. He believed that an actor must find a character within her if she is to act effectively. He believed in the communication between the actors onstage. Kazan did not allow himself to be limited by the Method, however. He had a strong visual sense, made more intense and more sophisticated by his film direction. He composed particularly powerful statements through the kinesic and pictorial codes of movement, gesture, and bodily pose in his productions. He likes to say that he learned nearly as much from Meyerhold, Vakhtangov, and Alexander Dean as from Stanislavsky, Clurman, and Strasberg.[33]

Most theatre practitioners agree with Arthur Miller that Kazan's great strength as a director is his ability to work with actors. Miller wrote that Kazan "does not 'direct,' he creates a center point, and then goes to each actor and creates the desire to move toward it. And they all meet, but for different reasons, and seem to have arrived there by themselves."[34] Kazan, he said, "pointed an actor and then walked along beside him with an arm over his shoulder in a gentle embrace of steel" (*T* 272). Kazan's approach to actors derived from the collaborative aesthetic of the Group Theatre and from his own sensitivity, as a former actor himself, to the terrors of the job. Miller described Kazan's work with the actors on *All My Sons* who had been with him in the Group Theatre as like that of "a football team, helping one another, advising, and criticizing" (*T* 275). In the Group, everyone had had a say about an artistic question, although the director had made the final decision.

Over the years, Arthur Miller has noted a number of qualities in Kazan's direction besides his uncanny ability to summon the best performance each of his actors is capable of, qualities that made him particularly effective in the *Death of a Salesman* production. One was the intensity he created in his productions, particularly in the actors' approach to the characters.[35] Another was what Miller considered his calculating, remorseless grasp of "an objectifying view at whatever cost. What counted was what came over to the audience, no excuses and no mercy to be expected . . . he drove the actors relentlessly" (*T* 272).

Through his extensive theatrical education and training, Kazan had also developed a sense of the theatre as part of a larger culture and society that Miller felt was essential to directing his plays:

> He had learned that a theatrical production is, or should be, a slice through the thickness of the culture from which it emerges, and that it is speaking not only to its audience but to other plays, to painting and dance, to music and to all forms of human expression by which at any moment we read our time . . . He identified himself with the idealism of the left and . . . his emotional and intellectual loyalties lay with the workers and the simple and the poor. (*T* 273)

Moreover, Kazan was a consummate showman, able, in his best work, "to find society in a gesture,"[36] a gesture that conveyed all of a play's cultural meaning to the broadest of American audiences.

Finally, Miller found in Kazan's direction a "dialectic inevitability . . . he always tries to make a whole of opposites."[37] For Miller, whose plays were built on the tension between contradictions, and the perhaps inevitable failure to resolve them except dialectically, this "organic dialectic sense" was crucial to any effective direction. Though their styles were anchored in psychological realism, and their politics in liberalism, both artists had a fundamentally modernist perception of the seemingly irresolvable contradictions in human experience and a similarly modernist impulse to try to find an organic form that would resolve or contain them.

Kazan worked out his approach to *Salesman*'s production between September, when he received the preproduction script from Miller, and the end of December, when rehearsals began. He has written that, in working out the meaning of the play that was to emerge in the production, he "came to believe that the point was far more lethal than anything Art put into words. It's in the very fabric of the work, in the legend itself, which is where a theme should be":

> The Christian faith of this God-fearing civilization says we should love our brother as ourselves. Miller's story tells us that actually – as we have to live – we live by an opposite law, by which the purpose of life is to get the better of your brother, destroying him if necessary, yes, by in effect killing him. Even sex becomes a kind of aggression – to best your boss by taking his woman! That contrast between the ideal and the practice specific to our time is the sense in which the play is a "social drama," and this theme, so shameful and so final, permeates the work's fabric and is projected through the example of human behavior so there can be no avoiding it . . . . The question remains: Why do we live by that law when we know – and Art shows us this – that the result is so humanly destructive?   *(K 358–59)*

Underlying this theme, Kazan thought, was the plot hinging on Willy and Biff. He wrote in his notebook: "This is a story of love – the end of a tragic love between Willy and his son Biff . . . The whole play is about *love* – Love and Competition. The Boy loves him. The only way Willy can give him anything back is thru the $20,000."[38]

In directing the play, Kazan's job as a Method director was to identify the "spine" or through-line of the play's action, around which the production would coalesce in order to express the meaning that he saw at the play's center. The play, he wrote, "has a line which is all down the inside of Willy's spine . . . this man goes crazy – right before your eyes – and commits suicide and Miller shows you the logic behind this series of acts" (KN 48). He reminded himself that "this play has to be directed with COMPASSION, which simply means with a quick and intense realization of the PAIN of each of the characters . . . and the real meaning of the 'SPINE,' which means the living and emotional meaning of the 'SPINE'" (KN 50). At the center of the play, in other words, was Willy, and Kazan saw his main directorial task as dramatizing Willy's experience in a way that would induce the audience's empathy and understanding.

In line with this view, Kazan saw the play clearly as a "tragedy, in a classic style, with the drive of an inner inevitability that springs from a single fatal flaw" (KN 44). Following Aristotle, Kazan noted that "Willy is a *good* man. He has worth. But he is a Salesman with a Salesman's Philosophy. Therefore he dooms himself" (KN 44). He also built on the neoclassical notion of the "tragic flaw" to complete his vision of Willy as tragic hero: "His fatal error (this is an Inevitable Tragedy . . . *our* Greek tragedy) is that he built his life and his *sense of worth* on something completely false: the Opinion of Others. This is the error of our whole society" (KN 45). Thus, in Kazan's view, a tragic structure underlay the play's social vision: "Modern man is *Always Anxious!* Because he is between two opposite fatal pulls: to best his neighbor, his brother vs. to be loved by his brother. These are mutually exclusive, an impossible contradiction. Inevitably it will end disastrously" (KN 47–48). For Kazan, this was the key to the play's dialectics.

The play's classical tragic structure was clear to Kazan, but it needed to be reconciled with its unorthodox style, its combination of realism and expressionism. Kazan found the core of the play's reality in the juxtaposition of Willy's subjective experience with the presumedly objective reality around him:

> This play takes place in an Arena of people watching the events, sometimes internal and invisible, other times external and visible

and sometimes *both*. The world is the world of Willy and the way he sees it . . . The people watching have an emotional relation to Willy, a reaching out to him. But by the end of the play, there is no one there for him to reach out to and he is living entirely within himself. The people watching this spectacle are horrified. The *man* simply isn't with them any more. *(KN 48–49)*

The key to the production's style was in the handling of the scenes in the past. In 1948, the chief theatrical and cinematic technique for moving between past and present was the flashback, a convention which implied that the events in past and present were equally and objectively real. This would not work for Willy, for whom the scenes set in the past are actually happening in the present, but in Willy's mind, not in objective reality. Kazan wrote in his notebook: "There are no flashbacks!" (KN 49).

As Kazan saw it, "The only laws of these scenes are the laws of Willy's own mind. And all the figures in Willy's mind are distorted by Willy's *hopes, wishes, desires*" (KN 49). Like Miller, Kazan referred to Willy's subjective experiences not as flashbacks, but as "DAYDREAMS. And daydreams are an action. What Willy is doing in these daydreams is justifying himself. He knows he's failed and he's living his life over in these daydreams in order to justify himself" (KN 49). The style followed naturally from this notion. Kazan concluded it "must be an activization in physical equivalents of the events of Willy's mind for the last 24 hours of his life. So it is *all* unrealistic, since it all happens *Willy's way* – as Willy feels it, experiences it" (KN 49). In other words, the play's action was all subjective, but the events in the present were real events as perceived by Willy and the events in the past were self-justifying fantasies whose origin might have been real events that had been reshaped by Willy's memory.

The implications for the actors of Kazan's view of the action were tremendous. Although their characterizations were never fully realistic, most of them had to create gradations of stylization depending on the level of subjectivity through which the character was to be perceived at any given moment. In planning the characterizations, Kazan noted, "*None of these dream figures are actually in the past! They are as much in the present. They are as Willy needs to think of them for his own reasons of personal dignity, self-esteem, etc.*" (KN 47). In other words, the images of the people that Willy conjures up in his daydreams are part of the daydreams' general function of justifying himself. Consequently, the figures in the past must be interpreted for the audience as Willy would interpret them at that moment.

The easiest character to deal with was Uncle Ben, because he exists only in Willy's daydreams and not in the play's present at all. Kazan noted that "Ben, *Altogether is in the Past*, is entirely subjective as Willie sees him: the embodiment of Success, Authority, Daring, Manliness, Enterprise, Fearlessness, Self-sufficiency. He is romanticized in Willy's memory and by Willy's necessity – into a God-like figure" (KN 46). It was as the embodiment of success that Kazan saw Ben, rather than as the representative of the absent father that was his main function in Miller's early scripts. As the production process progressed, Kazan was to persuade Miller to emphasize Ben's function as a symbol of success and competition, and to de-emphasize his role as father substitute. Some of Miller's most substantial revisions of the script were to focus on Willy's scenes with Ben.

Almost equally clear-cut in Kazan's mind was the function of Charley in the daydreams. "*Charlie in the past is convenient* too for the necessities of Willy's psychology. It's the way he *likes* to think of Charlie, needs to think of Charlie. Not in the past, necessarily, but as much in the present . . . Charlie in the past is an embodiment, a comic embodiment, of all the careless, ambitionless . . . " (KN 47). Although an attentive spectator could discern Charley's good qualities from his behavior in the scenes in the present – his tactful concern for Willy in the card game scene and his baffled but loyal friendship in the scene in his office – he needed to appear slightly ridiculous in the scenes in the past because that is how Willy would need to think of him.

Biff, Kazan noted, would also need to be a "stylized figure" in the past, but Willy's impulse toward Biff would be the opposite of his impulse toward Charley. Biff is "romanticized in Willy's imagination. Confident, easy, gorgeous, all the kids fawning on him, trying to steal the spotlight from him and no one succeeding" (KN 47). On the other hand, the Linda of the daydreams "is a figure fashioned out of Willy's guilt. Hard working, sweet, always true, admiring. 'I shouldn't cheat on a woman like that!' Dumb, slaving, loyal, tender, innocent. Patient with him. Always available for sympathy or even pity" (KN 47). Kazan contrasted Willy's image of Linda, the image that must be created in the daydream scenes, with the actual Linda, whose character emerges in the scenes with her and the boys alone: "In life, she is much tougher. She has consciously made her peace with her fate. She has chosen Willy! To hell with everyone else. She is terrifyingly tough. Why? She senses Willy is in danger. And she just can't have him hurt" (KN 47).

Kazan's view of Willy's character was based on the thematic dialectic that he saw at the core of the play. "Willy is one vast contradiction, and this contradiction is his downfall" (KN 45). The essence of Willy's being is seemingly irreconcilable contradictions brought about by the basic contradiction in his belief system. "He is torn between an absolute need to believe he is '*vital* in New England' and an absolute knowledge that he is not . . . he both hates and loves the same people and can neither really love nor really hate anyone" (KN 45). Kazan saw Willy as "a nicer guy than Charley" (KN 45). He is "neurotic, full of love and longing, need for admiration and affection, full of a sense of worthlessness" (KN 45), but also "haughty, proud . . . dominated by the dream of aggression, competition, pre-eminence" (KN 46).

In preparing for the production, Kazan's most important task was to find ways to physicalize on stage the qualities he saw in the characters and the play's meaning. One of the most important subtexts was built on a line of Linda's in the preproduction script. As she helps Willy on with his jacket in preparation for his meeting with Howard to ask for a New York job, Linda says, "I sewed the lining" (52). Miller had indicated a little business with the jacket in the scene, Willy starting to put it on, but getting distracted as he started to talk about Biff's prospects for the future. Using the jacket as a material signifier for business, and thus Willy's identity as a sales- man and his responsibilities as breadwinner, Kazan was able to encode an entire kinesic subtext which elucidated Linda's attitude toward both Willy and her sons, Biff's attitude toward Willy, and Willy's attitude toward his life and family.

In the play's opening scene, when Willy returns from his disas- trous trip, Kazan had Linda take off Willy's coat as she comforted him and put it on the bed while she helped him take off his shoes (7). When Willy worked up some temporary false confidence about being able to make a sale and started to put the jacket back on, Linda gently stopped him (8). When Willy went into the bath- room, Linda sat on the bed with the coat, examining its torn lining as if it were Willy's battered ego. Later, when Willy walked off in his slippers, leaving Linda alone with the boys, she sat at the table mending the coat as she protected him from Biff's accusations.

A material signifier of Willy, the coat became the site of conflict between Biff and Linda in the scene. As Biff tried to defend himself for not writing to his parents for three months, he put his hands on the coat and leaned across the table, almost seductively trying to win Linda away from Willy with the lines, "I was on the move . . . But you know I thought of you all the time. You know that, don't you, pal?" (39). Linda removed his hands from the coat as she insisted on naming Willy rather than herself as the object of Biff's responsibil- ity: "But he likes to have a letter . . . just to know that there's still a possibility for better things" (39). Linda stopped sewing and looked up at Biff directly when she confronted him with the question, "Are you home to stay now?" (39). And when Biff touched her hair in a gesture that tried to insinuate a special bond between them while he delivered the evasive line, "Your hair . . . Your hair got so gray" (39), Linda pushed his hand away and again turned her attention to sewing the jacket, denying his attempt at connection and keeping Willy the center of her attention.

When Linda finally approached the real subject of their conversation with the line, "Biff, if you don't have any feeling for him then you can't have any feeling for me" (40), Biff again leaned forward on the coat as he said, "Sure I can, Mom" (40). Accepting the challenge, Linda picked up the coat and hung it tenderly over the back of a chair as she delivered her ultimatum: "There's no leeway any more – either he's your father and you pay him that respect or else you're not to come here" (40). While delivering her line, "A small man can be just as exhausted as a great man" (41), she walked over to the chair and straightened the coat, and she again came over and stood smoothing it as she lamented the fact that Willy's friends were all gone (41). Through his use of the coat in the scene, Kazan was able to place Willy at its visual center and to express Linda's loyalty to Willy and his values in opposition to Biff's attempts to insinuate his own claims on her affection.

Kazan and Mildred Dunnock built the physicalization of Linda's character largely on props, the coat and the stockings she mended. Because Willy gave stockings to other women while Linda sat at home mending hers, the stockings were a material signifier of Willy's sexual guilt and his failure to provide for his family as well as he thought he should. As will be seen from the discussion of the revisions in the preproduction script, Kazan actually cut down on the use of the stockings from Miller's original suggestions, where they had brought out elements in Linda's character that Kazan chose not to develop. In relation to Linda, Kazan used them mainly to show her outward submission to Willy's desires and her secret rebellion. She hid the stockings in her apron or covered them with her hand when Willy ordered her to throw them out.

While her actions with the coat signified Linda's love of Willy and her loyalty toward his values, they also encoded a displacement onto

Willy of the nurturing, maternal energy which rightfully belonged to her sons. In his notebook, Kazan indicated that he believed Linda's basic toughness came from her absolutely single-minded devotion to Willy – "To hell with everyone else" – the kind of fierce protectiveness that is usually ascribed to a mother defending her children. Miller had suggested the basic outlines of her attitude in the script. One of her most assertive moments, for example, comes when she stops herself from picking up Hap's propitiatory flowers after she has knocked them to the floor, saying, "Pick up this stuff, I'm not your maid any more" (90).

While she insists that the boys are adults who must be responsible for their own messes, she treats Willy as if he were a small child, constantly waiting on him and trying to repair his mistakes. Kazan carried this to an extreme kinesically. At the beginning of the second act, for example, as the morning seems charged with hope, he had Linda stand watching Willy as he drank his coffee. When Willy motioned toward the stove, she hurried to get the coffee and pour him another cup. When he refused to let her make him some eggs, she went and got the saccharin from the top of the refrigerator, put it in his coffee, and stirred it for him. She helped him put his jacket on, and she ran and got the saccharin as he was about to leave, putting it in his pocket as she checked that he had his glasses and a handkerchief (53–54). When Willy came in from planting the garden that night, she wiped his hand with her handkerchief (94).

In contrast with the rather reserved and disapproving affect that Linda showed toward her sons, the series of nurturing gestures toward Willy encoded a statement that Linda's attitude went beyond that of the loyal and loving wife. Kazan's suggestion was that there was something extreme, almost unnatural, in Linda's allowing Willy to depend on her so completely, and that she exacerbated the opposition between Willy and Biff by her unquestioning loyalty to him and his values, however contradictory or distorted.

In his notebook, Kazan wrote, "it seems to be hard to find actions for Willy. What is a man who is anxious, worried, and swimming in

guilt, who is frustrated in his search for pre-eminence, etc. *Doing?*"
(KN 49–50). He answered himself in part: "He is defending himself
from imagined accusations and insults. He is justifying himself for
sins real and imagined . . . He is excusing himself for things he did
and couldn't help. He is overwhelmed by sudden feelings of
helplessness and seeking refuge in the sure and unmerited security
of his wife" (KN 50). Kazan's physicalization of these actions can be
found throughout the published script. Much of Willy's behavior is
built on the rhythms of approach–evasion and aggression–opposition–submission–retreat as he meets with an external contradiction
to the ongoing self-justification that is his inner life.

A good example of Kazan's kinesic encoding of Willy's action is
his scene with Linda in the past, when he returns from his trip and
they discuss the household finances. In his exuberance over the
upcoming Ebbets Field game, Willy picked Linda up and hugged
her, but put her down when she asked, "Did you sell anything?"
(24). He walked away from her as he lied about how much he had
sold, and she followed him, figuring the commission on his arm. He
shook her off his arm as he was presented with the fact that he
claimed to have earned an impossible $212 on the trip. As Linda fig-
ured his real commission, he again walked away from her, manufacturing in his mind the conditions that kept him from breaking
records. Linda followed after him with her line, "Well, it makes
seventy dollars and some pennies. That's very good" (25). Willy
responded, "(*Blaming her*) What do we owe?" (25), again walking
away.

Finding an excuse for an attack, Willy turned and confronted
Linda, demanding to know why, when she told him they owed $16
on the refrigerator, and he walked away again, with Linda following,
after she explained, "apologizing" (25), that the fan belt had broken.
The evasion and pursuit continued through the list of expenses and
Willy's accusations that he was being cheated until Linda gave him
the bad news of the total, comforting him with a hug and a pep talk
about how well he would do the next week. The kinesic text of

approach–evasion and aggression–opposition–submission–retreat
in the scene elucidated both the dynamics of Willy and Linda's
relationship and Willy's general approach to life as Kazan saw it.

In keeping with Miller's notion that the Loman men were sensuous and proud of it, and with his usual directorial tendency, Kazan
emphasized and increased the physical contact between the characters, particularly in regard to Willy. Partly, this expressed a sexuality
that was very close to the surface, as when Willy picked Linda up
and hugged her, or when he slapped The Woman on the buttocks as
he said "bottoms up!" (27). But Kazan also had Willy express his
need for connection and support from male characters physically.
During the card game he leaned across the table and grabbed
Charley's arm as he said, "Charley, I can't understand it. He's going
back to Texas again" (31). As he tried to reassure Biff and win him
back in the hotel room scene, Willy first put his arm around his son,
then knelt in front of him and hugged him as he pleaded, "She's
nothing to me, Biff, I was lonely, I was terribly lonely" (88). Finally,
he grabbed at Biff as he shouted in desperation, "I gave you an
order!" (88).

Placing Willy on his knees before Biff was part of a kinesic subtext of power and submission that Kazan encoded throughout the
production. Willy's sexual guilt and his betrayal of the idealized portrait of himself that he had drawn for his sons put him on his knees
to Biff. It was to Linda that Biff knelt, confessing his failures as a
son, as he said, "I've been remiss . . . I know that, Mom. But now I'll
stay, and I swear to you, I'll apply myself" (44). When Linda refused
to pick up the flowers, it was Biff who got to his knees and picked
them up, kneeling in front of her and holding the flowers as he
acknowledged his guilt for refusing to take responsibility for Willy
in the restaurant: "Didn't do a damned thing! How do you like that,
heh? Left him babbling in a toilet" (91). When Linda called him a
"louse," he got to his feet and threw the flowers away, making a challenge out of his acceptance of her censure: "Right! Now you hit it
right on the nose! . . . The scum of the earth, and you're looking at

him!" (91). Through this reversal of the visual trope of the courtly lover submitting to his mistress, Kazan encoded Biff's ultimate refusal to submit to Linda's values or to accept her distorted version of Willy.

With Hap, Kazan used the kneeling posture ironically to signify insincerity and manipulation. Hap, who never faces the truth, uses a feint of submission in order to get what he wants, but maintains the power in his relationships as fully as he can. Kazan encoded this proxemically when he had Hap kneel on Biff's bed as he tried to coax him into coming back to New York: "I think the fact that you're not settled, that you're still kind of up in the air . . . I mean . . . is there any future for you out there?" (14). His pose was submissive, but he was still maintaining the advantage of height over Biff that kept him in control. Similarly, in the restaurant scene, Hap knelt on a chair as he worked his line on Miss Forsythe, maintaining his height advantage as he used the false pose of courtly submission to gain sexual power over her.

With both of the boys, Kazan made use of several props and gestures that would both physicalize their most significant characteristics and encode the dynamics of their relationships with the other characters. This was especially true of Hap, whose self-conscious assumption of the role of New York playboy was central to his character. Hap used cigarettes as a shortcut to intimacy, both with Biff and with Miss Forsythe. In their bedroom, when Biff asked Hap for a cigarette, Miller had indicated that he toss him the pack. Kazan changed this so that Hap gave Biff the cigarette he had been smoking, a gesture that initiated the intimate conversation he has with Biff. In the restaurant scene, Kazan had Hap deliberately knock his cigarettes off the table toward Miss Forsythe as a gambit for meeting her. She took out a cigarette after Hap told her that he had gone to West Point, an invitation for him to come and light it, which of course he acted on. As she hesitated about whether or not to break her date in order to go out with him, Hap took a seductive drag on his cigarette, and she agreed to go with him.

Kazan and Cameron Mitchell developed two sets of gestures to signify Hap's creation of his playboy role, trying on his hat and combing his hair. He used the hat first in the scene with Biff when he was trying to impress his older brother with his conquests. As he prepared to tell the story of "ruining" his boss's fiancée, he took the hat off its hook and tried it on, posing narcissistically in front of the mirror while he talked. Later, when Linda told him to pick up the flowers, he pushed his hat forward over his eyes and turned his back in refusal. This gesture was a kinesic statement of his assertion of the playboy role, his refusal to see reality, and his refusal to submit to his mother, which Biff did when he picked up the flowers. Hap also assumed the playboy role to distinguish himself from Willy's failure, as he did when he took a comb from his pajama pocket and started combing his hair while Biff expressed his dismay that Willy had been taken off salary, commenting: "Well, let's face it; he's no hot-shot selling man" (48).

The two props Kazan and Arthur Kennedy used to characterize Biff were the football and the gold fountain pen, both of which had an obvious symbolic resonance. Kazan managed to employ them in sometimes intriguing ways, however. Biff, of course, threw the football around in the daydream scene of Willy's return, where it was a material signifier both of Biff's glory in Willy's eyes and, since he had stolen it, of his future demise. In the scene with Hap, Kazan had Biff find the old deflated football in a chest and carry it around as he told Hap of his confusion about his life. As he said the line, "I've always made a point of not wasting my life, and every time I come back here I know that all I've done is to waste my life" (15), he threw the deflated football into the chest, a kinesic statement of his desire to rid himself of the dead Loman dreams.

In the restaurant scene, the stolen gold pen became the material signifier of Biff's failure, which in Willy's eyes is a deliberate assault on him. Biff held up the pen as his words, "so I'm washed up with Oliver" penetrated Willy's daydream about Biff's flunking math (80–81). Willy picked up the pen as he slowly realized the significance of what Biff was telling him, and then tossed it from him, evading his sense of guilt as the Boston hotel room again intruded into his consciousness. Kazan had Hap go back and retrieve the pen as he and Biff left the restaurant with the women, a characteristic but significant gesture.

Kazan made similar use of other objects to encode a visual text that provided elucidation of the play's meaning and insight into the characters. When Bernard offered Willy a cigarette in Charley's office, Willy took his silver case and simply looked at it, forgetting to take a cigarette, signifying simultaneously Bernard's success and Biff's failure, Willy's bewilderment by both of these, and Willy's inability to accept them as real.[39] In the same scene, Charley came in with a bottle of bourbon and slipped it into Bernard's luggage without a word, signifying an easy-going, affectionate relationship between father and son that Willy could never have with his boys, but also a certain distance, as though Bernard were a friend or business associate of Charley's rather than his son.

THE REVISIONS

While Kazan was working out his interpretation and physicalization of the play, Miller was hard at work on the revisions that had to be made. Miller said in a 1964 interview that Kazan had at one time "had the idea of eliminating some or most of Willie [*sic*] Loman's memory scenes. We tussled for a couple of days and then gave that idea up."[40] In an interview given ten days after the opening, Kazan had said that "only two scenes had to be rewritten – the Uncle Ben sequences, which were too shadowy, not fully realized, and the restaurant scene."[41] These scenes were rewritten before and during rehearsals, but Miller had also made other substantial revisions in the preproduction script before the rehearsals began in December. The need for new transitions between scenes and the lengthening of Willy's monologue while polishing the car to accommodate the staging have already been mentioned. Miller also made some substantial changes that altered the characters and the play's meaning significantly.

In the preproduction script, each scene ends with the light dimming down to blackout and then coming up on the next scene, clearly marking the shift in time and place. The daydream scene in Howard's office about the Ebbets Field game, for example, originally ended with Charley's walking offstage into darkness, chuckling, and Willy following after him with his fists clenched while the music rose to a wild, mocking frenzy. During the blackout, Willy could be heard shouting about Biff from offstage, and then the light came up on Bernard and Jenny in Charley's office. Miller blended the scenes in revision so there was no blackout. Willy simply walked around behind the house, shouting his lines about Biff, and then appeared at the other side of the stage, entering Charley's office from the elevator. Most of the scenes were blended so there was no break at all. Linda's conversation with Biff on the telephone had originally ended with her standing in the kitchen smiling. The light dimmed out on her and then came up on the forestage, where the scene with Howard was to be played (R 2:8). In revision, the scene was blended so that Howard walked onto the forestage pushing his wire recorder while Linda was still talking, and the scene between Howard and Willy followed Linda's scene without interruption (54–55).

Miller also rearranged the order of the scenes and made some significant cuts in Act I. Originally, the light had come up on the boys' bedroom almost immediately after Willy's appearance. The boys had simply woken up, wondered what was happening, and gone back to sleep (R 1:1, Insert A). Miller cut this short scene, allowing the scene between Willy and Linda to run uninterrupted until Willy went down to the kitchen, waking the boys. The mood changes in the first Act were originally much more abrupt. Willy's daydream originally went from the joy of his return right to Bernard and Linda's warnings about Biff and an exchange about Linda's mending stockings that ended with her going off nearly sobbing and saying, "Why do you always yell at me?" (R 1:49). This was followed by a much shorter version of the card game between Willy and Charley (30–31), without the references to Uncle Ben, then the daydream scene about Willy's return (20–28), then a substantially different scene with Ben from that in the published version (33–35). In revising Act I, Miller made the transitions in Willy's mind seem more natural, and reworked the scene so that it introduced characters and information in a more thematically significant way.

Miller also made changes that altered his original characterizations. In the case of Linda, these changes tended to make her less of an individual and more of a representation of the nurturing loyal wife, the wife that Kazan thought she had to be in Willy's mind. Cutting Linda's emotional response to Willy's hounding her about the stockings is one example of this. She needed to represent the stoic wife who never lost patience with Willy, no matter how unreasonable his behavior. Miller also cut Linda's slightly testy response when Willy badgered her about not having bought a General Electric refrigerator. Linda had originally replied, "(*Angering, almost bursting out*) But would you *pay* for a General Electric?" (R 2:4). This was changed to the tentative "But Willy . . ." (52). Maintaining Linda's hopefulness to the end, Miller cut a significant line to Biff: "I've lost all hope, darling, that anybody is going to get me out of this" (R 1:63). He emphasized her preference for Willy over her sons by cutting a number of endearments such as "darling" and "dear" in her speeches to them. Interestingly, Miller almost cut the most-often-quoted lines in the play, Linda's "attention must be paid" speech, but thought better of it. He crossed the speech out in his preproduction script, but then wrote "stet" in the margin (R 1:67).

The most significant changes, however, involved the characters of Biff and Uncle Ben. Miller's conception of Biff seems to have been evolving throughout the production, perhaps partly in response to Kazan's ideas about the play, and partly as a result of clarifying his own.

In 1957 Miller wrote that he had attempted in *Death of a Salesman* to counteract what he called the "law of success," to which Willy succumbs, with "an opposing system which, so to speak, is in a race for Willy's faith . . . the system of love which is the opposite of the law of success" (*TE* 149). Miller suggests that the system of love "is embodied in Biff Loman, but by the time Willy can perceive his love it can serve only as an ironic comment upon the life he sacrificed for power and for success and its tokens" (*TE* 149–50). But Miller has also expressed his disappointment that Biff's "self-realization . . . is not a weightier counterbalance to Willy's disaster in the audience's mind" (*TE* 14), a problem that may arise from the play's representation of Biff's value-system in contrast with the powerfully presented success myth.

Whereas the law of success is omnipresent in the play, constantly reminding the spectator of its pervasiveness in the culture that has produced Willy and his sons, Biff's mature love for Willy emerges only in the climactic scene, when Biff embraces Willy and pleads with him to "take that phony dream and burn it before something happens." As Biff starts away, Willy says, "Isn't that . . . isn't that remarkable? Biff! He likes me!" and Linda responds, "He loves you, Willy!" (97).

Rather than moving to an Aristotelian recognition for Willy in the scene, Miller uses irony to suggest his continued blindness, as, "*choking with his love,*" Willy "*cries out his promise*: That boy . . . that boy is going to be . . . magnificent" (97). It is Willy's continued belief in the law of success, and in Biff's ability to fulfill it, that provides the immediate motive for his suicide – the $20,000 that will finance Biff's rise in business. Beneath this obvious irony is the inadequacy of the love that Biff is offering his desperate father. To prove his love, Biff plans to go away in the morning, never to return. Willy's faith in the law of success may have destroyed him, but Biff's form of love would leave his father to a bleak, perhaps poverty-stricken future, with only the feckless Hap to depend on. As a counter to the inhumanity of the callous business system that "eat[s] the orange and throw[s] the peel away" (59), Biff's value-system is far from adequate. One reason for this inadequacy is that

Biff did not originally function as a moral counterforce to Willy. In the preproduction version, Biff's character was far less virtuous and a good deal more like Willy's than it is in the published version, particularly in two ways, his sexuality and his compulsive lying to put the best face on his actions. He is also a compulsive thief and a convicted felon, characteristics that Miller and Kazan de-emphasized in the revision of the character and his representation on stage.

In the preproduction version of the first daydream scene, the young Hap and Biff tell Willy about a hike on which Biff has led the other boys. When Willy asks them what kind of "adventures" they had, Biff replies, "Well, we pitched camp in an apple orchard and . . . a girl came around, Dad" (R 1:37). Willy laughs, and Hap says, "Biff was with her in the tent," to which Willy replies, "(*Proudly, attempting a wry reprimand*) No! Biff!" and Biff says, "(*Smiling proudly*) She just wouldn't let me go, Dad." The scene continues:

WILLY: That so! (*Teeming with sensuous happiness*) Picked you out of all
    the boys, heh?
BIFF: Yeah, Dad.
WILLY: How old was she?
BIFF: Oh, about . . . forty.
WILLY: That so! How about Bernard, did he . . .?
BIFF: Oh, Bernard! He was blushing all the time, and anyway she
    wouldn't even look at him.
WILLY: (*With a joyous attempt at pity*) Bernard is not well-liked, is he?
BIFF: He's liked, but he's not well-liked. (R 1:37–39)[42]

The scene established several characteristics of the Lomans that are familiar from the published script: Willy's pride in Biff's popularity, his competition with Charley and Bernard, and the sensuality of the Loman men, coupled with their objectification of women. It suggests more overtly than any scene in the published play that Hap and Biff have absorbed their attitudes about sex and women directly from Willy. It also presents Biff as a much less innocent boy than he appears in the final script.

As he revised the script, Miller made a number of changes that set up a contrast between Hap's attitude toward women and Biff's. For example, in the earlier script, when Hap asks Biff if he is interested in Miss Forsythe, Biff replies, "I never speared anything like that" (R 2:39). And later in the scene, when he gets angry with Willy and wants to leave, he says, "Where's that woman? I'm going diving tonight" (R 2:54).[43] In the published script, Hap takes all the initiative with the women, and Biff seems to have been living an almost monastic life out West.

The most important change in Biff's character, however, was centered on the incident with Bill Oliver and Biff's narration of it. In the published script, Biff tells Hap in the restaurant before Willy arrives that Oliver had seen him for one minute and walked away after Biff had waited in his office for six hours. "He comes out, didn't remember who I was or anything," Biff says. "I felt like such an idiot" (76). Then Biff explains that he went into Oliver's office, took his fountain pen, and ran down all eleven flights to the street. When Biff tells Hap that he intends to tell Willy the truth about this, Hap persuades him to make up the story about having a lunch date with Oliver so that Willy will have something to hope for. When Willy arrives, Biff starts to tell him the truth, but is pressured by Willy's having been fired into using Hap's story. Biff tells Willy about stealing the pen, however, and says he can't keep the appointment with Oliver. When Willy quite naturally tries to persuade Biff that he can toss off his having picked up the pen as an oversight, Biff says, "Listen, kid, I took those balls years ago, now I walk in with his fountain pen! That clinches it, don't you see? I can't face him like that!" (82). When Willy continues to pressure Biff, he tells him he has no appointment.

One problem with the restaurant scene as it was finally done in production is Biff's motivation. If he agrees to go along with Hap's lie in order to ease Willy's anxiety about having been fired, why would he upset Willy needlessly by saying that he can't keep the appointment because he stole the pen? And since he has already told

Hap that Oliver didn't even remember him, the only motive for reminding Willy about the stolen basketballs would be to upset him further at a time when he was supposed to be setting his mind at ease. The inconsistency in Biff's motivation is partly due to Miller's extensive revision of the scene during rehearsals.[44] In the preproduction and early rehearsal scripts, Biff did not reveal that he was lying about seeing Oliver until his final climactic confrontation with Willy. Biff did not tell Happy the truth in the restaurant scene, but made up the lie about having an appointment with Oliver himself and told it to both Hap and Willy. He said that Oliver had remembered and welcomed him, that they had discussed the Florida deal, and that the only question remaining was the amount of the loan (R 2:41–49). Thus there was not the moral distinction between Biff and Hap that is made in the published version, and Biff's intention in the restaurant scene was to deceive Willy rather than to make him see the truth.

In the earlier version, Biff's stealing was much more central to the scene, to his character, and to his relationship with Willy. In telling about his meeting with Oliver, he said that he felt Oliver kept waiting for him to say something about his having stolen the basketballs. Then Oliver had gone to consult with his partner, and, Biff said:

> I waited two minutes, five minutes . . . and it's gettin' to be about
> ten minutes, see? And it's after five. So I started getting sore,
> y'know? Because nobody is going to treat me that way, I don't
> care who he is. And I could just see him out there with his partner
> laughing at the big dope coming back to the place where he stole
> a box of basketballs and having the nerve to ask for ten thousand
> dollars. I even thought I *heard* laughing in the next office. *(R 2:45)*

Biff said that he had been doing a crossword puzzle while he was waiting and that he'd taken the pen because he was angry at Oliver and, more importantly, because he'd remembered that Willy's pen was broken. The scene continued with Biff offering Willy the pen and Willy taking it. As Willy admired the pen, Biff burst out laughing:

BIFF: You don't care where I get anything, do you?

WILLY: You're not a thief.

BIFF: (*With a broad, vicious smile*) I found it, heh? You're already
        convinced that I found it on Forty-Second Street.   *(R 2:55)*

Then Biff told Willy that he had been in jail in Kansas City for stealing a suit and a hat, and "the suit I stole turned out to be your size. Isn't that a funny thing? The judge couldn't understand it and neither could I . . . but I'll be damned if the suit and the hat weren't your size" (R 2:56).

This scene linked Biff's stealing much more overtly to Willy than the published version does, giving a rather pat psychological explanation for it. Still trying to please Willy, Biff lied and stole like the other Lomans, and not only was he on the same moral level as Hap, but he was not as bright. As he said of Hap, "he's the same way in his heart, except he's too smart to do it that way. We're all thieves" (R 2:56). In the context of this characterization of Biff, the story of the pen and its revelation make more sense than they do in the final version. The restaurant scene has a clearer motivation. But there is no suggestion of an alternative value-system to Willy's in their final confrontation, an alternative that both Miller and Kazan thought Biff should provide.

In the published script, Biff approaches the final, climactic confrontation with Willy in the role of truth-teller. Twice, as Willy tries to resuscitate the saving fantasy of Oliver, Biff gently reminds him, "I've got no appointment, Dad" (93, 94). When Willy accuses him of cutting down his life for spite, Biff decides the time for basic truths has come. Laying the rubber tubing on the table in front of Willy, he says, "All right, phony! Then let's lay it on the line . . . you're going to hear the truth, what you are and what I am!" (95). Biff reveals that he has been in jail for stealing and has stolen himself out of every good job since high school. But this self-revelation is a lead into his deeper insight that the Lomans "never told the truth for ten minutes in this house" (96) and his attempt to get Willy and Hap to accept the fact that they are all "a dime a dozen" (97). That the others don't share his recognition is part of the play's tragedy, but Biff's self-acceptance and his rejection of Willy's phony dream suggest hope for the future.

In the earlier version, Biff's revelation was not that he had stolen – a fact that had already been established as central to his character – but that his appointment with Oliver was a fabrication. When Willy refused to believe him, Biff said:

> Once and for all, Willy . . . I got no appointment with Jonas [Oliver]. You know why? Because if I told anybody but you that I was going to ask a man for $10,000 they'd say I was crazy or a goddamned liar . . . I'm tellin' *you* now! Only you would listen to that nonsense . . . you and him [Happy]. Nobody else. Because only we don't know who we are. I'm a dime a dozen, Willy, and so are you. *(R 2:81)*

In some ways, the earlier scene was more dramatic. Coming presumably as a surprise to the audience as well as to Willy, the revelation that the Oliver story is a lie reveals the power of the Loman collective fantasy over Biff. The earlier version dramatized his freeing himself from its grip rather than presenting him as a self-appointed savior for the others. As a meeting of father and son, its emotional climax was also more authentic. But the earlier version did not serve Miller's and Kazan's thematic purpose. If Biff is to represent a hopeful alternative to the crushing law of success, he must have got beyond the tortured emotions and the moral confusion of the Loman family. He must seem cooler, more gentle, and in charge as he moves in to replace Willy and his values at the end of the play. Miller's revisions accomplished this and, on the whole, conveyed Biff's character more subtly and more effectively, but something of Biff's emotional immediacy might have been lost in the process.

In changing Ben's major function in the play from substitute for Willy's absent father to symbol of the success myth, Miller cut some lines and expanded others. In the preproduction script, Ben appears three times: during the first daydream about Willy's return; during the daydream in Howard's office; and in the garden. There is a running narrative in these three scenes. In the first, Willy asks Ben whether he found their father in Alaska, and when Ben tells him he had gone to Mexico instead, Willy asks him to look for their father on his current trip to Alaska, and Ben agrees. When Ben appears in Howard's office, Willy asks if he has found their father, and Ben says there is no trace of him in Alaska. At the end of the scene, Willy asks Ben again to look for their father, and Ben says he will look in Mexico, since he heard a rumor that he might have gone there. In the scene in the garden, Ben tells Willy that their father died in Mexico a long time ago.

Willy's futile search for his father in the earlier versions of the play made his affinity with Biff clearer. Both had suffered from the lack of a father's direction, Willy because his father had deserted him, and Biff because of Willy's confusion. Like Biff, Willy feels "like a boy" (15), "temporary" about himself (37), a theme that was reiterated more often in the earlier scripts. In the preproduction script, the discussion of the father is longer, ending with Willy's memory that he had sent their mother a barrel of salted fish from Alaska every Christmas for five years, and then it had stopped, and "that was all" (R 1:53). Pleading "*desperately*" with Ben to find their father, Willy twice repeats that he feels he could really get started if he could only talk to his father for an hour. When Ben reports in the second daydream that he couldn't find their father in Alaska, Willy says "*mournfully*": "I was really hoping to see him, I've waited for him so long, Ben. Everything's been so temporary . . . I've always wanted to have a talk with him" (R 2:17). Then he says that if his father had taken him along, he would have known what to tell his own boys. As Ben leaves for Mexico, he says, "Ben, find Dad, will you? If I could just get his advice for two minutes, I know that everything would clear for me" (R 2:19). In the garden scene, Willy says that their father would know what to do if he were there. In cutting most of the references to Willy's father, Miller not only condensed the role of Ben a good deal, but also de-emphasized the father–son theme somewhat by making the parallel between Willy's experience with his father and Biff's with Willy less overt. The downplaying of Willy's sense of desertion by his father also eroded one source for audience sympathy with him.

In the earlier versions, Ben's function as success symbol had been secondary to his function as father surrogate. In emphasizing the success theme, Miller wove several references to Ben's glittering wealth into the script (29, 31–33, 38). He also built up a conflict between Linda, representing the values that make for family stability, and Ben, representing the values of the jungle that are needed for success. He expanded the scene in which Linda angrily opposes Ben's attempt to get Willy to go with him to Alaska, telling him that Willy is doing well enough "to be happy" (62) in his sales job. He also replaced the discussion about Willy's father with the scene in which Ben demonstrates for Biff how not to fight fair in the jungle (35–36). The result was to make Ben a more distant, glittering, and fearsome figure, and a constant reminder of Willy's impossible and distorted image of success and its values.

THE REHEARSAL PROCESS

Kazan made the last entry in his *Salesman* notebook on 17 December. In the previous week, Mielziner had met with costume designer Julia Sze to finalize their design ideas, and with Alex North to discuss the arrangements for the music. Throughout the autumn, Miller had been faithfully sending his revisions of the script to the members of the production team, scene by scene. Although he had blended the scenes into one another, doing away with the clear demarcations between them that had appeared in the preproduction script, Miller had not attempted to indicate how the transitions would be made scenically.

Kazan and Mielziner met on 15 December to discuss this problem, deciding that the combination of projections and the minimal use of props, an abstract realism in style, would solve the problem. Thus, in the scenes to be played on the forestage, the props were to serve double and triple duty. Miller's script, for example, called for two desks, two chairs, and a hatrack to be used in the scene in Howard's office, and then for the scene to shift immediately to the Boston hotel room. Kazan and Mielziner decided that they could get by with one desk and one chair, and that these props could be used to signify both Howard's and Charley's offices (JM 46). Since the hotel room required no props, the whole environment would be created with lighting and projections. In the restaurant scene, the solution was to have Hap and the waiter Stanley carry on a table and two chairs when they entered, simply adding them to the table and chair already on stage for the scene in Charley's office (72).

On 27 December, the company met for the ceremonial first day of rehearsals on the roof of the New Amsterdam Theatre on Forty-Second Street, a former night club that now served as a rehearsal hall. The company sat on chairs and benches set in a shallow semi-circle facing the table at which Miller, Kazan, Bloomgarden, and the three stage managers sat with their scripts and notes. After the formal round of greetings, Kazan gave his opening speech, which Mielziner has described as brief and earnest, "both a welcome and a pep talk as he warned them that it would not be an easy production" (JM 49). Then Mielziner explained the design concept, translating as best he could for the actors his model of the set into the space that had been marked out on the rehearsal floor, and showing the actors where the sightlines would be.

The participants have varying memories about Kazan's work with the actors during rehearsals. Miller has described more than once his trepidation as day after day went by and Lee J. Cobb seemed to make no progress in creating the character of Willy: "He sat for days on the stage like a great lump, a sick seal, a mourning walrus. When it came his time to speak lines, he whispered meaninglessly. Kazan, the director, pretended certainty, but from where I sat he looked like an ant trying to prod an elephant off his haunches" (*TE* 48–49). He has also described his delighted astonishment as suddenly one day, Cobb stood up and started to speak, "and the theater vanished. The stage vanished. The chill of an age-old recognition shuddered my spine; a voice was sounding in the dimly lit air up front, a created spirit, an incarnation, a Godlike creation was taking place; a new human being was being formed before all our eyes" (*TE* 49). Miller remembered press agents and lighting men weeping at that moment and Kazan "grinning like a fiend, gripping his temples with both hands" (*T* 188). Miller's recollections are clearly a playwright's subjective vision, though. Alan Hewitt, who played Howard, did not remember Cobb's having "'sat there like a lump' and opening up suddenly 'ten days before the opening,'" noting, "to be sure, Cobb did a lot of talking, not to say arguing over anything and everything, but he could not have held back on 'acting' the play, because, after the first two weeks of rehearsal, we staggered through complete run-throughs every evening, a Kazan method which I enthusiastically endorse."[45]

Another Kazan characteristic was suiting the directorial approach to the actor. First he had to know what he was dealing with. Since he had already worked with the other principal actors, he knew how to approach them, but Mildred Dunnock was as yet unknown to him. She has commented, "as soon as he'd accepted me for the part, he began probing and probing at me, asking the most personal questions. I wasn't insulted, because I realized he was just trying to familiarize himself with the material with which he had to work."[46] In rehearsal, he took a different approach to Dunnock, whose training was classical and technical, than he did to Cobb or Kennedy. Cobb, he would take "away in a corner and whisper to him and then get just the portrayal he wanted."[47] He got at Dunnock's personality through her vocal training. Miller remembers that Kazan "straightened her spine" in the "Attention must be paid" scene by having her deliver her long speeches to the boys at double and quadruple her normal speed, until she "was standing there drumming out words as fast as her very capable tongue could manage," slackening off only after he had elicited the "outrage and protest" that he wanted from her (*T* 189). Dunnock remembered that Kazan carried a fencing foil at rehearsals, and that he would "stab that foil at me and scream and swear, 'You've got more and, damn it, you'll give it to me! You're a tigress defending her cub! Now, attack that scene – again, again!'"[48] Dunnock, who jumped at the chance to work with Kazan several times after *Salesman*, marvelled that somehow he "seems to get whatever he wants from you," because he had an instinctive sense of the most effective approach to each actor.[49]

As Hewitt noted, Kazan had the actors running through the entire play after two weeks. Mielziner wrote that, at a run-through of the first act on 13 January, just sixteen days after the first rehearsal, "most of the actors knew their parts fairly well, although some carried their type-written sides for occasional help" (JM 50). The rehearsals continued at the New Amsterdam Theatre while the production was slowly taking shape in preparation for the Philadelphia previews.

On 14 January, the scenery, electrical equipment, and props were loaded up and shipped to the Locust Street Theater in Philadelphia. During the next two days, the stagehands set up the platforms, put together the scenery that was connected to them, and hung the borders, the masking wings and the all-important backdrop (JM 51). Simultaneously, the electricians were hanging the lights. When this was completed, Mielziner's assistant, John Harvey, directed the angling and focusing of the lighting equipment, based on the blueprints and plans that had already been drawn up. On 18 January, Mielziner arrived in Philadelphia and quickly tested the leaf projections to make sure they were going to work (JM 52). On the next day, he held the first lighting rehearsal, and the 141 lighting cues were painstakingly marked up. On 20 January, Kazan took the actors through their first run-through on the actual set, and on the next day, conducted the first dress rehearsal (JM 59).

Opening night in Philadelphia was Saturday, 22 January 1949.[50] On the afternoon before the performance, Kazan and Miller took Lee J. Cobb to a performance of Beethoven's Seventh Symphony by the Philadelphia Orchestra. Miller remembers, "we sat on either side of him in a box, inviting him, as it were, to drink of the heroism of that music, to fling himself into his role tonight without holding back" (*T* 190). Mielziner has reported the production team's reaction to that night's performance:

> The first public performance of *Death of a Salesman* gave us all the feeling that the play had it. There were scenes that didn't go well; others seemed a little long, and would later be cut or changed. But from the very beginning, long before any applause, there was a sense that the play really held the audience. (*JM 60*)

Miller was astounded by the audience's reaction: "With the curtain down, some people stood to put their coats on and then sat again, some, especially men, were bent forward covering their faces, and others were openly weeping . . . It seemed forever before someone remembered to applaud, and then there was no end to it" (*T* 191). It was a scene that would be repeated many times at performances of *Death of a Salesman*.

THE CRITICAL RESPONSE

The critics seconded the audience's reaction. "'Death of a Salesman' is a truly great play, admirably acted. It is the theater at its best," wrote R. E. P. Sensenderfer.[51] Edwin Schloss called it "an infinitely moving and bitterly splendid play – a triumph of the craft and magic of the theater, and a first rate work of dramatic art."[52] Even the jaded, "show-biz" *Variety* reporter called *Salesman* an "emotional rhapsody," observing:

> Regardless of what new thrills the new year may bring to the stage,
> the top drawer position attained at this preem stage by *Death
> of a Salesman* puts Miller's new play in a class by itself. All the
> superlatives a tub-thumper ever dreamed up apply perfectly to this
> opus. And it's a sure-fire bet that they can never print up enough
> ducats to satisfy the demand this is going to create at the box
> office.[53]

The "ducats" started flowing immediately as word reached New York that a truly exceptional play was on its way. Not only were there long lines at the Philadelphia box office, but Bloomgarden was flooded with mail orders for advance ticket sales in New York (JM 61).

When *Salesman* opened in New York on 10 February 1949, the audience was just as responsive as it had been in Philadelphia. Critic Louis Kronenberger commented that New Yorkers had "waited for *Death of a Salesman* with the expectation of seeing a masterpiece":

> Whoever you met that had caught the show out of town had clearly
> seen a masterpiece already, and behaved a little as if he had seen a
> ghost. Few things in Broadway history can have had so sensational
> a build-up: fewer still – which is far more wonderful – have been
> so breathlessly received when they arrived.[54]

One reviewer called the play "emotional dynamite," noting that "sobs were heard throughout the auditorium, and handkerchiefs were kept busy wiping away tears."[55] Clearly prepared to see the play as a major event in the modern theatre, the first-night critics were rhapsodic in their praise. From his authoritative position at the *New York Times*, Brooks Atkinson wrote:

> Arthur Miller has written a superb drama. From every point of
> view "Death of a Salesman," which was acted at the Morosco last
> evening, is rich and memorable drama. It is so simple in style and so
> inevitable in theme that it scarcely seems like a thing that has been

written and acted. For Mr. Miller has looked with compassion into the hearts of some ordinary Americans and quietly transferred their hope and anguish to the theatre. Under Elia Kazan's masterly direction, Lee J. Cobb gives a heroic performance, and every member of the cast plays like a person inspired.[56]

In an attempt to indicate the play's potential significance as a literary drama, Atkinson went on to call it "a suburban epic that may not be intended as poetry but becomes poetry" and "a wraith-like tragedy." Ward Morehouse wrote in the New York *Sun*: "When the living theater soars it dwarfs all competitive mediums. It soared last night at the Morosco. Miller's new play is a triumph in writing, in acting and in stagecraft."[57] Richard Watts asserted that, "Under Elia Kazan's vigorous and perceptive direction, 'Death of a Salesman' emerges as easily the best and most important new American play of the year."[58] In his first-night review, Robert Garland wrote, "Arthur Miller's 'Death of a Salesman' at the Morosco is my personal prize-play of the 1948–1949 New York season. Here and now, I beat the Pulitzer people and the Critics' Circle to it."[59] *Salesman* was to win not only the Pulitzer Prize and the Drama Critics' Circle Award, but the Donaldson Award and Tony Awards for best play, best direction, best scene design, and best supporting actor, Arthur Kennedy. It ran for 742 performances on Broadway. The published script was a best-seller, and it is the only play ever to be a Book-of-the-Month Club selection. *Death of a Salesman* had clearly found a wide and appreciative audience.

Some of Miller's most cherished responses to the play came not from critics but from businessmen. He tells with pride the story of Bernard Gimbel, head of one of New York's largest department stores, giving orders on the night he saw *Salesman* that none of his employees were to be fired for being overage (*T* 191). He saved among his papers from the period a letter from the president of the National Council of Salesman's Organizations, written in May, 1949. It informed Miller that he had been named the outstanding individual spokesman for the selling profession in America, noting that every salesman had witnessed a tragedy like Willy's in his own experience.[60] Howard A. Fuller, the president of the Fuller Brush Company whose door-to-door salesmen seemed ubiquitous in the forties and fifties, wrote an article for *Fortune* magazine in which he praised Miller for having demonstrated that "in peacetime the professional salesman is the real hero of American society." Fuller went on to depict the salesman as "the cutting edge of a free competitive economy who cheerfully exposes himself to the slings and arrows of outrageous fortune in order to present to the public new ideas embodied in the innumerable products constantly being produced by industry," a description worthy of Willy himself.[61] Miller also recalls that "a lot of salesmen were very upset by" the play, however, and he has told the story of one church bell salesman in Waterbury, Connecticut, who got up and walked to the other side of the room when Miller told him he had written *Death of a Salesman*.[62]

While the first-night critics were unanimously lavish in their praise for every aspect of the play and the performances, there were some negative reactions later on, some of which were inspired as much by Miller's politics as by his play. In the *Partisan Review*, Eleanor Clark found in the play "an intellectual muddle and a lack of candor that regardless of Mr. Miller's conscious intent are the main earmark of contemporary fellow-travelling."[63] One other out-and-out attack, by Federick Morgan in the *Hudson Review*, seems to have been motivated more by a general hatred for the New York theatre than anything else. Noting that *Salesman* had won all of the year's prizes and awards, he wrote, "it is, not surprisingly, a miserable affair; and it would be unfair to single it out here from among the many Broadway productions which are completely devoid of merit were it not for just this excessive publicity which it has received."[64] He continued in a vitriolic style more characteristic of nineteenth-century newspaper critics than of writers for distinguished quarterly reviews:

Miller had the makings of some sort of play; but he was
unfortunately unable to bring a single spark of dramatic intelligence
to bear on his material. The terms in which he conceived of his
theme are so trite and clumsy as to invalidate the entire play and
render offensive its continual demand for the sympathy and
indulgence of the audience. It proceeds, with unrelieved vulgarity,
from cliché to stereotype. The language is entirely undistinguished
(the personages are continually grunting, groaning and vehemently
repeating the tritest colloquialisms); the tone of the play can best
be described as a sustained snivel.[65]

While there was nothing approaching Morgan's viciousness
in the other reviews, there were some more gentle expressions of
his complaints. In a conscious reaction against the "raves" of
the New York reviewers, the critic for *Time* asserted that *Salesman*
was "no more than an altogether creditable play," and complained
that it "is written as solid, sometimes stolid prose. To its credit,
it has almost no fake poetry; but it has no real poetry either."[66] In
a generally favorable review, Joseph Wood Krutch wrote in
The Nation that the play was "prosy and pedestrian." Comparing the
dialogue to that of a Theodore Dreiser novel, he complained that
it was "almost as undistinguished, as unpoetic, as unmemorable,
and as unquotable."[67]

Most critics recognized from the beginning, however, that
Death of a Salesman is no less important as dramatic literature than
as theatre. From the time of its premiere, the play has been the
subject of a spirited critical debate, centering on some of the most
significant issues in the discussion of modern drama. The issue
that received the earliest, and the most sustained, attention was the
play's status as a tragedy. To the opening-night newspaper critics,
there was no question that what they were seeing was, as one called
it, "a soaring tragedy."[68] Another wrote that *Salesman* "is composed
of essentially the same materials used by the Greek tragedians
of the Golden Age."[69] A third wrote that "'Death of a Salesman' is
a play written along the lines of the finest classical tragedy. It is

the revelation of a man's downfall . . . whose roots are entirely in his own soul."[70]

There was no time for sustained analysis of the play's tragedy in the opening-night reviews that were pounded out in newsrooms immediately following the performance in order to be in time for the morning editions. A number of more thoughtful follow-up pieces appeared in the weekend newspapers, however, several of which examined Miller's unusual creation of a modern tragedy in detail. In one of the most perceptive of these, John Beaufort wrote:

> In "Death of a Salesman," Mr. Miller is writing once more about moral responsibility and the misconception of what constitutes moral responsibility. He is writing about the conflict in people and between people. It remains for Biff, who alone perceives the significance of the conflict, to claim his ultimate freedom. Therein lies the catharsis of the play, the journey through "pity and fear" to a heightened sense of what the individual must mean to himself and to others, a repudiation of the false measurements of success. This is not the whole answer. But it is more than Willy Loman perceived.[71]

Beaufort was raising here what was to become one of the central issues in the critical debate over the play. Could *Death of a Salesman* be a tragedy if its hero underwent no "recognition," in the Aristotelian sense, no fundamental process of learning and transcendence as a result of his experience? In offering Biff's new perception as a substitute for Willy's, Beaufort was raising a critical issue that has never been resolved conclusively.

Another aspect of the debate was raised by John Mason Brown, writing the next week in the *Saturday Review*. "Miller's play is a tragedy modern and personal, not classic and heroic," he wrote, "its central figure is a little man sentenced to discover his smallness rather than a big man undone by his greatness."[72] Brown seemed to have been anticipating an article by Miller himself that appeared the next day, 27 February 1949, in the *New York Times*. Despite the fact that the early critics had assumed his play was a tragedy, and several had placed it alongside the classical tragedies of the Greeks, Miller used the rhetorical strategy of answering a putative attack on the concept of modern tragedy in his own piece:

> In this age few tragedies are written. It has often been held that the lack is due to a paucity of heroes among us . . . we are often held to be below tragedy – or tragedy above us. The inevitable conclusion is, of course, that the tragic mode is archaic, fit only for the very highly placed, the kings or the kingly, and where this admission is not made in so many words it is most often implied.[73]

As a challenge to this point of view, Miller asserted, "I believe that the common man is as apt a subject for tragedy in its highest sense as kings were" (*TE* 3), and in the short space of his newspaper article he proceeded to outline a description of modern tragedy that reversed some of the central assumptions about the genre which had been in force since Aristotle had described it more than two thousand years earlier. Unlike classical descriptions of tragedy, which hold that the hero is punished for his challenge to the gods, a rebellion impelled by overweening pride and followed inevitably by guilt, Miller's held that tragedy "is the consequence of a man's total compulsion to evaluate himself justly" (*TE* 4). Where the classical theory located evil in the hero's violation of a transcendent order and found him justly punished for it, Miller located evil outside the hero: "if it is true that tragedy is the consequence of a man's total compulsion to evaluate himself justly, his destruction in the attempt posits a wrong or an evil in his environment" (*TE* 5). In an extraordinary rejection of the traditional notion of tragedy as an affirmation of a transcendent order through the hero's submission to his punishment for violating it, Miller asserted:

> The tragic right is a condition of life, a condition in which the human personality is able to flower and realize itself. The wrong is the condition which suppresses man, perverts the flowing out of his love and creative instinct. Tragedy enlightens – and it must, in that it points the heroic finger at the enemy of man's freedom. The

> thrust for freedom is the quality in tragedy which exalts. The
> revolutionary questioning of the stable environment is what
> terrifies. In no way is the common man debarred from such
> thought or such actions. (*TE* 5)

While the emphasis in earlier tragic theory had been on the individual's guilt for his violation of a higher order, whether supernatural or social, and the subsequent expulsion of the hero so that order could be restored, Miller's was on the individual's right to self-actualization and to personal freedom, rights which he assumed were inherently human. Miller's notions of good and evil and of the individual's relation to society were entirely in keeping with the values of the post-World-War-II United States and entirely at odds with the prevailing notions of classical tragedy.

Miller also rejected the notion that the hero's enlightenment should come through punishment, submission to authority, and repentance for his violation of the higher order. Instead he wrote, "no tragedy can . . . come about when its author fears to question absolutely everything, when he regards any institution, habit or custom as being either everlasting, immutable, or inevitable. In the tragic view the need of man to wholly realize himself is the only fixed star" (*TE* 6). Furthermore, it is "from this total questioning of what has previously been unquestioned" that "we learn" (*TE* 4).

Reprinted many times, Miller's brief essay proved to be a seminal document in the discussion of tragedy in the second half of the twentieth century. Not surprisingly, and as he no doubt intended, it became a starting point for the more sophisticated critical discussions of *Death of a Salesman*. Several influential critics, including George Jean Nathan, Eleanor Clark, Eric Bentley, and John Gassner, took Miller's article as a challenge, debating the nature of tragedy and its relation to *Salesman* in the monthly magazines.[74]

The question of *Salesman*'s social statement was also a major issue in the early criticism of the play apart from the issue of tragedy. Several of the early critics simply assumed that Willy was, as Wolcott Gibbs put it, "a failure, a man who has finally broken under the pressures of an economic system that he is fatally incapable of understanding."[75] The play was very quickly submitted to partisan analyses by both right and left, however, both of which found in the play a Marxist attack on the capitalist system. Eleanor Clark, who called Miller a "fellow-traveller" in her *Partisan Review* essay, asserted that he was trying both to "present" and "evade responsibility for" the idea that "the capitalist system . . . has done Willy in; the scene in which he is brutally fired after some forty years with the firm comes straight from the party line literature of the 'thirties, and the idea emerges lucidly enough through all the confused motivations of the play that it is our particular form of money economy that has bred the absurdly false ideal of both father and sons."[76] On the other hand, Harold Clurman, in one of the most overtly Marxist analyses he produced, wrote that *Salesman* was "a challenge to the American dream," or more precisely, "the American dream . . . distorted to the dream of business success."[77] Historically, Clurman said, the ideals of hard work and courage had been replaced in the United States by salesmanship, "the ability to put over or sell a commodity regardless of its intrinsic usefulness." He went on to describe the alienation of the worker under this system in which the salesman was divorced from the production and use of his product.

In 1957, in the Introduction to his *Collected Plays*, Miller asserted that "a play cannot be equated with a political philosophy" (*TE* 150), and he took some pains to argue against the view that "a work of art is the sum of its author's political outlook, real or alleged, and more, that its political implications are valid elements in its aesthetic evaluation" (*TE* 151). But he also made it clear that "Willy Loman has broken a law without whose protection life is insupportable if not incomprehensible to him and to many others; it is the law which says that a failure in society and business has no right to live" (*TE* 149). This law, he wrote, "is by no means a wholly agreeable one even as it is slavishly obeyed, for to fail is no longer to belong to society . . . therefore, the path is opened for those who wish to call Willy merely a foolish man even as they themselves are living in obedience to the same law that killed him" (*TE* 149). While Miller refused to allow his play to be reduced to its political implications, he made those implications clear whenever he had the opportunity.

The question of *Salesman*'s juxtaposition of realism and expressionism in style and of past and present in the narrative was also controversial from the start. Most of the early reviewers did not fully apprehend the play's experimental approach to time. Eric Bentley complained that the play's "chief formal device is the flashback."[78] In a May interview, Thomas Mann said that he had seen *Salesman* and been "very much impressed," but "if there is a fault it is in a kind of stylistic instability. There are times when the play moves on a plane of symbolism and other times when it is exactingly realistic. This I would call stylistic confusion, instability, and is the only criticism I could make of the play."[79] Clearly this sophisticated spectator had not apprehended the production's subjective realism. On the other hand, Eugene O'Neill was quick to see the play's experimental quality: "'Miller's bolder than I've been,' O'Neill said. 'I'm not so sure he hasn't written a great American play.'"[80]

Several critics also perceived that there was more going on in *Salesman* than a series of flashbacks. Richard Watts of the *New York Post* called it a "stream-of-consciousness technique."[81] In an unusually perceptive first-night review, William Hawkins wrote:

> Often plays have been written that crossed beyond physical actuality into the realm of memory and imagination, but it is doubtful if any has so skillfully transcended the limits of real time and space. One cannot term the chronology here a flashback technique, because the transitions are so immediate and logical.[82]

In perhaps the most sophisticated analysis of the play's formal use of time, John Mason Brown wrote: "What we see might just as well be

what Willy Loman thinks, feels, fears, or remembers, as what we see
him doing. This gives the play a double and successful exposure in
time. It makes possible the constant fusion of what has been and
what is. It also enables it to achieve a greater reality by having been
freed from the fetters of realism."[83]

The criticisms of the dialogue and the form, debated by critics of
the play ever since, were the only serious questions about its artistic
quality raised in the wake of *Salesman*'s first production, but there
were a few complaints about the acting. Miller has said that Cobb's
performance became somewhat self-indulgent during the play's run,
so that one "could drive a truck through some of [his] stretched out
pauses," and that Cobb had taken to "re-directing Arthur Kennedy
and Cameron Mitchell and to enjoying rather than suffering the
anguish of the character" (*T* 194). Several of the magazine reviewers, who did not necessarily see the show during its first performances, while Kazan was keeping a tight rein on the actors, complained about what Harold Clurman saw as "grandiosity" and
"histrionic bravura" in Cobb's performance.[84] Krutch called it "as
heavy-footed as the dialogue itself,"[85] and Gilbert Gabriel said he
"wished that Lee Cobb could be more of a schnook and less of a
Caesar."[86] This was partly a result of Elia Kazan's refusal to "police
the show" once it was established on Broadway. Unlike other directors of long-run plays, he did not return to see performances at regular intervals, giving notes to the actors about their performances,
and holding occasional rehearsals to remind the company of the
original concepts and objectives. With a strong-willed actor like
Cobb in the lead, the performance was bound to change without
some directorial supervision.

Lee J. Cobb withdrew from *Salesman* "before he should have," in
Kazan's opinion (*K* 362), pleading exhaustion, which is understand-
able considering the demands of the part, one of the longest in
modern drama, and the intensity of his approach to it. According to
one newspaper report, "Cobb's very intense identification of himself
with the failure of Willy Loman" was considered by "Mr. Cobb's

friends to have contributed to the illness which [was] forcing him to take a prolonged vacation."[87] He was replaced by Gene Lockhart on 6 November 1949. In contrast to Cobb's "big and powerful" Willy, Brooks Atkinson wrote, Lockhart's was "pudgy and crumpled. But he plays with the knowing versatility of an experienced actor and also with an intimacy and sincerity that bring Willy's anguish very close to the hearts of the audience."[88] Lockhart said in an interview that he conceived of Willy as a "little bantam rooster that keeps getting up and hitting the wall again after every knockdown,"[89] the first approach to the character as "little man" that was to be taken by Hume Cronyn, Warren Mitchell, and, perhaps most prominently, Dustin Hoffman.

Former understudy Albert Dekker took over from Lockhart on 4 May 1950 for a four-month summer stint before Thomas Mitchell, who had played Willy for over a year in the touring company, replaced him in September. Atkinson described Mitchell as a "hearty and wholesome actor who is now giving one of his most animated and flexible performances," noting that "Mr. Mitchell breaks up Willie's [sic] tragic ordeal into its component parts more thoroughly than Lee Cobb or Gene Lockhart did. In the course of the evening, Mr. Mitchell analyzes the intellectual structure of Mr. Miller's requiem for the repose of Willie's broken soul."[90] In Atkinson's opinion, Mitchell's more analytical approach to Willy had lightened the production's tone:

> Mr. Mitchell's method comes at the expense of the flowing, tired tragedy of previous performances. Especially in the early scenes. Mr. Mitchell is too hearty, too bluff, too active and decisive. "Death of a Salesman" becomes at times too much like a folksy comedy.[91]

Kazan has commented that "Tommy Mitchell was a bit on the Irish side, and there was a certain slyness in his performance," but thought "he was very effective."[92] In an interview, Mitchell admitted the ethnic basis for his Willy:

"I'm Irish," Mitchell grinned – as though there were any doubt of it. "I don't know whether Miller was writing about a Jewish or an Irish or any other family. (I don't think it's a British family – and neither did London.) Anyhow, Lee Cobb, who created the role, showed us a whole legion of Willys. I play him more individualistically because that happens to suit my style – and because I couldn't have done the other as well as he, even if I tried."[93]

In his review, Atkinson made an unusual direct plea to Kazan:

> What the current performance needs is fresh direction. From Mr. Mitchell down the line, the actors are all right individually, but they have lost contact with the original tragic mood. Without the security of proper direction, they substitute violence and excitement for the spiritual anguish of Willie's private ordeal. The program still describes this performance as "Elia Kazan's Production," adding "Directed by Elia Kazan," a few lines down the page. Well, Mr. Kazan's personal services are presently needed. The finest part of a superb drama is being wasted. Call for the old maestro.[94]

Kazan, whose attention was focused on film projects at that point, still refused to return to *Death of a Salesman*. Kermit Bloomgarden, however, was persuaded to hire another director, Daniel Mann, to come in and work with the actors for a week early in October 1950. Since only four of the original actors remained at this point, three of them in minor roles, the production was now very different from the one that had been performed in February of 1949. *Death of a Salesman* had assumed one of many new lives.

CHAPTER 2

PRODUCTIONS IN ENGLISH

The touring company of *Death of a Salesman*, directed by Harold
Clurman on a set designed by Jo Mielziner, opened in Chicago at
the Erlanger Theater on 20 September 1949, while the New York
production was still going strong. The touring cast included
Thomas Mitchell as Willy, June Walker as Linda, Paul Langton as
Biff, and Darren McGavin as Hap. The traveling company left
Chicago on 18 February 1950 for a tour that included Detroit,
Cleveland, Pittsburgh, Columbus, Cincinnati, Indianapolis, St.
Louis, Kansas City, San Antonio, Denver, Salt Lake City,
Vancouver, Seattle, Tacoma, Portland, San Francisco, Los Angeles,
Pasadena, Long Beach, San Diego, "and just about every city
USA."[1] By February 1950, productions had already been mounted
in Great Britain, Denmark, Sweden, Switzerland, Argentina, Italy,
France, Austria, Greece, Germany, and Israel.[2]

Since its premiere, there has never been a time when *Death of a
Salesman* was not being performed somewhere in the world.
What follows is a brief discussion of some of its most significant
professional productions in English.

LONDON, 1949

Except for the actors, the London production was as close as possible to a duplicate of the Broadway production. The producer,
H. M. Tennents, engaged Elia Kazan as director and Jo Mielziner
and Julia Sze as scene and costume designers. Mielziner's design for
the set repeated the New York design, with some modifications for

the shallower stage at the Phoenix Theatre in London. The production was to hinge on the performance of Paul Muni as Willy. In 1949, Muni was already a veteran stage and film actor, having come to the New York stage as a star of the Yiddish theatre in the 1920s. He had won an Oscar for his film portrayal of Louis Pasteur in 1936, and had a well-earned reputation as an accomplished character actor. At 54, he was seen as an ideal choice to play Willy Loman.

There was some tension between Kazan and Muni from the beginning of the production, however. As was his custom, in preparation for the rehearsals which were to begin early in July 1949, Kazan had written Muni a letter at the beginning of May outlining his interpretation of Willy. Muni responded courteously on 10 May, replying that he thought he understood what Kazan was after for the character, but that he was concentrating on the words themselves. He suggested that, since the characters were so sharply drawn, it would be a mistake to give them any emphasis beyond the inherent values already "shrieking" out from the script.[3] Making it clear from the start that he did not believe in theorizing about acting, he stated his intention of trying to understand the character and projecting that understanding as simply and sincerely as possible. On that premise, he wrote, he was looking forward to a talk with Kazan, which, he hoped, would not be a labored one.[4]

The implicit message of Muni's letter was clear. Having long since established his own system of preparing a part, he was not interested in any complicated Method theorizing about this play. Always adaptable to his actors, Kazan backed off a bit. In an interview at the end of May, he said:

> I don't know what Paul has in mind . . . but it will be his own creation, and as far as I'm concerned, the more he brings to the part the better. He's been thinking about the play for the last three weeks, but I don't expect to find out what he plans to do with the part until we get to London.[5]

As it turned out, Muni's preparation was less than thorough. One reviewer noted that, although Muni played Willy with "great feeling," on opening night, 28 July 1949, "he seemed to be endowing the little man with a hesitating manner which for a time passed muster as a piece of characterization, but in the end came under suspicion of being the artist's cloak for an imperfect acquaintance with his words."[6] The response to Muni's portrayal of Willy was positive for the most part, and Kazan was politely complimentary about his performance. In a 1957 interview, he said, "Paul Muni was very good indeed. There was something of a Chaplinesque quality in his performance. He is a man of unique talent."[7] Arthur Miller was clear about his disappointment in Muni, however. "He didn't do it right," Miller said in a 1970 interview:

> He had come to a time in his career when he was listening to his own voice – he was a very good actor but his style had been superseded twenty years earlier really. The style was too studied, too technical. There was too little real inner life in his performance.[8]

Miller reported in *Salesman in Beijing* that Muni had gone so far as to "record the entire role on a gigantic reel of tape under his wife's tutelage and then imitate himself in a rendition of the 'American Salesman,' with the wooden smile and the 'glad hand.'"[9]

Muni was also plagued with illness throughout the six months of the London run. When he made the decision to leave the show after six months, forcing it to close on 28 January 1950, he gave his ill health as explanation: "I began with a bad throat . . . and the strain of playing this long and exacting part has just worn my health down."[10] Of course Muni was not alone in being worn out by the formidable role of Willy Loman. As we have seen, Lee Cobb also left the show early, to be succeeded by Gene Lockhart, Albert Dekker and Thomas Mitchell before the New York production closed. Even the athletic and comparatively youthful Dustin Hoffman insisted on cutting his performances back from eight shows a week to seven, and finally to six, when he played Willy in 1984.[11]

5. Ralph Theodore, Katherine Alexander, Kevin McCarthy, and
Paul Muni in the first London production, 1949

Despite Muni's problems, the production was a moderate success. After an opening night with fifteen curtain calls from the
traditionally reserved British audience, the reviews had been overwhelmingly positive.[12] The London *Times* called *Salesman* a "mas-

sive and relentless play," "beautifully produced" and "meticulously well acted."[13] As has been the case with actors who followed him, including John Malkovich and Mel Gibson, the part of Biff established Kevin McCarthy, who also played the role in the 1950 film, as a significant actor. The response to the conception and the staging of the play was sophisticated and appreciative. One reviewer, T. C. Worsley, noted that "Mr. Miller in this play has joined the school of American playwrights (Saroyan, Thornton Wilder, Tennessee Williams) who are trying to break out of the constrictions of the naturalistic play form while at the same time retaining the realist contemporary subject . . . an attempt to make a poetic approach to every day life without using poetry."[14] While applauding this "poetry without words," however, Worsley objected to what he saw as the "self-importance" permeating the play's atmosphere, noting that "the little theme is made to take itself much too seriously."[15] The experiments with time and place Worsley put down to the needs of American audiences "who, when they are in the theatre, would much rather be in the cinema."[16]

Disapproval of Willy Loman as an exemplar of the defects of the American way of life pervaded the critics' response, even while they recognized the play's merit. One critic confessed that he "could not help wishing that Mr. Miller had used satire and not sentiment in his approach to a way of life whose standards and atmosphere are really – to those at any rate who are not yet in danger of having to live that way – a matter for laughter rather than for tears."[17] Another took it upon himself to explain the British attitude toward Willy Loman in the *New York Times Magazine*, noting that perhaps the British audience had not responded as emotionally to the play as the American because "we're suspicious of popularity hunters" and "the British are likely to despise Loman for an outlook on life (smiles into diamonds) which other nations regard as quite natural."[18] One of several letter-writers expressed agreement that Britons could not find Willy "worth the tears" because he was "a cad and a mental bounder, apart from his business life."[19] Whatever the critics' views of Willy or his values, however, the critical consensus was voiced by the London *Daily Express*: "This play seems to lay the soul of America bare, throws across the footlights, flat in your face, all the hopes, fears, frustrations, inhibitions and terrible yearnings of a nation."[20]

DUBLIN, 1951

By the time *Death of a Salesman* reached Dublin, Arthur Miller was a target of McCarthyist attacks in the United States for his "Communist sympathies," a fact that was quickly conveyed by the Catholic press to anti-Communist groups in Ireland. The production of *Salesman* presented by Gate Theatre Productions, the Irish National Theatre's experimental theatre, and directed by Hilton Edwards, who also played Willy, was picketed by anti-Communist demonstrators. According to the *Irish Independent*, theatre patrons were handed leaflets by "a number of young men, members of the Catholic Cinema and Theatre Patrons' Association."[21] The newspaper also reported that six gardai (policemen) were posted outside the theatre.

The "leaflet," a single printed sheet, quoted an article in the American Catholic magazine, *The Sign*, stating: "Some shows are hotbeds of left-winged agitation and the focus of comrade acclaim out front. The current *Death of a Salesman* is a good example."[22] It then listed a number of organizations to which Miller was alleged to belong and which were cited as subversive by either the US Attorney General or the California Committee on Un-American Activities. It also quoted J. Edgar Hoover and Pope Pius XI on the dangers of Communism. Stage designer Mordecai Gorelik, who sent one of the circulars to Miller, wrote that they had been distributed by a group known as "Maria Duce," the local equivalent of the Christian Front. According to Gorelik, plainclothesmen were posted inside the theatre expecting trouble, but none emerged, and the play was very well received.[23]

Despite the audience's enthusiastic reception of Miller's play, the political demonstrators had managed to set the tone for its discussion in the Dublin press. One reviewer, who thought the play "a brilliant bit of writing to which Mr. Edwards, as director and actor, and the rest of the large cast did full justice,"[24] felt it necessary to justify his evaluation in ideological terms:

> Variously described as Communist propaganda and as an indictment of capitalism, either description can fit only remotely, and there are contributory factors that acquit it of either charge. The play is rather a scathing criticism of certain facets of the American way of life which have their roots, particularly in big cities, in the worship of money and the pleasures that money can and does buy at the expense of family life and decent living.[25]

Responding even more directly, Gabriel Fallon wrote a lengthy article addressed directly to the demonstrators, accusing them of misquoting the *Sign* article to distort its statement about *Salesman*, and launching his own ideological defense of Miller's play. What Miller presents in Willy, he wrote, is "a human being pursued by the furies of his own making, flaggelated [*sic*] by his sins, and finally succumbing to a planned despair in a last effort to achieve through his ill-taught sons an earthly immortality in place of that immortality which his materialistically conditioned vision fails to see."[26] In the end, he said, the play must "stir our deep pity for the millions of Willy Lomans fooled by 'earthly allurements and insidious error.'"[27]

His ideological defense dispatched, Fallon went on to praise the play's "imaginative realism," to note the "tragic hush – so distinguishable from the hush of mere attentiveness" which had enveloped its audience, and to judge the production "the most memorable I have experienced in the modern theatre."[28] The other critics agreed that the theatrical experience had been a powerful one, although they differed from Fallon about the play's tragic nature. The *Irish Times* called it a "terrifying Twentieth Century morality play"[29] and the *Sunday Press* reviewer complained that it was "harrowing without being tragic."[30] All of the reviewers had praise for both Edwards's direction and his acting, and for Tony Inglis's multi-level set. Gorelik, himself one of the finest designers in the early twentieth-century theatre, thought the setting and lighting excellent.[31]

SOUTH AFRICA, 1951

Death of a Salesman was first produced in South Africa by the Sarah Sylvia company in Cape Town on 20 November 1951. The role of Linda was the first performance in English by Sylvia, a star of the Yiddish theatre. To play Willy, she brought in Jacob Ben-Ami, a distinguished actor in both the Yiddish and the English-language theatres. Ben-Ami and Leon Gluckman, who played Biff, served as producers, and they had their troubles with the two theatres in which the production was mounted, the Labia Theatre in Cape Town and the new Reps Theatre in Johannesburg. The curtain at the Johannesburg opening on 18 January 1952 rose quite late because the complicated lighting system, based on the Mielziner original, had been incorrectly wired, and Ben-Ami was forced to fly in a lighting man with more technical expertise than was available locally.[32]

Despite the technical problems, the production was an overwhelming success in both cities. The *Cape Argus* said that the Cape Town opening night audience's verdict was "a great actor in a great play,"[33] but was quick to give credit to Sylvia, to Gluckman, and to designers Joseph Cappon and Elli Swersky as well as to Ben-Ami for the production's power. The *Cape Times* critic wrote that Ben-Ami's was "one of the greatest performances I have ever seen in the theatre, but it did not blind me to the fine work done by Madam Sylvia as his patient wife."[34] Summing up the praise that had been heaped on play, actors, and production in the four days since the opening, another critic wrote that "no superlative that has been lavished on the Labia Theatre production of *Death of a Salesman* is too extravagant. This is magnificent theatre and one of the most moving plays I have ever seen."[35]

Physically, the production was pretty much a copy of the Broadway and London design. The acting was somewhat broader and more stylized, however. Both Ben-Ami and Sylvia wore rather heavy make-up, and Sylvia's costume, accent, and gestures clearly suggested the Yiddish tradition she came from. The contrast of these two with the rather aggressively "American" look of the actors who played the boys made for an interesting generational subtext in this production. Making Biff and Hap the sons of immigrants emphasized the pressure they were under to succeed in the American system.

For the most part, South African audiences were as enthusiastic as the critics. Thousands were reportedly turned away from the box office in Johannesburg until the run was extended from three to eight weeks. The opening night in Johannesburg had proved something of an embarrassment, however, to critics who admonished their readers for their rude behavior. One critic reported that, "before the late rise of the curtain there were three rounds of ironic applause," and "the entry of hundreds of leisurely moving people after the curtain went up on the second act had to be seen to be believed."[36] Another noted that, "except for the few nincompoops who started walking out as the curtain fell, the house stood up and acclaimed the performance as the curtain rose and fell time after time."[37] Ben-Ami took it all in his stride. He told an interviewer that first-night audiences were bad everywhere, and that, "on most nights of the play's eight-week run in Johannesburg, there was dead silence in the auditorium, and in the atmosphere of rapt concentration he was able to lose his own identity."[38]

AMERICAN PRODUCTIONS, 1951–1975

Wishing to maintain control over any production of his play that might be seen as an official "revival," Arthur Miller did not allow professional productions of *Salesman* within 100 miles of Broadway for twenty-five years, until he authorized a production by the Philadelphia Drama Guild in 1974 that was to be directed by George C. Scott and designed by Jo Mielziner, with Martin Balsam and Teresa Wright as Willy and Linda. At the time, Miller said that he had refused earlier requests because "anything that could be classified as a revival would be reviewed as professional, whether it warranted it or not. I think this group has the capacity to do the play. I wasn't satisfied in the past that this was the case with other groups."[39]

Even with this distinguished group of artists, Miller was hesitant to give up control of the production, reserving final directorial approval over Scott's work to himself. At the beginning, all parties seemed amenable to this arrangement. Martin Balsam tried to dismiss the issue of directorial control in an interview: "All I know . . . was that Miller was here on the first day of rehearsal, shook all of our hands, and said go to work and waved good-bye." Teresa Wright added, "I know he's very interested in the production . . . and I suppose it's only natural for him to stop by and take a look at the final results."[40] Balsam commented that the cast could feel "that George is slowly imposing a certain sense of style on the production and that is very exciting."[41] As was perhaps inevitable with two such strong-willed artists as Miller and Scott sharing directorial control, however, trouble erupted, and Scott ended up leaving, with Miller taking over the direction of the production a week before its opening.[42]

Reviewers traced the production's problems directly to the change of directors. One noted that the actors were "frequently a beat off any sense of effective pacing, and usually a tone away in getting a credible sound to their dialogue," and that Martin Balsam's conception of his role was but "partially built."[43] Another commented that "the physical action – the blocking – is somewhat clumsy at times and the show's pace was uneven on opening night."[44] Interestingly, the Mielziner set, so lavishly praised in 1949, had clearly become dated by 1974. The multi-level set was seen as "overly busy" with "too much to see and too little space in which to move." And the use of lighting to separate past and present, a daring innovation in 1949, was viewed as "an obvious device but a helpful one."[45] The American theatre had changed in twenty-five years, and so had *Death of a Salesman.*

Despite the ban in the New York area before 1974, the play had been produced hundreds of times, by university, community, and professional theatres throughout the country. Cleveland, Indianapolis, San Francisco, Columbus, Rochester, Baton Rouge, Boston, Des Moines, Hollywood, Cambridge, Chicago, Philadelphia, Washington, Baltimore, and Minneapolis are just a few of the cities where local productions were compared with the touring company and found superior by local critics.

A few amateur productions were also mounted in the New York area. In 1954, one community theatre production by the Glen Players of Glenwood Landing, Long Island, achieved notoriety when its star, a national officer in the anti-Communist American Legion walked out on the production one week before it was to go on because the local American Legion post had received "information from various North Shore residents linking the playwright with left-wing groups."[46] The local Legion commander supported his actions, saying, "after all, this play was written by a man who was brought up before the House Un-American Activities Committee, even though he hasn't been proved guilty."[47] After a lengthy meeting, the Glen Players adopted a resolution reaffirming their judgment that the play was "excellent theatre" and contained nothing "un-American or offensive to anyone,"[48] and they decided to go ahead with their production. With Charles H. Gerald, Jr. imported from the Town Theatre in Columbia, South Carolina, to play Willy, the play was produced on 9 December to a standing-room-only audience.[49]

In 1951, a Yiddish version, translated, directed, and starred in by Joseph Buloff in Brooklyn, provoked a debate over the language of the play, with critic George Ross contending that "what one feels most strikingly is that this Yiddish play is really the original, and the Broadway production was merely – Arthur Miller's translation into English."[50] According to Ross, hearing and seeing the play in Yiddish demonstrated clearly its fundamental Jewishness. Charging Miller with trying to "ignore or censor out the Jewish part" of his American–Jewish experience, Ross remarked that Buloff had "caught Miller, as it were, in the act of changing his name, and has turned up the 'original' for us."[51] Even Ross noted, however, that the play's style was alien to the traditional and rather convention-bound Yiddish theatre. He reported that the Brooklyn audience had laughed at "the famous stage set which requires Willy to walk around through a skeleton doorway into his kitchen instead of by short cut through the imaginary wall."[52]

The issues raised by these two productions – the political and ideological implications of the play and its relationship to Jewish–American culture – are significant, and they have been the subject of continuing critical discussion over the years. Even more provocative, however, were the productions by the Guthrie Theater of Minneapolis in 1963 and the Center Stage of Baltimore in 1972. The Guthrie's production, mounted fourteen years after the original, and in repertory with *Hamlet, The Miser,* and *Three Sisters,* inevitably prompted questions about *Death of a Salesman's* status as literature. In his *New York Times* review, Howard Taubman asked directly, "is Arthur Miller's play a classic?"[53] He waffled on the answer, but other critics referred to the play's "exalted position in the American theatre" and to Willy as "a classic figure in American drama."[54] Clearly, *Salesman* was on its way into the canon of American literature, if not modern drama, but critics were still hesitant to confirm its position in the early sixties.

The production itself was an attempt to modernize what had become the already dated "American style" of the late forties and fifties, a style that had been greatly influenced by Jo Mielziner's orig-inal design for *Salesman*. Director Douglas Campbell and designer

Randy Echols stripped away what Miller has called the "layers of gauze" from the Mielziner design, doing away with the backdrop of apartment houses and the elaborate lighting effects that Mielziner had used to create the past, and using simple multi-leveled platforms, skeletonized stairs, and a few items of furniture for the set. This stripped-down set proved controversial, and the judgment of its effectiveness seemed to depend on the individual spectator's approval of the Guthrie's then new open-stage design. Taubman suggested that the production "makes a virtue of the open stage of this new theater."[55] Another critic wrote:

> Though its original staging was for the proscenium stage and had scenery, the play is far more effective on the Guthrie's open stage, with a starkly simple scaffolding construction at the rear and with only lighting to define areas and change scenes. Nothing exists to distract the imagination from the fluid movement of the action in and out of reality, recollection and hallucinatory dreams.[56]

Henry Hewes suggested in the *Saturday Review*, however, that the staging had not solved the problem of representing "the constant surrounding pressure from [the house's] big-city environs"[57] and another called the production "a daring disappointment," complaining that "the limitations of his stage and his apparent desire to strip this American tragedy to the bone have led Campbell to mount the play in a stark, expressionistic manner that demands of its audience an imagination not all will feel compelled to summon."[58] Hume Cronyn, who played Willy, was ambivalent about the production. He wrote to Miller that, although he admired Douglas Campbell's courage in reconceiving the play as he did, he thought that it did not entirely work, and it might have been better to follow the original stage directions.[59]

The critics were similarly split over another issue brought about by the physical requirements of the production, that of Willy's size. Played by Hume Cronyn, Willy Loman was necessarily a "little man," and his characterization took the opposite direction from that of the hulking Lee J. Cobb. Cronyn's interpretation was based on the role as Miller had originally conceived it, with Willy as a "shrimp" rather than a "walrus." Most critics were able to accept this conception of the role. As one noted, "there are excellent reasons why Miller's hero, archetype of the 'little man,' should be played by an actor who is physically small."[60]

Nevertheless, there were those for whom Willy Loman was identical with Lee J. Cobb. Hewes suggested that, because Cronyn's "physical size is markedly less than that of the role's creator, Lee J. Cobb . . . the temptation to regard the play as a tragedy is eliminated." Cronyn's Willy, he suggested, "emerges as a neurotic little man who never was much good as a salesman, and whose suicide at the end is simply one more self-deluded act." In Hewes's view, the play's stature itself "owes a great deal to the playwright's decision to revise his original concept"[61] of the character to fit Cobb's interpretation. Seldom has the function of the actor's body as a signifier of the character's status been quite so clearly stated, but it has been a perennial factor in productions of *Salesman*. The "little man" interpretation has been dictated by the stature of actors such as Warren Mitchell and Dustin Hoffman as well as Cronyn, and big actors like Fredric March and George C. Scott have reached for a massive stature as Lee J. Cobb did.

The Center Stage production in 1972 brought to the fore the issue of race and ethnicity in casting the play. Although it was the first professional production cast with African–Americans, it was not the first to raise the color issue. As early as 1960, Miller had turned down a request from Terry Carter to do a "Negro version" of *Salesman* Off-Broadway. Although Carter assured Miller that care would be taken to avoid interracial casting that might "distort" the play – the entire Loman family, as well as The Woman, Miss Forsythe, and Letta were to be played by black actors – the request was refused, presumably because of Miller's ban on professional productions in New York.[62] According to Miller, however, he approved a production in New York

6. Hume Cronyn, Jessica Tandy, and Ken Ruta in the Guthrie Theater production, 1963

during the sixties that would have featured African–American Frederick O'Neal as Willy, although the production never materialized.[63] O'Neal had played Willy in a 1962 production directed by Esther Merle Jackson at Clark College in Atlanta with an all-black cast.

The Center Stage production featured Richard Ward, who had been a hit in *Ceremonies of Dark Old Men* at the theatre in the previous year. Miller attended the opening night of the all-black production, and contributed a note to the program, saying:

> I have felt for many years that particularly with this play, which has been so well received in so many countries and cultures, the black actor would have an opportunity, if indeed that is needed anymore, to demonstrate to all his common humanity and his talent.[64]

The production was not particularly successful, chiefly because some inexperienced actors were cast in the minor roles. In several interviews, Ward made it clear that he had wanted to do the play with an integrated cast, particularly with Charley played by a white man, showing that "a white man and a black man can live next door to each other and care for each other . . . their children can grow up together and love each other."[65] Miller also was quoted as saying he would like to see the play done with an integrated cast, "just because it would allow a greater selection of players."[66] The producers reported that they had thought about an integrated cast, but decided that it "might be an attempt to make a statement that's not in the play." They had wanted to make Charley white, "but some black leaders in Baltimore pointed out that the neighbor ends up successf[ul], and that a 'be white, be a success' message might come across."[67]

Not surprisingly, the production was analyzed almost exclusively in terms of the race issue. Mel Gussow asserted in the *New York Times* that "Black time has caught up to *Salesman*," and contended that "what makes this more than just an intriguing experiment, but an exciting concept, is not only what it tells us about *Death of a Salesman*, but what it tells us about the black experience."[68] In Gussow's view,

"Willy Loman's values are white values – the elevation of personality, congeniality, conformity, salesmanship in the sense of selling oneself," so that in the context of an all-black production, "Willy becomes a black man embracing the white world as an example to be emulated."[69] Hollie West of the *Washington Post* found the concept less revealing. Putting black actors "in roles written for whites," she contended, required the actors to "shed the badge of their color. Without the nuances of black dialogue and a consciousness reflecting the unique customs and traditions of black life, such actors may ask the question: Am I playing a white black man?"[70] West did not think the production succeeded in transferring the circumstances of the lower-middle-class white family in New York during the 1930s and 1940s to "the black circumstances of the same period."[71] Although she found Ward's performance as Willy entirely convincing, she found historical and social reality impinging on the dramatic illusion of the other characters: "Have black women been willing to play secondary roles when their husbands were failing, as in the case of Mrs. Loman?" she asked. "Would Biff have been considered an outcast among thousands of similar black men a generation ago?"[72]

Despite his support for Richard Ward's desire for interracial casting in the Baltimore production, Miller made it clear three years later that he found the question of race in casting an extremely complex one. A year after taking over the direction of the Philadelphia Drama Guild production from Scott, Miller approved an Off-Broadway revival of *Salesman* at the Circle in the Square Theatre that Scott was to direct, with himself in the title role. When he learned that Scott was planning to cast a black actor as Charley, Miller wrote him a four-page single-spaced letter, warning him to consider carefully what the implications of this casting would be. So-called "color-blind" casting, he believed, only worked when it was entirely color-blind, with Biff black and Happy white, for example. This, however, took the play out of the realm of realism, and made its relation to the social reality it depicted purely metaphorical, a conception which needed to be thoroughly thought through.[73]

as director, must bear the blame for the essentially mediocre production":

> A star who doubles as director is like a concerto soloist who also conducts the orchestra. He is too busy with his own job to be more than perfunctory with the others and cannot stand outside the performance and be objective. Even the scenes that do not involve Scott seem directed by the actors themselves.[80]

Douglas Watt articulated the consensus when he wrote that, "while Scott has a keen concept of Willy, and of the play as a whole, he should probably never have tried to stage it himself . . . you have the feeling that the others were largely left to shift for themselves."[81]

While James Farentino earned some praise for his role as Biff, and at least one critic thought Teresa Wright "superb" as Linda,[82] most found the supporting actors somewhat aimless and wooden. Miller, who had contributed an extensive set of notes after viewing a rehearsal three weeks before the play opened, was particularly concerned about Harvey Keitel's portrayal of Happy, so much so that he thought Farentino's performance was hindered by his having nothing to play against in his scenes with Keitel.[83]

There was no doubt, however, about the magnitude of Scott's performance. The normally reserved Clive Barnes wrote in the *New York Times* that it was "a performance to bate your breath . . . that kind of a performance – exciting beyond words, and almost literally leaving criticism speechless."[84] Christopher Sharp suggested that "the difference between Lee J. Cobb's Loman and Scott's version is the distinction between the general and the particular":

> Scott's gnome-like Loman is such a distinct individual that there is no mistaking him for a universal failure . . . Scott's Loman is an animal to be gazed at through bars; it is possible to sympathize with the creature, but it is all but impossible to empathize with him. This Loman touches us not because he is like what we are, but because he is so unlike what we are.[85]

Speaking of Scott's Loman as "a harsh, not very lovable man," Martin Gottfried suggested that "this coldness makes sympathy difficult, but it provides a bigger payoff at the end. It is easy to pity a likable man. It is overwhelming to learn, too late, of the soul beneath a cold man's exterior and to watch him being crushed unawares."[86]

The horseshoe-shaped Circle in the Square Theatre proved a less than ideal performance space for *Salesman*, at least as it was conceived by Scott. One critic noted that "movement on the long oblong stage . . . requires something like traffic control to keep the actors from drifting out of rapport with the audience."[87] Another put the case succinctly: "Scott's use of this theater's peculiar, oblong, arena was doomed from the start. The play was born to a proscenium stage."[88] Rather than making use of the abstraction that had been the Guthrie's approach to the open-stage performance space, Marjorie Kellog's design placed a solid construction representing the house at one end of the stage, even including some exterior walls. Although most of the house was open platform, it was fully and realistically furnished.

At least one critic thought the realism went too far for the production, complaining of its "unsparing drabness" and calling it "heavy-handed naturalism in which the literal predominates over illusion."[89] Another complained of the lack of a suggestion of apartment houses hemming the house in.[90] The problem was that the oblong shape of the stage made "the action seem as if it's occurring in the neck of a giraffe," as one critic put it.[91] The sightlines of the oblong theatre also dictated the placement of the actors, to some deleterious effects. Harold Clurman, who had directed the original road company, noted that the effect of the Requiem scene was undermined by the fact that the sightlines made it impossible for the actors to stand in a line together over Willy's grave. "The characters are, therefore, dispersed on the stage in a manner which makes the funeral ceremony casual and haphazard rather than solemn, as it should be."[92]

In general, although Scott's performance was extraordinary and his interpretation of Willy Loman unique, the production itself was

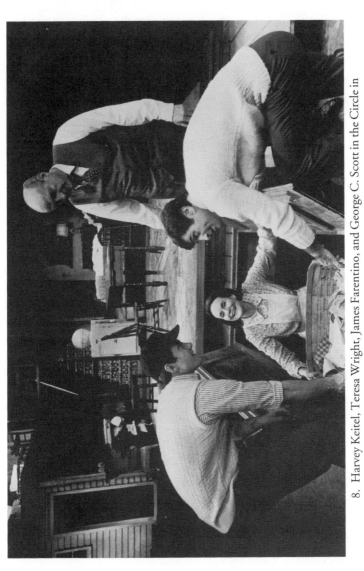

8. Harvey Keitel, Teresa Wright, James Farentino, and George C. Scott in the Circle in the Square production, 1975

not a success. The physical space of the theatre required a radical reconception of the play, visually and kinesically, which Scott did not provide, and the actors required more attention than he was able to give them. It was clear, however, that the play had reached the status of unqualified eminence that reviewers had not been ready to accord it in 1963. One critic called it "THE great American tragedy."[93] Another said it was "one of the greatest plays ever written by an American; a major tragedy; a classic."[94]

LONDON, 1979 AND SYDNEY, 1982

Death of a Salesman was produced by the Cambridge University Amateur Dramatic Club in 1965 and by Bolton's Octagon Theatre in 1970. But when London's National Theatre opened its revival at the Lyttelton on 20 September 1979, after previews in Leeds and Norwich, the occasion was clearly seen as the rediscovery of both the play and Arthur Miller for the British stage. The late seventies was a period when the British theatre was taking a fresh look at American drama generally, and when *Salesman* appeared at the Lyttelton, Kaufman and Hart's *Once in a Lifetime*, Odets's *Winter Journey*, and Williams's *Cat on a Hot Tin Roof* were all being revived in the London area. Two weeks before *Salesman* opened in London, Michael Billington took the occasion to write an article suggesting that "there has for a long time been a British resistance to non-musical American theatre and that, particularly in our present rather jittery state, there are things in American drama we might look at with an envious respect."[95]

The opening itself proved a tremendous event in the history of the play, and of Miller's reputation. One critic wrote that "no play written in English since the war has the emotional impact of Arthur Miller's *Death of a Salesman*."[96] Another wrote that the "superbly acted and directed revival at the National confirms *Death of a Salesman* as one of the greatest plays in the English language since the war – indeed I can't think of a greater one – and puts Miller in contention with O'Neill as the greatest of American playwrights."[97] A third wrote simply that *Salesman* is "one of the great plays of our time."[98] Arthur Miller was judged "incontestably the finest postwar American playwright."[99] Summing up the revival's impact, one critic wrote, "it is a triumph for Miller, America's post-war Ibsen, who is resurrected as a playwright of enduring relevance. We have missed him and his kind of drama."[100] Not since *Salesman's* extraordinary first-night reviews in 1949 had the play or Miller received such universal and such enthusiastic praise.

The occasion provided a similar rediscovery for Warren Mitchell, who had become completely identified with the part of the obstreperous bigot Alf Garnett in the long-running television series, *Till Death Do Us Part*, the role that *All in the Family's* Archie Bunker was modeled on. As one critic noted, "it's a quaint business for an actor to be totally identified with the worst part he ever played, and quite possibly the worst performance he ever gave, but that is clearly the fate of Warren Mitchell, of whom it seems to have been forgotten that, long before 'Alf Garnett', he was the best character actor in the land."[101] Another marveled, "It's amazing that a man who has for the past dozen years gained considerable success from a comic role that verged on caricature should have attempted the part [of Willy Loman]. That he should turn it into a triumph is near fantasy. But in Warren Mitchell's hands a triumph is what it is."[102]

Like Hume Cronyn before him and Dustin Hoffman after him, Warren Mitchell had no choice but to play Willy as a "little man." In London for early September rehearsals, Miller had obligingly prepared the London audience for this interpretation with some well-placed interviews. He told one reporter:

> I'd never seen or heard of him before but when I walked into a room where all the actors were, I knew he was Willy. The main character is a bantam cock, full of juice with a lot of fight in him. What moves you about Willy is his intrepid, crazy kind of faithfulness towards those bad things he believes in. Warren Mitchell has got that.[103]

He told another reporter that, "meeting Warren Mitchell, who is not tall, he thought: 'Good God, they've finally found Willy. It took thirty years and another country!'"[104] Ten years later, after witnessing both the London and the Broadway revivals, Miller said:

> There have been three chief players, as far as I am concerned.
> One was Warren Mitchell, who played it marvelously in London.
> I didn't know Warren and I just saw him in the play and we chatted
> for a while but his Willy and Dustin Hoffman's are related. They are
> both small men, feisty fellows. They've got a large world that's
> trying to kill them and a small man reacts with a kind of nervosity.
> That's in the part. It is obvious that Willy is leaping from one
> contradictory attitude to another very rapidly, sometimes with
> hardly a line in between, and to me that also was the characteristic
> of a little man, a physically small man. And I wrote it for a small
> man, if I wrote it for anybody.[105]

Warren Mitchell had just finished playing Willy in Perth when Michael Rudman, a transplanted Texan who had become affiliated with the National Theatre, was casting the Lyttelton's *Salesman*. According to Mitchell, they were playing tennis when each found out about the other's involvement in the play. Mitchell did a scene for Rudman after the match was over. And, although "there was much debate at the National"[106] about casting a TV comedy actor in such a role, Mitchell was given the part. Minimalist director Rudman and Method actor Mitchell worked well together, Mitchell noting modestly that "learning the lines was my main problem and really it is the only problem if you are me playing Willy Loman. I knew the man. My Dad was a commercial traveller. I am a father and have dreams for my children. I really can't schepp any nachas (see Arthur Miller for translation)."[107] Interestingly, according to Mitchell, Rudman considered putting him in the role "casting it Jewish."[108] Although Miller has never accepted the idea that Willy is a "Jewish role," quite rightly pointing out that the play has been interpreted successfully all over the world

and in all kinds of ethnic contexts, his three favorite Willys – Lee
J. Cobb, Warren Mitchell, and Dustin Hoffman – have all been
Jewish.

Mitchell's approach to the character differed from Cobb's in
more than physical terms. His whole interpretation of the trajectory of the action was different. As one perceptive reviewer
described it:

> Warren Mitchell's Willy Loman is a bespectacled, gray, weary
> little man. Mitchell does not present the salesman in strength
> at first, and then strip him to his frailties, as American actors have
> tended to do. From the moment he enters, limping and searching
> for his door key, we know he's already dead. His attacks on his
> family, his bravado, his jokes, his last hopes are only camouflage.
> He is an old bantam rooster scratching frantically for the last
> grain of life.
>
> As a result, when his anger finally flares fully, in the scene in
> which his long-time employer casually fires him, Mitchell shows
> us not only the failure Willy is, but the success he could have
> been had he not needed so desperately to be "well-liked."[109]

Mitchell explored elements in Willy's character that had been left
out of the exhausted rage in Cobb's and Scott's portrayals. One critic
noted "a jauntiness about his movements."[110] Another said Willy
was "a very funny man" in Mitchell's interpretation.[111] Rather than
the tragic portrayal of the American productions, one critic suggested, this one showed that "America and its ruthless success ethic
have produced in [Willy] a not very nice guy whom the secret of
success has eluded. Mitchell has you identifying with Willy as with a
cornered rat."[112]

Although the rediscovery of the play and of Warren Mitchell's
acting ability tended to overshadow the rest of the production, it
clearly owed its success to Rudman's unobtrusive but forceful direction of a very talented ensemble cast. One critic summarized the
whole effect:

> Rudman's is a company production in which Mitchell takes his
> place alongside Doreen Mantle as the wife, David Baxt and Stephen
> Greif as the sons and Harry Towb as the long-suffering Charley.
> There is no blazing star turn here, rather a successful bid to keep
> Willy in his home and office environment until at the last his
> relatives and neighbors are left staring into whatever crater is
> reserved for burnt-out cases.[113]

Often singled out for praise were Harry Towb, and Doreen Mantle, who gave what one critic called "one of the great performances of the generation,"[114] and another "a performance of enormous beauty and depth, a study in pale radiance and fragile gallantry, of acting of infallible balance and perception."[115]

In designing the set for Rudman's production, John Gunter used the Lyttelton's proscenium stage to create a set that was reminiscent of Mielziner's original design, but less self-consciously "poetic." The house had three platforms: the parents' bedroom at stage right was highest, the boys' bedroom at stage left, a few feet lower, and the kitchen raised about a foot off the stage level at the center. Minimal props were used, capturing the abstract realism of the Mielziner original. The house was surrounded by threatening apartment walls, with "perilous fire-escapes, threads of rust and black, against grimy red-brick,"[116] representing the threatening urban landscape in more solid detail than earlier productions had done.

The rest of the set, however, was more abstract and more expressionistic than the original. The rear wall was a backdrop showing the blank wall of an apartment building with large, blank, rectangular windows, and the sightlines were open at the top to reveal two large steel girders above the backdrop. The shape of the house was indicated only by a very abstracted roof-line, showing a windowframe above the boys' bedroom. The frame of a kitchen door was set at an angle to the right of the kitchen platform, but there was no surrounding wall. The house was set on a "raft" which was moved downstage when in use. The house was moved upstage when not in use, and sets for the other scenes were moved in on trucks. With the time changes managed by replacing the tenement walls with backdrops showing open country, and for the Requiem scene, a cemetery, the set provided a fluid if rather heavily expressionistic environment for the play's action.

When Warren Mitchell repeated his role as Willy in 1982 under George Ogilvie's direction for the Nimrod Theatre of Sydney, Australia, he did it as a visiting star. Suffering like other theatre companies from the cut-backs in Australian funding for the arts during the early eighties, the Nimrod unabashedly presented *Death of a Salesman* as a "curriculum play." *Salesman* was a set text for High School Certificate students in 1982. Mounting a production with Mitchell, who was known not only as a significant Willy Loman, but as Alf Garnett, and with Mel Gibson, fresh from his movie triumphs in *Gallipoli* and *Mad Max*, was a sure money-maker. The stars demanded and got enormous salaries for a Sydney production – a reported 5,000 Australian dollars a week for Mitchell and $2,000 a week for Gibson.[117] But the gamble apparently paid off. As one critic put it, "students are attending by the bus load."[118]

Salesman had been produced in Sydney twice before, in 1953, and in 1970 by the Old Tote Theatre Company. In 1982 the play was considered more relevant to Australian life than at either of the earlier times, "with ghosts, long thought exorcised, again stalking the land, unemployment, recessions, and the rest, and with insecurity eroding all the inherited assumptions of materialism."[119] Mitchell's acting of Willy was universally acclaimed. Gibson's performance as Biff received mixed reviews. One critic described his performance admiringly as "a long, most delicately judged crescendo. Its climax concentrates the play's power in one explosion."[120] Others noted, however, that Gibson did not appear "entirely comfortable in the role,"[121] that he was "too loveable, too bewildered, too puppy-like and too romantic,"[122] and that "there is much more to the troubled Biff than Gibson is able to capture and convey."[123] With the exception of Judi Farr as Linda, the supporting cast was not considered to be up to Mitchell's level, which naturally made for an uneven production.

Another problem the production team faced was the thrust stage of the York Theatre in the Seymour Centre, where the production was mounted. Facing many of the same problems as those who had staged the play in the round, director George Ogilvie and designer Kristian Fredrikson had difficulty in dealing with the time changes and the fluid action.[124] At least one critic, however, found that "Fredrikson's tall, architectural design serves at once as an imposing backing to the action . . . and as a reminder of the play's nature and its theme."[125] And despite its flaws, the production was clearly "Sydney's theatrical event of the year."[126]

BROADWAY, 1984

The history of the 1984 New York production of *Death of a Salesman* reveals a major change that had taken place in the American theatre between 1949 and 1984. The original production of *Salesman* was in one sense the endpoint of Elia Kazan's battle as director to achieve creative hegemony over his theatrical productions. Although his method of working was collaborative, he clearly called the shots in the end. As he has written, Kazan believed that the director "should be the overlord of a production. I and those like me were the 'Young Turks' who took over the theatre of the forties and fifties."[127] The first half of the twentieth century became the "age of the director," precisely because directors like Kazan had seized creative control of the production away from the producer. The only effective way for an actor like George C. Scott to gain artistic control of a production during this period was to direct it as well as act in it. And unless a playwright took extraordinary steps, as Miller had in insisting on final directorial say in the Philadelphia Drama Guild production, a play very quickly moved from being the playwright's to the director's in production.

The 1984 production of *Salesman,* however, was definitely controlled by playwright Miller and actor Hoffman. The idea had begun with casual post-tennis discussions in Connecticut, where they lived near one another, and had developed quickly. Flush from the financial and critical success of the movie *Tootsie,* and in control of his own company, Punch Productions, Hoffman was in a good position to create the production that he wanted. His admiration for Miller and the play went all the way back to his adolescence, when his brother had given him the play to read:

> Something happened to me when I read that play that had never happened to me before. It had nothing to do with acting, it had to do with my family, and I simply could not talk about that to anyone. I would just go off into corners and start weeping. The play is still an emotional experience for me. In a sense I can't talk about the play without mourning Willy Loman.[128]

In 1990, Hoffman wrote that Miller "is what I look up to as an artist. He's my artistic father."[129] Both Hoffman and Miller have often told the story of their first encounter in 1964, when the young Hoffman was assistant director to Ulu Grossbard for an Off-Broadway revival of *A View from the Bridge.* Grossbard told Miller that one day Hoffman should play Willy Loman. Miller says he thought to himself, "Well, it looks like I'll just have to wait a few years to see about that."[130] Shortly afterward, Hoffman played Bernard for the Caedmon recording of *Salesman* that Grossbard directed, sitting next to Lee J. Cobb as often as he could, "as if trying to memorize his art,"[131] during rehearsals.

When it was time for him to play Willy, Hoffman's apprenticeship was clearly over. Together with Miller's long-time associate, producer Robert Whitehead, Hoffman and Miller set up a production deal with CBS, in which, according to Whitehead, CBS agreed to put up $600,000 of the needed $850,000 investment in exchange for the rights to the television version of the play which was to be taped after the Broadway production. Miller, Hoffman, and Whitehead put up the remaining $250,000.[132] Under this arrangement, Miller and Hoffman each received 45 percent of the weekly profits of the Broadway production and Whitehead 10 percent.[133] Creative control was shared by Hoffman and Miller, who hired Michael Rudman to direct, and proceeded to do four months of auditions, in which they heard at least 500 actors, before settling on Kate Reid as Linda, Stephen Lang as Hap, David Huddleston as Charley, and John Malkovich, who had played Biff in the 1980 Steppenwolf production in Chicago, to repeat his role, even though they had to wait several months until he had finished with film commitments. The stage was set to repeat the 1979 London triumph on Broadway.

Miller predicted in an interview that "Dustin will create a new Willy. It ain't going to be the other one. It'll be his Willy."[134] The "other one" was of course Lee J. Cobb's Willy, a phantom that Hoffman had to exorcise before he could create his own interpretation. After listening over and over again to Miller's own spoken introduction to the Grossbard recording in order to catch his New York rhythms, Hoffman finally left the record on and listened to Cobb's performance:

> "I hadn't listened to it since we cut the record," Hoffman said.
> "It recalled to me all the times I had hung around rehearsal and watched him. His Willy was like Rodin, and it depressed me." Gradually, he realized, "I don't have his kind of power, his guns – and that was a liberating thing. I was going toward the opposite. Instead of this 'walrus,' I was going to be a spitfire."[135]

Hoffman's conception of the role became the key to the production. The "small man" interpretation familiar to Rudman from his work with Warren Mitchell would be set against New York's memory of Cobb's monumental Willy. As he had in London, Miller was careful to mention in the preproduction publicity interviews that his original conception of the character was being restored in the production, "walrus" turned back to "shrimp." "I had always seen him as a small man with a bantam-like quality married to a larger woman and with these two big sons,"[136] he said. And indeed this is the way Willy is described in the early drafts of the script. As Mitchell had done, Hoffman was to realize on stage the image that had been displaced for most Americans by Lee J. Cobb and George C. Scott.

Hoffman's creation of Willy's physical aspect was meticulous. He shaved his head so he could wear a thinning grey hairpiece. Rather than create the sense of age with flabbiness, he lost weight: "I want to be just skin and bones," he said, "Willy has been trying to kill himself for six months. The play is the last 24 hours in his life. Willy can't sleep, can't eat. He's wired."[137] He experimented with age spots and the proper facial make-up until he was satisfied, although the make-up's rubber-and-glue base expanded during a show "like bubble gum," and had to be patched up at regular intervals.[138] He created a gravelly "old man's" voice for the part, and made his body into the aging spitfire that he wanted Willy to be.

The production opened in Chicago on 19 January 1984, moving on to the Kennedy Center in Washington, DC, at the end of February. Although the Chicago critics saw the production's promise, they thought it still had a long way to go. One critic noted that both Hoffman and Reid fluffed their lines on opening night, that the Alex North music was played too loud, and that the production worked "only in powerful fits and starts."[139] By the time the production opened in Washington, it was clear that Hoffman had control of his performance. David Richards wrote in the *Washington Post*:

> This is not the huge, lumbering salesman that tradition (and residual memories of Lee J. Cobb) might lead you to expect. Hoffman plays Willy as a sharp, birdlike creature with flapping arms and a piercing voice. He is the quintessential little guy, straining to look bigger than he is, trying for that extra cubit of stature by tilting

his chin up and rocking back and forth on his heels. But his suit
invariably appears too big for him, and when the light catches the
lenses of his wire-rimmed glasses, he looks momentarily dazed. He
is not without his comic aspects.[140]

Hoffman, he wrote, "projects the feistiness of the mutt, the arrogant
bluff of the adolescent who yearns to pal with the big guys on
the block . . . Hoffman possesses a spindly urgency. He doesn't
run down . . . he revs up – his delivery becoming increasingly
staccato, his gestures slicing the air with growing frenzy."[141] When
the production opened on Broadway, the London *Times*
critic noted that Hoffman had "done an Olivier, truly transforming
his voice and body. As if coming from a pit strewn with stones,
the voice retains an actor's strength and range while expressing
a prematurely old man's rage and exhaustion. Looking like
any suit would be too large, Mr. Hoffman resembles a clothed
skeleton."[142]

While the critical consensus was overwhelmingly that Hoffman
had come up with a brilliant reconception of Willy Loman and exe-
cuted it flawlessly, there were a few dissenters. One critic thought
that "watching Hoffman's Willy is watching a blazing struggle:
some will see it as giving a unique force to his portrayal of the most
deeply divided character in American drama."[143] Although there
was the usual sniping from critics like Robert Brustein and John
Simon, the only bad review the production received in New York
was from Howard Kissel of *Women's Wear Daily*, who complained
that "Dustin Hoffman's Willy is a collection of mannerisms – a
grumpy, perpetually hoarse voice, a self-conscious Brooklyn accent,
a wanly ingratiating smile and physical movements that often suggest a maladroit child trying to amuse his elders."[144] He suggested
that "one admires Hoffman's ingenuity and energy, but one wonders
if the performance would be more touching if it were
less effortful."[145]

Michael Rudman's role as director was downplayed throughout

9. Kate Reid, Dustin Hoffman, John Malkovich, and
Stephen Lang in the 1984 New York production

the production. Although he occasionally participated in preproduction publicity interviews, it was Hoffman and Miller who dominated them, while Rudman stayed in the background, allowing
the production to be perceived as "Dustin Hoffman's *Death of
a Salesman.*" Rudman's direction was unobtrusive and, under
Miller's watchful eye, true to the play as written. Brustein called it
"respectful" and "deliberate."[146] John Simon thought it ranged
"from uninventive to pedestrian."[147] Nonetheless, perceptive
spectators noted the importance of Rudman's direction in building
a coherent production around Hoffman's Willy. Richard Schickel
wrote that Rudman's "fluid, driving production is not just a revival
and a restaging, nor even a reinterpretation of the play, but a virtual
reinvention of it."[148] Lloyd Rose suggested that Rudman had created a production "that is modern in the best sense: text-oriented,
focused on the psychology of relationships rather than of individual

characters, commenting not on the original production but on what that production foreshadowed, what we understand it to mean when we look back."[149]

The set design, by veteran Broadway designer Ben Edwards, paid homage to the original by Jo Mielziner, a fact that was not lost on older critics who had seen the original 1949 production. Brendan Gill found the set "agreeably reminiscent" of Mielziner's, and Clive Barnes thought it added its own "tenement dignity" to the original design.[150] Although it lacked the backdrop of apartment houses, the design maintained the basic three-level set of the house. Edwards employed the same abstract realism Mielziner had used with props. A revolving wall was used for set changes, replacing the kitchen's refrigerator with a water cooler for the office and a jukebox for the restaurant, achieving the same fluidity as the original with a less minimal approach to the sets.

While Hoffman's performance was the clear focus of attention, this production made John Malkovich a star. Nearly every review singled him out as "the revelation" in the production, marveling at the range he was able to achieve in the part of Biff, from a tentative, soft-spoken delicacy in the opening scenes to an explosion of sheer fury in the final confrontation between Biff and Willy. While over-shadowed by Malkovich, Stephen Lang was praised for his subtle, insightful performance, as was Reid for her "ferocity and warmth."[151] Reid was the only cast member who also received negative reviews. One critic suggested that she missed "the internal nuances in the tough role of Willy's wife."[152] Another said hers was "an adequate performance from an actress capable of being admirable."[153]

The production was a tremendous hit, reportedly earning Hoffman and Miller $63,000 each per week after its initial investment was recouped.[154] As it had on previous actors, the role of Willy Loman took its toll on Hoffman. At the end of April, he requested that he be relieved of the Saturday matinee performance.[155] The theatre owner objected, because of the revenue that would be lost, and a fight ensued, which ended in Robert Whitehead's resignation.[156] The production continued until 30 June, took a summer hiatus, and then reopened for another engagement from 14 September to 21 October, this time with only six performances per week. To cover the lost revenue, ticket prices were raised from a top of $37.50 on weekend nights to $42.50 for all performances.[157] Hoffman and Miller maintained their control of the production, and their income from it. In the basic terms of money and power as well as the more important ones of artistic conception and control, actor and playwright had succeeded in eclipsing producer and director.

CHAPTER 3

PRODUCTIONS IN
OTHER LANGUAGES

Death of a Salesman has been produced on six continents, in every country that has a Western theatrical tradition, and in some that have not. It has been played in Yiddish in Argentina and in English by actors from the Yiddish theatre in South Africa. It has been played before a native audience in a small Arctic village, with the same villagers returning night after night to witness the performance in a language they did not understand. There is no need at this point to demonstrate *Salesman's* universality, but the range of its appeal and the rapidity with which it has been established as one of the significant works in the world's theatrical repertoire makes a fascinating story.

At the end of 1949, a report was prepared for *Salesman's* New York producers, listing the foreign productions that had been authorized so far. It included a production to be produced and directed by Peter Brook in Paris, which unfortunately never materialized; productions in Berlin, Munich, Vienna, and Zurich, all to open within a few days of each other in the spring of 1950; productions in Greece, Israel, and Italy; both Spanish and Yiddish productions in Argentina; and in Scandinavia, five productions in Sweden as well as productions in Oslo and Copenhagen.[1] Important productions were soon mounted in Belgium, France, and the Netherlands. From this first European base, the play moved into Eastern Europe and Asia, with major productions eventually being mounted in Leningrad, Moscow, Beijing (Peking), and Tokyo. Each of these productions had its problems related to culture and language, but very seldom did the play fail to move its audience, given adequate actors and a decent production. A few examples will have to represent the universality and the differences in *Death of a Salesman* that have been revealed as it has been produced throughout the world.

The first European production of *Salesman* other than Kazan's London production opened in Vienna at the Theater in der Josephstadt on 4 April 1950. It was directed by Rudolph Steinboeck and designed by Otto Niedermoser, with Anton Edthofer as Willy, Adrienne Gessner as Linda, and Kurt Heintel and Hans Holt as Biff and Hap. Its highly praised translation by Ferdinand Bruckner quickly became the standard German version of the play. Describing what was to become the universal indicator of a successful production of *Salesman*, Paul Barnett wrote that "the first-night audience – many had tears in their eyes – sat for a long moment in awed silence, and then acclaimed the play in swelling applause that did not cease until the actors had appeared and reappeared on the stage for twenty-two curtain calls."[2] The *New York Times* correspondent could not disguise his pleasure as he wrote, "seldom has an American play been received in Vienna with more universal critical acclaim than the German version of Arthur Miller's 'Death of a Salesman.'"[3]

The production raised the three perennial issues that permeate discussions of the play almost everywhere it is produced: the question of its tragic nature, the question of Willy's significance as a hero, and the question of the play's cultural relevance to countries that do not fetishize business success in the way America does. Barnett noted that the success of the play "was not a foregone conclusion" in Vienna because of its "Americanisms":

> The Willy Loman type, the "go-getter" that measures success in
> terms of dollars, is not common in Austria. In fact, the average
> Austrian usually speaks with condescension, if not contempt, about

"the American business man." Thus there was the danger that Willy Loman would be a curiosity from America rather than a deeply moving figure.

Bruckner deleted some of the most obvious Americanisms – "he's liked, but he's not well-liked" – from the translation and Biff's identity as a sports hero was played down in the production. Willy's final advice to Biff about the Ebbets Field game as he goes off to kill himself was cut, and probably wisely so. As Barnett put it, "a good football player in Austria is looked upon as a good football player, not as a potential 'leader of men.'"

The most significant change, however, was in the conception of Willy himself. Although the notion of the traveling salesman meant little to an Austrian audience, Austrians had an immediate recognition of the "little man," the "Beamte," or petty bureaucrat who was the central character in a strong tradition of German expressionist plays by dramatists such as Georg Kaiser, Ernst Toller, and Walter Hasenklever. Anton Edthofer's Willy was very much in this tradition. In contrast to Lee J. Cobb or Paul Muni, he "gave Willy more quiet dignity and intelligence and played on a lower, more subdued level than is actually allowed by the text."[4] What he lost in energy, particularly in portraying the more youthful Willy, he seems to have gained in identification with the audience: "The Viennese were soon able to believe that their own circumstances were being treated there among the skyscrapers. The fate of the Everyman from across the ocean became a fate that concerned them."[5] There was finally no doubt expressed by Viennese critics that Willy Loman's experience was tragic.

In 1950, *Salesman* was produced in Düsseldorf, Munich, Frankfurt am Main, Berlin, Oberhausen, Hannover, Kassel, Mainz, Mannheim, Bochum, Esslingen, Heidelberg, Neuwied, Regensburg, Münster, Hamburg, and Dortmund, for a total of 199 performances. Between 1950 and 1961, it received fifty-nine professional productions throughout West Germany, for a total of

722 performances.[6] Important revivals were staged in Augsburg in 1965 and in Mainz in 1972. Over the years, the issues changed somewhat, but central to the German view of *Salesman* were its critique of "the American way of life" and its treatment of the family. Writing in the *Sueddeutsche Zeitung* in Munich, Hans Brun expressed surprise in 1950 that "capitalistic America could produce a story in which the hero . . . 'goes to the dogs.'"[7] Sounding much like Miller in the 1957 preface to his *Collected Plays*, Brun said that Willy is not destroyed "because of his wife or because of wrong decisions but because the 'laws of prosperity' were stronger than he, a mere human being." Claude Hill suggested that the play's theme, "the pitiless thrust of the old and exhausted man through a profit-obsessed world,"[8] represented in its realistic critique of capitalism, a "fresh wind" blowing through a European theatre dominated by stereotyped dramatic characters and the beglittered figures of the operetta.

While German critics were quick to note the play's critique of capitalism, however, most avoided the reductionism of seeing it only in those terms. As one critic observed in 1965, one might be tempted to take the play as a Marxist "Lehrstück," its social statement being so strong, but that Miller clearly indicates that "the dreamer Loman is not simply a victim of the capitalistic milieu."[9] He is a man of weak character, who has it in his power to make something decent of his son Biff, but fails to do so. In 1972, Walter Busse noted that, although Miller was successful in revealing the dangers of the capitalist system, he was no Marxist who found salvation in the transformation of society. Although no social drama has unleashed more discussion of human happiness, he suggested, "it is universal."[10] Willy's fate evokes sympathy because it is essentially tragic, and not dependent on specific social circumstances.

Although the unrealistic form of the play and its time changes were noted with interest by German audiences, they were absorbed without difficulty into the German tradition of theatre. One critic called the play "a combination of medieval passion play and modern movie."[11] More common was the opinion that Miller combined Ibsenist social analysis with the cinematic flashback technique ("einer filmartigen Rückblendung"[12]). Reviewers regularly noted the play's affinity with Ibsen, Tennessee Williams, Thornton Wilder, and Eugene O'Neill. One of the most interesting ideas was that the play represented a new form of Realism, which had a "mystical–irrational" undercurrent springing rather from an idealistic than a materialistic world view. Noting that the new style of Miller, Williams, and Wilder combined elements of Naturalism, Neoromanticism, and Expressionism, Claude Hill named it "magic realism" ("Magischen Realismus").

For the most part, the German designers took their lead from the stage directions in designing the set. This description of the set designed by Eugen Wintterle for the Tübingen production in 1952 is typical: "The scene, Willy Loman's little transparent house with the New York apartments in the background, remains the same throughout the play."[13] The reviewer noted that the curtain fell only once during the play, and the spotlight moved with Willy as he changed positions and time periods on the simple set. The 1951 Bielefeld production made heavy use of lighting effects to move the production out of the realm of realism. In the opening scene, the skeletal house that was the center of the simultaneous set was lit in phosphorescent green. A spotlight threw a circle of reddish light on the background apartment houses with their distorted windows, casting an expressionistic implication over the scene.[14] The Augsburg production in 1965 also showed a clear expressionistic influence, with a menacing landscape of towering skyscrapers, such as never could have been imagined in Brooklyn in the 1940s, lowering over the open platforms that represented the Lomans' house.

The German productions tended to be faithful renditions of the play as written, and as their creators imagined Miller intended, but interpreted within the German theatrical tradition. Seeing Miller's play through a history informed by Ibsenist social drama, expressionist conceptions of the "little man" who is at the mercy of the capitalist system, abstract expressionist staging, and the new American tradition of subjective realism, they produced a version of *Salesman* that emphasized Willy as a social being and de-emphasized his individuality and the play's family dynamics.

FRENCH LANGUAGE PRODUCTIONS

The first production of *Death of a Salesman* in French was by Jacques Huisman at the Théâtre du Vieux Colombier for the Théâtre National de Belgique in 1952. Encouraged by Raymond Gerôme, who was to translate the play for him, Huisman obtained the rights from Miller's Paris agent and began preparing for the production. He was surprised by a phone call from the agent "with the shattering news that Mr. Miller did not want us to do the play. At least, not unless Peter Brook agreed to supervise it."[15] Huisman has said in an interview that his admiration for Brook's work was such that he "had every reason to welcome this suggestion."[16] The outcome was that Peter Brook came to Brussels for the last four or five rehearsals of the National's production, and made what Huisman considered very useful suggestions, primarily directed toward making the production more natural, doing away with "mannerisms or artifice." After a successful premiere engagement in Brussels, the production was moved to Paris, where to everyone's surprise, the French critics overcame their anti-American sentiments and their contempt for provincial Brussels to give the play their enthusiastic approbation, and to ensure a two-month run.

Huisman has said that he produced *Salesman* "as a strictly contemporary play": "In 1952 the problems of Willy Loman, who loses his grip on reality and is subsequently thrown out of his job, were real enough for any member of our audience." It was only gradually that the universal significance of the play was revealed to him, as both Belgian and French critics "seem to have discerned immediately that beyond his American-ness, this 'commis-voyageur' was rather the archetypal Voyageur, the existential traveller, a modern version of Everyman."[17]

In keeping with his rather pragmatic view of the play, Huisman and designer Denis Martin devised uncomplicated and clear scenic solutions for the changes in time and space. An outsize calendar in the Lomans' living room made the shifts between past and present clear to the audience, and intense white-blue light in the scenes with Ben "indicated that the action was midway between dream or reminiscence and reality."[18] Although audiences adapted quickly to the production's semiotics, the French critics were slower to accept the new stage language because they were unable to categorize it to their satisfaction. In *Le Figaro*, Jean-Jacques Gautier called *Salesman* a "pièce américaine néo-réaliste," recognizing its pedigree through O'Neill, Williams, and Wilder.[19] He accepted the single set, since he felt the writing indicated the locales specifically enough, but he had trouble accepting the synthesis of realism and symbolism that he saw in the set, complaining that the director seemed undecided about the question of style. At some times, he wrote, the production seemed to move toward realism, but at others, it had an "insufficiently suggestive symbolism" which reminded him of the post-war German theatre. In the end, he wrote, the production suffered from "a certain regrettable imprecision" in style. On the other hand, Robert Kemp wrote that the set was "convenient, evocative, and somber, like the play."[20]

Although the Belgian production was highly praised, and ran for two months in Paris, Arthur Miller was not entirely happy with its reception. He said in an interview that the production had opened "with very little effect. It wasn't a very good production, I understand."[21] In 1965, he wrote that the Paris production had been "hardly noticed" because in 1950, "Willy Loman was a man from Mars," a view that is not borne out by the mostly favorable critical reception. Miller had higher hopes, however, for the production about to be mounted by Gabriel Garran at the Théâtre de la commune d'Aubervilliers in suburban Paris, noting that "today, the

French are up to their necks in time payments, broken washing machines, dreams of fantastic success, new apartment houses shading out the vegetables in the backyard, and the chromed anxiety of a society where nothing deserves existence that doesn't pay."[22] The French audience did seem more ready to receive *Salesman* this time. The highly enthusiastic reviews did not question the play's style or its staging. One reviewer noted that the Aubervilliers theatre could not have chosen a more opportune moment for the revival of Miller's play after fifteen years. He predicted that 1965 would be a watershed year in the history of the French theatre, when the moribund commercial theatre would be replaced by "an art turned once again toward life."[23] By 1965, *Death of a Salesman* was recognized in France as "one of the great tragedies of contemporary dramaturgy."[24]

As Miller had predicted, French life had caught up with Willy Loman. One critic spoke of Willy as a man dominated by his obsession with the "mythe du standing."[25] Jean-Jacques Gautier, who found Claude Dauphin "astonishing, moving, remarkable, inimitable"[26] in the role of Willy Loman, remarked:

> What an actor, indeed, but also what a character, this Loman!
> He is Mr. Mediocrity, Mr. No Matter Who, Mr. Nobody, Mr. Everyone, in a universe of life on credit, of death on credit, of capitalism, of bills, of life insurance, and more bills, and always bills, in the United States – even more than here.[27]

The French critics were also well prepared for the style of the play. Gautier described the style offhand as "réalisme mythologique." No longer put off by the synthesis of realism with expressionism and symbolism, the critics had high praise for Garran's staging of the play and André Acquart's set design. Jean Paget found the staging remarkable in every aspect, giving a great deal of credit to Eric Kahane's adaptation as well as to the director and designer. The total effect, he said, was "an admirable tragic tension, in time and space," supported by Acquart's "very beautiful, nearly futuristic" set.[28] In brief, he wrote, the set represented "all the horror of the Americanized world, dominated by the abominable god of money."[29] In *Le Figaro*, Claude Baignères pronounced that Garran and Acquart had acquitted themselves with "une virtuosité imaginative d'une exceptionnelle efficacité."[30] The staging was abstract, largely composed of scaffolding and scrims, upon which were projected a night sky, trees, or skyscrapers to indicate changes in time and place. The critics agreed that it was completely appropriate to this "modern" theatre and its contemporary rendering of *Salesman*.

The 1965 production was so successful that it was revived in 1970, in a production directed by Garran and designed by Acquart, with Claude Dauphin and Héléna Bossis in the leading roles. The production opened on 30 November 1970 at the Théâtre des Variétés in Paris, the first professional production of *Death of a Salesman* in central Paris. The production and Dauphin's performance were well received the second time around, but the play was not looked upon with as much reverence. Dauphin's performance tended to move Willy's character away from the tragic, and toward the pathetic, "making the crumbling four-flusher an appealing figure, underlining the entire performance with a wistful pathos," as one reviewer put it.[31] Without the earlier shock of recognition that the play depicted French values and social conditions as well as American, the production seemed sentimental rather than tragic. One French critic wrote that, rather than calling the play a modern tragedy, it would be more precise to call it "mélotragique."[32] The reviewer for the *International Herald Tribune* asserted that, although "on its original appearance, made during a dull New York season," it was acclaimed an American tragedy of the first order, "this it is certainly not":

> Willy Loman, victim of false standards and incurable self-deception,
> a liar, a coward and a relentless fraud, suffers no awe-inspiring
> casting down but a painful, sad decline. Rather than a tragedy, we

have a hard-luck story told with shrewd observation, unswerving honesty and sympathetic understanding.[33]

HISPANIC AND ITALIAN PRODUCTIONS

The production of *Death of a Salesman* by La Compañía Lope de Vega in Madrid opened on 10 January 1952. While the play itself was somewhat controversial with the Spanish audience, there was nothing but praise for the direction of José Tamayo, the scene design of Sigfredo Burman, and the translation by José Lopez Rubio. The set was called "original and spectacular, ingenious and efficient,"[34] and the whole production "a lesson in good theatre."[35] While some Spanish critics considered Willy's problems specifically "yanqui" problems, and were not interested in them, most agreed with the reviewer who said that nothing happens in the play that could not happen in Spain or Switzerland, and that in reality, there existed "muchos millones de Willy Loman."[36]

The 1953 production of *Death of a Salesman* in Mexico City featured the highly respected Alfredo Gomez de la Vega, who was given credit for having "the eminent position not only as our most accomplished actor and director but also as the sponsor of the finest in the world's contemporary dramatic art, as a stalwart and somewhat solitary leader in the renascent trend of our theatre."[37] Gomez de la Vega had secured the Mexican rights to the play after seeing it in New York and London, and translated it himself, waiting over a year until Mexico City's Palacio de Bellas Artes was available for the production, which he produced and directed, as well as playing Willy Loman. The production, which opened on 18 April 1953, was seen as an occasion for promoting cultural interchange between Mexico and the United States. As one critic explained, "it is a very effective means of promoting in this country a sound appreciation of North America's values which extend beyond technology or purely material advantages and comforts."[38]

The perennial cultural question of the audience's responding to a tragedy about a traveling salesman in a country where they hardly existed was raised here, but quickly dismissed, with the recognition that Willy's is the universal middle-class experience:

> It is the final frustration of a man whose sole practical asset was that of being "simpatico," whose entire life rested on a myth, who had formed a cog in a machine that wore itself out in the grind and became useless. It is the tragedy of the average "little man" who fails to achieve a real, a fruitful and rewarding life because the nature of his task and means of livelihood are based on unreality. Traveling salesmen are not as common in Mexico as they are in the United States, but Willy Loman, under the name of Juan Fulano, is a readily recognizable person. Here he is the glib and "simpatico" fellow who squanders away his life as a hanger-on in politics, or as a minor bureaucrat, eternally hoping that he might secure the right kind of "pull," as a "coyote," fixer or factotum, or indeed as a traveling salesman – a little man clinging to a dream, buying his bits of lottery tickets, assured that some day he'll hit the big prize.[39]

Mexico had no trouble identifying with Willy Loman, or understanding the significance of his experience.

Salesman was produced in Italian at the Eliseo Theatre in Rome on 16 February 1951 in a production directed by Luchino Visconti, and with a young Marcello Mastroianni in the role of Hap. Visconti's was a particularly striking visual production, a combination of almost constructivist abstraction in the house and almost operatic luxuriance in its environment. The trees in Willy's backyard spoke more of Florida than of Brooklyn. The play was revived in 1975 in a production directed by Edmo Fenoglio, with the massive Tino Buazzelli as Willy. This production was mounted in the Teatro Grande in Pompeii, where critics delighted in pointing out the startling effect of an abstract set dominated by a symbolic white refrigerator in a theatre that was constructed between 200 and 150 BC. In 1975 the Italians saw Willy's fate as stemming from his domination by "consumismo," an unthinking materialism that was recognized in Italian society as well as American. Buazzelli, Massimo De Francovich, who played Biff, and Gabriella Giacobbe, who played Linda, received high praise for their intensely emotional performances.

EASTERN EUROPE AND ASIA

Considering the dominant American presence in the country as a result of World War II and the Korean War, it is not surprising that *Death of a Salesman* was produced in Seoul, South Korea, in 1957, although it may be remarkable that it was done with local actors. More remarkable for the fifties, however, was *Salesman*'s production, in a translation by E. Golyshev and B. Isakov, at Leningrad's Pushkin Theatre by the Leningrad Academic Dramatic Theatre in July 1959, directed by Rafail Suslovich. One of the major hits of the theatre repertory in that year, the production was moved to the Vakhtangov Theatre in Moscow later in the month, where customers were lining up to buy tickets a week before the show's opening.[40] Gala Ebin, who saw the production on 13 July in Leningrad, reported to Kermit Bloomgarden that the Soviet production made the play into an outright condemnation of the capitalist system. According to Ebin, the act curtain, a loud, ugly painting of New York skyscrapers, theatening to crush the stage and the audience, set the mood for the production.[41] It was a step-by-step exposure of the faulty, inhuman American economic system, which relentlessly destroyed Willy Loman's dreams. As is always the case when the social criticism in the play is stressed, Suslovich made the production's climax the scene in Howard's office when Willy is fired, treating the final confrontation scene between Biff and Willy as a long denouement. In Ebin's view, Biff's final rejection of Willy's dreams was treated in the production as the act of an ungrateful, heartless son, the final cross for the hero to bear. He also felt that the scene with the women in the restaurant was overdone, and that the

10. The 1957 production in Seoul, South Korea

dream sequences, in which Biff and Hap were played by younger actors, were ineffective.

G. Kapralov's review in *Pravda* for 29 July 1959 confirms Ebin's view of the production's interpretation. The play, he wrote, is "imbued with the author's torturous reflections on the fates of the simple people of America."[42] Speaking of Willy Loman's story as "one of the deepest social tragedies of modern America," he said, "the dramatic fate of the salesman stands out in the production as the natural consequence of the inhumane laws of the capitalist world." Although he noted that Willy has many good qualities – "he loves his work, is enthusiastic about it, he has a sensitive heart, he can be kind and selfless" – the tragedy is that "Willy's consciousness is poisoned by the false bourgeois propaganda that in America all have equal opportunity." Kapralov found the central message of the play in Linda's plaintive repetition over Willy's grave that they were free of debt ("We're free ... We're free ... We're free" [101]): "In these words the dramatist invested profound philosophical meaning. In the capitalist world it is only at the cost of his life that man buys his illusory 'freedom.'"

Kapralov saw in the production the exposure of yet another failure of modern bourgeois society:

> the absence of ideals, man's oppressive sensation of the meaninglessness of existence. This theme is unfolded through the images of Charley and Happy. The actor V. Iantsat in the role of Charley found a true picture of the role, showing a man, whose life, despite material sufficiency, flows monotonously and aimlessly. The excessive revelry of Happy, Willy's son (actor V. Medvedev), his chase after pleasure, disguises the feeling of loneliness and emptiness which is gnawing at him.

As a result of Miller's apparent inability to offer socialist solutions to these capitalist problems, the play did not quite measure up to Kapralov's standards:

> Arthur Miller sees no exit from the contradictions he so sharply depicted. Therefore his play is pessimistic; the dramatist is not always consistent in his criticism of capitalist society and its customs. But as a whole his work is the artist's honest witness to the "American way of life."

This use of the play to mount a simplistic critique of capitalism and "the American way of life" was typical in Eastern bloc countries where art was expected to advance the cause of socialism. *Death of a Salesman* was one of very few American plays to be given a number of productions in the Soviet Union throughout the cold war. Given this kind of production, it is not difficult to see why.

When Arthur Miller set out to direct the play at the invitation of Cao Yü, a well-known playwright and head of the Beijing People's Art Theatre, and Ying Ruocheng, one of China's most distinguished actors and directors, in 1983, he already had a good idea of the simplistically Marxist aesthetic expectations he would be up against. During his trip to China in 1978 with his wife, photographer Inge Morath, to work on their book *Chinese Encounters*, he had met many Chinese artists, writers, and theatre people, who had explained to him the devastating effect of the recent Cultural Revolution on drama and theatre. Under the rule of Mao's widow Jiang Qing and the rest of the infamous Gang of Four, all of the actors, writers, and theatre artists with any claim to distinction had been jailed or assigned to "re-education" jobs as menial workers or farm laborers. Jiang Qing had enforced the simplistic aesthetic of the "Three Prominences" in all art forms, in which, as Miller learned from the eminent actor and director Jin Shan:

> There had to be a Bad Element, who is actually a spy or agent of imperialism, a group of worker-peasant heroes or Number Two Heroes, and finally a Number One Hero, or Hero of the Heroes. The Number One Hero, of course, can have no inner conflicts, no personal weaknesses, and naturally no character.[43]

Although distinguished artists like Cao Yü and Ying Ruocheng, as well as a younger generation of writers and directors, were trying hard to open the Chinese theatre to new forms and ideas, the shadow of the Three Prominences still hung heavily over it in the early eighties. Everyone connected with the production agreed that it would be very difficult to get a Chinese audience to accept a play in which there was no Number One Hero, and no villain. One of Miller's greatest difficulties in directing the play was getting even Ying Ruocheng, who played Willy, to conceive of him as a sympathetic character even though he was "not Good."[44] Similarly, from the Chinese point of view the play had no "message," in the sense of the clear social moral they were used to. In rehearsal, it took a long time to establish the essential interpretive through-line that Miller used in his production, which was essentially filial love. As he explained to his actors: "This is a love story . . . away from home [Biff] sometimes feels a painfully unrequited love for his father, a sense of something unfinished between them bringing feelings of guilt" (B 79). As he explained in a later interview, Miller dismissed the usual predictions that the play would not be understood because there were no traveling salesmen in China: "Of course, it doesn't depend on the salesman; it depends on the father and the mother and the children. That's what it's about. The salesman part is what he does to stay alive. But he could be a peasant, he could be, whatever."[45]

Nevertheless, Miller was relieved to find, as he explored the play with the actors and studied the Chinese culture around him, that there were salesmen in China in 1983, and even a nascent insurance business, and that there were Beijing neighborhoods where single-story houses like Willy's were being engulfed by six-story apartment buildings. Most important was the recognition early in the rehearsal process of the family dynamics in the play. As the young actor who was to play Hap put it: "One thing about the play that is very Chinese is the way Willy tries to make his sons successful. The Chinese father always wants his sons to be 'dragons'" (*B* 7). The rest of the cast laughed in agreement. Here was an anti-Maoist sentiment at the heart of Chinese culture that had persisted despite all the leveling efforts of fifty years of Communist rule. Miller had found a way into the play from which his interpretation could be realized on stage.

A number of cultural and aesthetic differences had to be overcome before director and actors could achieve a unified aesthetic entity, however. The traditional Chinese acting style, derived from Chinese opera and the traditional Chinese theatre, was a style writ large, with actors turned toward the audience rather than the other characters, and with a great many large and emphatic gestures. From a Western point of view, and in a Western play, this style appeared as over-acting. Although the training school of the realistic Beijing People's Art Theatre acknowledged a debt to Stanislavsky, Miller came to see the Chinese acting technique as the opposite of the American Method:

> By virtue of training and temperament the Chinese actor creates feeling by acknowledging his debt to his objectifying techniques. He does not "throw himself into the part" but builds a performance by pieces of knowledge, as it were, of story, character, and specific circumstances. He doesn't start with frenzy but hopes to end with it. (*B 251*)

Throughout the six-week rehearsal process, Miller worked with the actors to internalize much of what their training taught them to externalize, and to communicate with the other actors onstage, moving toward an ever greater psychological realism in the production. These accomplished actors adapted quickly to the new style, with Zhu Lin, who played Linda, in particular making a remarkably quick shift from a weeping and "warbling" wife to a strong Linda who was deeply concerned about her husband and angry at her sons for abandoning him. Zhu Lin told a critic that she had at first found it difficult to understand the basis of Linda's love for Willy. When Miller suggested to her that Linda and Willy had eloped when they were young and that "Linda loved Willy not only for his intelligence, diligence and ambition, but also for his boasting and his affection for their sons," she was able to find a way into the character.[46] Her Linda suffered a constant emotional dilemma, "finding it very hard to take sides during a family conflict. To support Willy against their sons would not be justified, but to support the sons against their father would hurt her husband."[47]

While the actors showed amazing ability to adapt their acting techniques to the more realistic style of the production, they were not as quick to drop the conventions of the Chinese theatre. One of Miller's perennial headaches throughout the production process was dealing with the convention that Chinese actors playing Westerners had to wear wavy, light-colored wigs and heavy white make-up, a convention that would wreak havoc on the carefully calibrated psychological realism of the acting. His ongoing battle with the wig-makers and his efforts to coax the actors to forego the security of the wigs makes an entertaining subtext in *Salesman in Beijing*, his account of the production. He had a similar problem with the make-up which, as he noted, "is a mask" in China, "not an emphasis of the expressiveness of the face. The stage is an artificial place where ordinary-looking people have no business" (*B* 207). In short, Chinese actors felt naked on stage without heavy make-up and wigs. It took a good deal of persuasion to get most of them to dispense with these props, but it was vital to the new view of Western drama that Miller and Ying Ruocheng were trying to introduce to the Chinese theatre with this production. In the end, Miller felt that the effort was successful. For Chinese audiences, the absence of make-up on actors playing foreigners turned out to be the most startling element of the production: "Many viewers had said that for the first time 'it made us feel like *them*,' meaning Westerners." Miller felt that this audience response had major cultural significance:

> If this turns out to be the case for the audiences in the future, it alone will justify the production of *Salesman* here, at least for me. It can really open the world repertory to China, not merely as a curiosity, but as an experience in which they can participate, and one that would do much to penetrate their isolation as a culture, a major accomplishment whose resonances can roll out in many surprising directions. *(B 233)*

One of the basic aesthetic questions that had weighed on Miller from the beginning of the production was its cultural locale: "Exactly where is this play supposed to be taking place? In China? America? Where?" (*B* 4). It was only through the process of the production that the answer to this question emerged. As he gradually worked the actors away from "imitating Americans" and into realizing their characters, Miller came to believe that "by some unplanned magic we may end up creating something not quite American *or* Chinese but a pure style springing from the heart of the play itself – the play as a nonnational event, that is, a human circumstance" (*B* 155). By 22 April, a month into the rehearsal process, Miller had forgotten that the ethnic question was ever a problem: "By now [the actors] simply are the Lomans-as-Chinese-looking-people. This places them in some country of the mind, I suppose, certainly not in any earthly geography" (*B* 172). The audience's response showed that Miller was right, and the ethnic consciousness that had constrained both his and the actors' conception of the play had indeed been transcended in the production. It was an important event for the contemporary Chinese theatre.

When Yang Shipeng directed *Death of a Salesman* at The Performance Workshop of the National Theater in Taipei, Taiwan, in April of 1992, there was no evidence of heavy make-up or wigs. *Salesman* had already been established as a play that had relevance to Chinese culture. And of course it was far more relevant to the Taipei of the 1990s than it was to the Beijing of the 1980s. At Arthur Miller's insistence, Yang used the Ying Ruocheng translation, but with his own emendations, substituting Taipei idiom for that of Beijing. According to critic Catherine Diamond, in both his alteration of the translation and his directing style, "Yang strove for what he believed would appear most natural to the Taipei audience, neither emphasizing the play's Americanisms nor trying to adapt the story to a Taiwanese local [*sic*]."[48]

While Yang "had a clearcut goal of presenting an American play without any concessions to the Chinese actors or the Chinese audience,"[49] he seems to have been less successful than Miller at adapting the Chinese acting style. According to Diamond, although Li Lichun as Willy and Deng Chenghui as Linda employed an effective restraint in their acting, in the rest of the cast, "the male actors in particular engaged in a great deal of demonstrative acting – pointing, waving their hands around, and touching each other to get attention."[50] Yang followed Miller's lead in his interpretation of the play for the Chinese audience, however. He avoided emphasizing the obvious parallels between forties America and nineties Taiwan: "Out-of-town extramarital affairs, children suffering from parental expectations, the high cost of housing, overcrowding, disappearance of green spaces, job obsolescence, increasing competition for jobs, and the struggle to maintain the esteem of others while facing failure."[51] As Miller had, he focused on the family, moving the audience to tears with Linda's closing speech as so many productions in so many countries had done before.

A similar identification with the success myth occurred in Japan. John Dillon, who directed *Salesman* in Tokyo in 1984, has written that a Japanese professor told him that, "when he first encountered the play thirty years ago he saw it as a damning portrait of far-away materialistic America. Now he sees it as a portrait of present-day Japan."[52] When Dillon arrived in Tokyo, during the slowing Japanese economy of 1984, the press was exposing an "epidemic" of suicide among older Japanese businessmen. Although suicide is seen in Japan as an honorable solution to a problem rather than the ultimate defeat it is in American terms, Dillon used this fact of modern Japanese life to serve as the cultural link between the play and the audience. He decided to look for "what American in the play was essential to its flavor and texture, then find what about the play was Japanese, the suicide and saving face, then bring together the best of both worlds."[53]

Like Miller, Dillon found the Asian acting style, deriving in this case from Kabuki, exaggerated. He solved the problem of over-emoting and "scenery chewing" by giving the actors a good deal of stage business. "*Do* more, suffer less" became the watchword during rehearsals.[54] Like Miller, Dillon also had to restrain his actors' desire for wigs. In a way that Miller never would have, however, Dillon used the Kabuki tradition's preoccupation with madness in his characterization of Willy Loman. The pervasiveness of madness and suicide in traditional Japanese theatrical forms tends to predispose both actors and audience to see Willy as mad. As Dillon has commented: "Ask an American what *Salesman* is about and he or she will probably say it's a play about a man who loses his dreams, or struggles to be 'well-liked' by his sons and his society. Ask a Japanese and he or she may tell you it's about a man who goes mad and kills himself."[55] He decided to use this perception of the play to shape his own production, rather than imposing a more "American" interpretation on his Japanese company, building it around the characterization of Willy by Akira Kume. As Dillon saw it:

> The triumph of American acting, partly because of the infamous "method," is the ability of our actors to *relate* to one another. But since madmen don't relate, some American actors edge away from the arias of madness. Kume, so proud, so hopeful and so sad as Willy, is also the most insane Willy I've ever seen, but without diminishing his character's humanity.[56]

No doubt Miller, who dismisses the 1950 Columbia film of *Salesman* with scorn because he feels that Fredric March played Willy as a "psychopath," would have trouble with this interpretation, but it was very effective with its Japanese audience.

Many of the cultural problems and solutions in the Chinese and Japanese productions have been similar, however, right down to the problem that directors have with the Asian aversion to public displays of affection. Staging the Boston hotel scene between Willy and The Woman is always a problem. In both Miller's and Dillon's productions, the actors embraced and turned their heads away from the audience, simulating a kiss. When Dillon wanted his Willy to kiss Linda on the forehead, Kume had to begin by kissing the air, working his way up to actually touching her forehead only on opening night. Dillon had to fight Keiko Niimura's impulse to play Linda as an obsequious wife, and making the "attention" speech "a tragic lament, rather than a call to action."[57] On the other hand, the added Japanese subtext of Willy's loss of face as a consequence of having to admit his failure to his sons added depth and power to the restaurant scene in this production.

Cultural differences have been evident in every translation, adaptation, and foreign production of the play. What is most notable, however, is the ease with which audiences all over the world have understood and sympathized with the plight of Willy Loman, and have grasped the issues of the play. As Arthur Miller has said, "once you get past the etiquette, get past the cultural differences . . . you arrive at Homo sapiens – Willy Loman."[58]

CHAPTER 4

MEDIA PRODUCTIONS

The film rights to *Death of a Salesman* were sold to Stanley Kramer. By 1951 Kramer had made a name for himself as one of the most successful of a new breed of independent Hollywood producers who had broken away from the control of the studio system in order to make the pictures they wanted to make in the way they wanted to make them. As an independent, he had established a method of working in which director, designer, and actors were brought together for rehearsals and script revision in a collaboration that went far beyond the usual Hollywood "story conference."[1] In 1950, Kramer had produced two films that were considered artistically as well as financially successful, *Cyrano de Bergerac* and *The Men*. *Death of a Salesman* was the first film he produced under a new and unprecedented arrangement with Columbia Pictures. For $25 million, he had agreed to deliver thirty pictures over five years, taking on a new "bottom-line" financial pressure that had not been present during the making of his earlier films.

The new financial pressure showed in Kramer's choice of writer and director, and in his approach to the film. Director Laslo Benedek was a Hungarian who had left his psychiatry studies in Vienna to work for producer Joe Pasternak in the thirties, and had directed his first Hollywood film, *The Kissing Bandit* with Frank Sinatra, in 1948. *Salesman* was to be his fourth film. Stanley Roberts, the screenwriter, was a studio hack who had been writing screenplays such as *Pals of the Saddle*, *Who Done It?*, and *Hi' Ya Sailor* since 1937. The only significant screenplay he was to write besides *Salesman* was *The Caine Mutiny* (1954). For a play that would require as imaginative an approach to screen adaptation as *Death of a Salesman*, these two were not the most likely choices for director and screenwriter.

Kramer's concern about money was evident from the first. Laslo Benedek has written that Kramer admitted "there was undoubtedly a risk involved" from "a box office point of view" in taking on the project, and that, "in order to give the picture a chance financially, it would have to be made on a very short schedule and without any waste."[2] For Benedek, the implications of this position were clear. He had to work fast, and he could afford to take no risks. The film's production, from the beginning of rehearsals to the first finished print, took fourteen weeks. After two weeks of rehearsal, Benedek shot the film in twenty-six days, with only one shot retaken for technical reasons. Looking back, Benedek wrote, "I confess that, once I saw the picture put together, I'd like to go back to 'fix up' a few things that one always knows better by hindsight. Unfortunately, this was not possible" (LB 96).

Kramer was cautious about the casting. To play Willy he chose Fredric March, an established movie star who had been an early choice for the stage role.[3] As Linda he cast Mildred Dunnock, who had clearly made the part her own. As Biff, he cast Kevin McCarthy, who had played the role in London, and as Hap, the original, Cameron Mitchell. Howard Smith and Don Keefer were also engaged to repeat their Broadway roles of Charley and Bernard. Although there was some room for a new chemistry to develop among the actors, other than the choice of March, Kramer opted for safe, established interpretations of the characters rather than new ones.

Kramer's cautiousness directed the production team's artistic approach as well. Benedek wrote that "the fundamental decision regarding the concept of the picture" was made "simply and coura-geously by Kramer," and that "there was never any question of altering the play's meaning or content . . . our task was to transform a play into a picture and our duty to stay true to it" (LB 82). Still, he wrote, "I wanted to make *Death of a Salesman* into truly a motion picture in its own right, not let it be stagey but make it, without permitting it to become arty, as cinematic as possible" (LB 82). Not surprisingly, Benedek found his biggest challenge in the approach to the concept of time and the treatment of the scenes in Willy's mind. Like Miller and Elia Kazan, he was absolutely clear on one thing: "There are no flashbacks here," he wrote (LB 83). "It is simply that the past keeps flowing into the present, bringing its scenes and its characters with it – and sometimes we shall see both past and present simultaneously" (LB 83).

Benedek's approach to representing the simultaneity of time differed radically from that of Miller and Kazan, however. In contrast to the stylization of the stage production, he wrote,

> the realistically trained eye of the camera demanded real sets, furnishings, and props. This in turn raised the question of the settings for the fantasy sequences. How "real" were the backgrounds and surroundings in Willy's memories and fantasies? And now we realized that the demands of the camera coincided with the demands of psychology and of the drama itself. The very point Miller made was that for Willy the past merged with the present, fantasy was as real as reality and his mind slipped from one to the other without being aware of a dividing line.
>
> This is a mental process in the film's own idiom – one the film can truthfully reproduce. *(LB 82–83)*

The result was that the film did not distinguish between Willy's subjective experience and his experience in objective reality. Each was treated with an equally conventional realism, although the film had a stylized, film noir approach to lighting.

Benedek's question about the subjective scenes was how real to make them. "How would the characters act, think and speak: as they really had done or as Willy remembered them? Seeing Willy having breakfast from close, what would he eat: cereal or ham and eggs?" (LB 84–85). Benedek's answer to this "all-prevailing problem of ham and eggs versus stylization" was an attempt to be consistent: "We would have to see exactly as much of life, and exactly in such a way as Willy saw in any particular state of mind" (LB 84). In other words, the camera's gaze was to be purely subjective, from Willy's point of view. In a scene that was shot in a subway tunnel, "there were extras walking along with him as long as Willy would be aware of them – when he became submerged in the fantasy about his dead brother, he was alone with him in the endless tunnel" (LB 84).

For the most part, this convention is adhered to consistently in the film, but there are crucial times when it is not. When Willy starts talking to himself while sitting in a subway train, for example, the camera's gaze is relentlessly objective, framing him with other passengers who react to his strange behavior. The woman passenger sitting next to him edges further and further away, until she finally gets up and changes seats. Lost in his daydream and mumbling away, Willy is aware of none of this. The effect is to invite the audience to share the perspective of the passengers, losing its engagement with Willy's subjective perception of things. In this scene, the audience identifies with the passengers rather than with Willy, objectively judging him to be crazy, and certainly losing its empathy with him.

Roberts's approach to the screenplay was workmanlike, essentially adapting Miller's dialogue to the changes in location that were decided on. While the play takes place on a single set dominated by the house, the film was opened out spatially to include several locations. It begins with a shot of Willy in his car. The first scenes with Willy, Linda, and the boys were shot realistically in the separate rooms of the house, and on the staircase. In Willy's first daydream about the boys polishing the car, he opens the kitchen door and goes outside to a back yard flooded with sunshine, and to Hap and Biff at work on a real car. Willy helps Linda with the wash and carries it into the kitchen, now brightly lit in contrast to the dimness of the kitchen in the "present" scenes. For the first daydream about The

Woman, Willy moves away from Linda, who is seated at the kitchen table, and into the next room, which is decorated to look like a Boston hotel room. He then goes back to Linda in the kitchen, which is dimmed down into its "present" look when Hap comes down the stairs and Charley comes in for the card game.

Willy and Charley remain at the kitchen table playing cards while the superimposed image of Ben seems to come from nowhere. The daydream with Ben and the boys was filmed outside the house, with the boys running off to a "real" apartment building under construction to steal building materials. The appearance of Ben, the one "daydream" character who is treated expressionistically in the film, made for one non-realistic set. To create the sense of an infinite distance as Ben walked away from Willy, the wall of the living room was stretched to a distance of 180 feet on the set.[4] The immediately following "attention must be paid" scene with Linda and the boys was filmed rather claustrophobically in the kitchen.

The card game and the first daydream about The Woman were two of the few scenes where Benedek used a cinematic device to achieve the juxtaposition of past and present, subjective and objective reality, that is constantly present on the stage. During the card game, the spectral, larger-than-life figure of Ben is placed at the center of the frame, flanked by the hunched figures of Willy and Charley playing cards in the present. As Willy comes out of the daydream about The Woman and back into the kitchen with Linda, all three are caught for a moment in a single frame, Willy hesitating between his sexual and his domestic needs.[5]

The second day, Act II in the play, begins with Willy in the garden, catching a ladybird. The scene shifts to the kitchen, and then directly to Howard's office. Before Willy goes from Howard's to Charley's office, he calls Charley and tells him he will be taking the subway. The biggest change in location is the filming of the second daydream about Ben in the subway tunnel and the Ebbets Field sequence in a subway train rather than in Howard's office. The scene then shifts to Charley's office for the scenes with Bernard and

Charley, and then to the restaurant, the house, the back yard, and a very realistic cemetery.

Roberts's greatest alteration was to cut about 15 percent of Miller's dialogue. Some of the cuts were just to make the movie "less talky," or to simplify the narrative. For example, Linda's phone call to Biff, Bernard's description of his fist fight with Biff, and Charley's discussion with Willy about putting up a ceiling were all cut. Several thematically significant cuts were made as well. The most important was the deleting of Ben's references to Willy's father, cutting out all vestiges of his role as father-substitute and transforming him completely into an expressionistic representation of Willy's success myth. Another was the deletion of Willy's questions to the waiters in the restaurant about seeds and his lines, "I've got to get some seeds, right away. Nothing's planted. I don't have a thing in the ground,"[6] an important if heavy-handed thematic reference.

Miller has written that his only participation in the film was "to complain that the screenplay had managed to chop off almost every climax of the play as though with a lawnmower."[7] As an example of Stanley Roberts's obtuseness in adapting the play, Miller described Roberts's cutting of Biff's explosive line to Linda, "I hate this city and I'll stay here . . . now what do you want?" (42), an emotional climax that leads into Linda's explanation that Willy has been trying to kill himself. According to Miller, Roberts objected to the line because he didn't want Biff shouting at his mother.[8] Roberts also de-emphasized Biff's negative qualities. He cut his lines about having stolen the suit in Kansas City, and he gave the line Biff says to Letta about having been in front of a jury to Hap, making it into a simple joke. Rather than going out with Hap and the women, Biff simply leaves the restaurant in the film. When Hap arrives at home, he finds Biff sitting on the front steps, where he says he has been all night. His lines in the scene with Linda, in which he says he walked off and left his father and that he is "the scum of the earth" (91), were also cut.

Hap's part was cut even more severely than Biff's, so that he emerged neither as the neglected younger son nor as the intrepid believer in Willy's dream that he is in the play. His lines about Willy's dream in the Requiem scene were cut, as were his constant claims that he is losing weight in the daydreams and that he is getting married in the present scenes. Although he was still depicted as morally inferior to Biff, almost all references to his sexual activity were deleted. His story about "ruining" the fiancees of his bosses was cut, as were the references to the brothers' sexual exploits as young men. Although his "pick-up" scene with Miss Forsythe in the restaurant remains, Hap is not shown deserting Willy in order to leave with the women, and his perhaps most revealing line, "that's not my father. He's just a guy" (84), was cut. Rather than resisting Linda's demand as he does in the play, Hap picks up the flowers after she throws them on the floor. The overall effect of the changes was to make Hap into a rather bland bystander to the film's action rather than the foil to Biff that he is in the play.

Several critics have complained that the camera work in the movie is unimaginative. In an early essay on the film, Robert Warshow contended that the opening shot in the car is the best use of the camera in the film, asserting that "once the camera has brought Willy to his home – that is, to the point at which the play begins – it abdicates in favor of the playwright, and we never really get back to the figure in the car."[9] As Warshow noted, for most of the film the camera concentrates "obstinately on the figures of the actors."[10] Close-ups and two-shots prevail, as the director clearly tried to take every advantage of Fredric March's extraordinary facial expressiveness.

There was a thematic thrust as well, however, in keeping the camera focused so relentlessly and so closely on Willy. As Miller has complained several times, March played Willy "as though he were insane" because the director and the screenwriter "saw the play in totally psychiatric terms – in part I think because they were afraid of the subject matter at that time."[11] In Miller's view, the reason was that the political climate in the United States had shifted so completely between 1949 and 1951 that even as mild a critique of American society as *Salesman* made was risky in a film. Hence, the focus had to be on the individual, and his ordeal had to be treated not as American social reality but as an individual psychological problem. As Miller puts it:

> The misconception melted the tension between a man and his society, drawing the teeth of the play's social contemporaneity, obliterating its very context. If he was nuts, he could hardly stand as a comment on anything. It was as though Lear had never had real political power but had merely imagined he was king.[12]

In keeping with the interpretation of Willy as psychotic, Benedek made use of a number of conventional expressionistic camera techniques to signify Willy's madness to the movie audience. The distortion of the room, as in the Ben scene, and the slanting of the floor in the scene with The Woman were familiar indications of psychological disturbance, as was the speeding up of the dialogue and the closing in of the camera as Linda and Bernard delivered their warnings about Biff's not studying and being rough with the girls in the first daydream sequence. In the climactic scene when Willy drives off to his death, Benedek placed Ben beside him in the car, talking to him, as Willy's perception of the lights in the city became a single phantasmagoria of diamonds and then the screen blacked out, signifying his death.

Benedek made use of some interesting camera angles to convey at least a subtext of the Lomans' oppression by American conditions and values, however. Willy's "I was right! I was right! I was right!" line (37), spoken when he feels that Ben has validated the way he has brought up his sons, is delivered by March in a seemingly victorious pose, arms flung up to the sky as he shouts the line in the back yard. Benedek ironized this gesture by shooting March from the back, facing the towering, blank brick wall of the apartment building, which dwarfs Willy, rendering his gesture pathetic against the reality of his social environment. During Linda's "Attention" speech, the camera registers Biff's perspective as he sits at the kitchen table while Linda stands over him, forcing him to confront her vision of his duty to Willy, and Hap stands behind her. From this distorted angle, Linda appears huge, her maternal demands dominating the scene as the ceiling looms just above Hap's head. As Biff makes his final plea for truth to be spoken in the Loman house, Benedek's camera frames the whole family, Willy with his back to the camera, Biff facing the camera as he confronts Willy, Linda and Hap gazing at Biff and Willy as silent witnesses. Benedek's visual statement, that for the single moment when they face the truth instead of manufacturing saving myths, the Lomans are a family, is a strong underlying theme in the film, despite its focus on Willy's dissociation from reality.

One consequence of keeping the main focus on the individuals is that the film is surprisingly static. In contrast with the tense energy that is achieved in many of the scenes in the stage production, the characters in the film tend to stand or sit still, while they converse in tightly framed two-shots. In the first daydream scene when Willy returns from his trip, for example, Kazan had created a rather complex kinesic subtext of approach–evasion and aggression–opposition–submission–retreat in the dynamics between Willy and Linda. In the film, Benedek had Willy help Linda hang the wash, and then carry it inside. The rest of the scene is almost completely static, with Linda sitting at the table and Willy standing in the kitchen doorway as they discuss finances. This de-emphasis of movement and of the environment focused more attention on the dialogue in the film than it had received in the stage production, an unusual situation to say the least.

Arthur Miller has made no secret of his feeling about the *Salesman* film. His anger permeates his discussion of it even forty years after it was made. "I hated that movie," he said in 1990.[13] Miller has been making the reasons for his dislike clear since the fifties. Aside from the approach to Willy's character, which he thinks robbed the play of its social statement, Miller contends that it was a mistake to open the play out spatially and that the film failed to create the sense of tension between past and present that is central to the play's narrative dynamics. Exaggerating slightly, Miller has complained that the film makers moved the film "all over New York City. As a result they had to cut out pieces of dialogue and then create filmic devices to bring them back in, because the story is so intense you can't drop it out. It's a botch, that's all."[14]

In a more thoughtful analysis in the Introduction to his *Collected Plays* in 1957, Miller wrote:

> The dramatic tension of Willy's memories was destroyed by transferring him, literally to the locales he had only imagined in the play. There is an inevitable horror in the spectacle of a man losing consciousness of his immediate surroundings to the point where he engages in conversations with unseen persons. The horror is lost – and drama becomes narrative – when the context actually becomes his imagined world . . . The setting on the stage was never shifted, despite the many changes in locale, for the precise reason that, quite simply, the mere fact that a man forgets where he is does not mean that he has really moved.[15]

The basic failure of the film, Miller felt, was formal. The film makers failed to find a way of "keeping the past constantly alive, and that friction, collision, and tension between past and present was the heart of the play's particular construction."[16]

Miller's other consistent complaint is about the way the film was handled by Columbia Pictures. In 1951, McCarthyist paranoia was reaching a peak in Hollywood, as the House Committee on Un-American Activities (HUAC) called witness after witness to undergo the ritual it required of former Communists or "Communist sympathizers" in order to avoid blacklisting. The witness had to admit to his or her activities that might have advanced the Communist cause, to name the names of others who had been involved in these activities, and to renounce Communism. In order to keep working in movies, many were willing to report on their own activities, but balked at naming others. This was the course that Arthur Miller took when he was called before the Committee in 1956. His action got him convicted of Contempt of Congress, a conviction that was later overturned in the courts. Some named the names, and were ostracized by their colleagues on the left. Others refused to answer questions at all, invoking the protection of the constitutional amendment against self-incrimination, but were then blacklisted, their careers in motion pictures destroyed.

In the autumn of 1951, as *Salesman* was being made, Stanley Kramer's partner and the script writer for *Champion, Home of the Brave*, and *The Men*, Carl Foreman, was called before HUAC and refused to testify. Unwilling to continue his association with Foreman, Kramer bought out his interest in the producing company in October, two months before *Salesman* was released. Meanwhile, productions of *Death of a Salesman* were being picketed by the American Legion because of Miller's well-known leftist sympathies. Fearing a public reaction against the film for its failure to affirm the values of American capitalism, Columbia made a short film meant to accompany *Salesman* when it was shown in theatres. The film, shot at the Business School of the City College of New York, consisted, according to Miller, of

> interviews with professors who blithely explained that Willy Loman was entirely atypical, a throwback to the past when salesmen did indeed have some hard problems. But nowadays selling was a fine profession with limitless spiritual compensations as well as financial ones. In fact, they all sounded like Willy Loman with a diploma.[17]

Miller was understandably outraged by this seemingly perverse intention to subvert the meaning of the film, and threatened a lawsuit if Columbia distributed the short with it.[18] The end result was that *Salesman* was distributed without the short film, but Miller felt that the film's misguided interpretation of Willy as psychotic was a direct result of the political pressure that Kramer felt from HUAC and the American Legion through Harry Cohn and Columbia Pictures.

Salesman's reviews were mixed. Although some enthusiastic reviewers thought it "great," and even better than the play,[19] others found it downright boring.[20] Most, however, gave it respectful if qualified praise.[21] Although one critic named Fredric March "the greatest Willie [*sic*] Loman of them all,"[22] March received more blame than praise, with the *Time* reviewer calling him "one of the film's worst drawbacks."[23] Voicing irreverently in *The New Yorker* the opinion of the majority, John McCarten wrote that "as Willy Loman, Fredric March struck me as being a man so extraordinarily balmy [*sic*] that in anything approximating reality he'd have been quickly netted for Bellevue [Hospital]."[24] While one critic thought Roberts's screenplay "sharper and more moving than the stage version" and that "the considerable wordiness of the play has been clipped and brought under control,"[25] others called the film "loquacious" and "talky."[26]

Most of the critics found the adaptation unimaginative and uncinematic. One complained that "we have largely been given not much more than the photographed play."[27] Another suggested that the adaptation might have been better if Kramer "had taken a few enterprising liberties with Miller's original."[28] The perceptive *Time* reviewer thought that Benedek had made a mistake in modeling the memory sequences on the stage production, rather than using the conventional movie flashback. He thought the use of the stage technique of physically walking from one time and locale into another clashed "oddly with the everyday realism of the movie sets."[29]

Hanging over all of the critical reaction to the film was the sense that, as one writer put it, "'Salesman' is pretty grim stuff."[30] Noting that the film's release in December 1951, just in time for the holiday season, was not particularly appropriate, he wished rather plaintively for "some softening humor to relieve its lengthy tension."[31] Voicing the general sense among the reviewers that a great work of art must be depressing, and perhaps vice versa, Bosley Crowther wrote in the *New York Times* that "'Death of a Salesman' is dismally depressing, but it must be acclaimed a film that whips you about in a whirlpool somewhere close to the center of life."[32]

CBC RADIO, NBC STAR PLAYHOUSE, 1954

Two radio adaptations of *Death of a Salesman* may represent the two ends of the spectrum of aesthetic quality for the radio play. Although considerably shortened and simplified, the adaptation done by Alan Savage for the Canadian Broadcasting Company (CBC) attempted to capture something of the play's unique quality by representing the disintegration of Willy's mind and the simultaneity of experience in the play through radio techniques. Turning the play into a simplistic domestic melodrama, the adaptation by Robert Cenedella for NBC radio was unabashed popular entertainment.

Both radio plays cut away the social themes of the play as well as its depiction of the Lomans' sexuality, making it a play about the family, and specifically about the father–son relationship. In the CBC version, Alan Savage left the action in the first act substantially intact, although he cut a great many of the lines. He inserted an act break, beginning the second act with The Woman's first appearance (26) and the third with Linda's first scene with the boys (38). He cut the second act severely, eliminating the scenes in Howard's and Charley's offices entirely, and moving from the breakfast scene immediately to the restaurant scene, where Willy simply tells the boys that Howard has fired him. Eliminating the "business scenes" left Willy's work life to be suggested entirely within the context of the family, considerably reducing the play's social implications. Savage also cut the references to the boys' experience with women, eliminating Hap's talk about women in the boys' bedroom scene and the whole incident with the women in the restaurant. This emphasized Willy's relationship with The Woman, making it a single betrayal rather than a behavioral pattern, and thus more the stuff of melodrama than of psychological realism.

In shortening the play, Savage reduced the parts of Linda, Biff and Hap considerably, giving Willy an even greater focus than he has in the text and reducing both the complexity of the family relationships and the significance of Biff's final realization. Interestingly, Savage cut Biff's story about stealing the pen, both from his conversation with Hap in the restaurant and from his talk with Willy, making his speech about the pen in the confrontation scene the first revelation that he had stolen it. This returned the revelation of Biff's action to the earlier version in Miller's preproduction script, making a melodramatic climax out of the revelation and eliminating the psychological preparation in the final version of the play. These cuts foregrounded the two revelation scenes – Biff's discovery of Willy with The Woman and Biff's revelation about the pen – giving the play a sharper and more conventional structure, and placing Willy's failure with his sons at the center of the play.

In line with this development, the part of Linda was cut severely. Her first scene with the boys, with the "Attention" speech, was left pretty much intact, but her story of Willy's suicide attempt was greatly shortened, and her hopeful conversation and phone call to Biff at the beginning of Act II were cut, along with her appearance in the first scene with Ben, reducing her character to that of long-suffering defender of her husband. Linda's confrontation with the boys after they have left Willy in the restaurant was cut almost entirely, eliminating the evidence of Linda's fierce preference for her husband over her sons and the toughness with which she will fight for him.

Savage also cut Ben's part considerably. In cutting the scene in Howard's office, he also cut the Ebbets Field daydream sequence, but he took the Ben part of the sequence (61–63) and added it to the first Ben sequence, during the card game (31–38). This made for one, considerably shortened, chronological sequence for Willy's daydream of Ben, making the experience clearer to the audience, but diminishing the sense of fragmentation in Willy's consciousness. Ben did not appear after the card game scene in this version except as a kind of echo of his epigrammatic formulations for success as Willy plants the garden and plans his suicide. Ben's sparring with Biff and his lesson about how to get out of the jungle were cut. As he did with the other characters, Savage preserved the aspects of Ben that were necessary in depicting Willy's failed dream for his family, but cut the psychological and social implications from his speech and actions.

Savage's use of the medium of radio was efficient and unobtrusive for the most part. He used the sound of doors closing to suggest entrances and exits, particularly in the daydream scenes where these could be confusing. He established scene shifts by simple devices such as Happy's asking Biff if he is awake when the scene shifts from the parents' bedroom to the boys'. He did suggest that Ben's voice in the early part of his daydream sequence be produced "with what ghostly effect possible" (31), becoming "a definite presence" after Charley leaves and Willy is free to enter completely into his daydream (34).

Savage took the hint from Miller in his use of music, using "Willy's theme," "Ben's theme," and "Bernard's theme" as "bridges" both from one scene to another and from scenes in the present to daydream scenes. The music also helped to create character, theme, and mood. "Bernard's theme" introduced the troubled daydream about Biff's flunking math into the restaurant scene. At the end, the music conveyed the building crisis. The flute was to become high and shrill, suggesting "the whistle of the boat of the Styx" (62) as Ben said, "the boat. We'll be late" (99), leading Willy off to his death. It was the music that Savage used to end the play, locating the Requiem in a flute theme that "whispers around in the clouds for a brief moment and then fades out and away. No strings. No orchestra. Nothing but silence. The end."[33]

Although simplified and made over from tragedy to melodrama, the CBC radio version was a sincere attempt at adaptation. It preserved at least one of Miller's major thematic concerns, that of the family, and it represented through the medium of radio what Miller has described as Willy's "disintegrating personality," the play's great contribution to the concept of character. The NBC version made none of these attempts. It reduced the daydream scenes to two, Willy's return from the trip in Act I and Biff's discovery of Willy with The Woman in Act II. Uncle Ben was cut completely from the play, along with all references to Willy's father. All references to the Lomans' sexuality except the Boston hotel-room scene were cut, including The Woman's appearance in Act I, Hap's talk about women with Biff, and the incident with the women in the restaurant scene. This made Willy's sexual guilt into a single incident of adultery, which was used to explain both his and Biff's failures. Biff did not mention stealing the pen except in a passing reference. In short, all complexity was removed from the characters and their motives.

This adaptation turned the play into a simplistic melodrama. The script built to two climaxes: the revelation of The Woman as an obvious motivation for Biff's problems and Willy's guilt, and the suicide, prepared for by the overly dramatized disclosure of the rubber pipe.[34] There was no psychological complexity, no social statement, no use of the musical motifs, no development of the play's thematic implications. Everything was literalized and reduced to its least common denominator.

A sense of what Miller's play became in this radio version can easily be gained from the speeches by the Narrator, introduced to make this simplified version even more simple. The Narrator's heavily literal opening sets the tone for the play:

> There is a home in Brooklyn – a small, fragile–seeming home surrounded on all sides by the towering angular shapes of apartment houses. It is night now . . . late at night, and in one bedroom of this home are two young men, the sons. Neither one lives here any longer, but they are both here this night. They sleep, but not too soundly. And in another bedroom a woman – the wife and the

mother in this home – lies also in bed, but does not sleep at all. Perhaps she hears the front door open downstairs. (DOOR OPENS OFF . . . AND CLOSES) Perhaps she hears the thud . . . (THUD OFF) of two heavy cases set down heavily on the floor. But if she hears these sounds, she does not stir. Perhaps she tries to tell herself that she does not hear them, that those footsteps on the stairs . . . (FOOTSTEPS ON THE STAIRS) are imagined footsteps. But then the bedroom door opens, softly . . . (DOOR OPENS SOFTLY).[35]

This radio play moved ploddingly and literally through Willy's last twenty-four hours, from home to much shortened scenes in Howard's and Charley's offices to the restaurant and back to home, the significance of Willy's downfall tied exclusively to his one incident of sexual guilt. The result was a poor approximation of Miller's play.

TELEVISION VERSIONS, 1957–1966

The first television version of *Death of a Salesman* was produced by Granada Television and aired on 27 November 1957 by Britain's fledgling commercial television network ITA, its first attempt at a two-hour program. The adaptation by Stanley Mann was directed by Silvio Narizzano. Granada had tried to get Lee J. Cobb to play Willy, but Cobb, for personal reasons including his recent marriage, had refused.[36] Albert Dekker, whose long association with the play had begun with his substituting for Thomas Mitchell in the original road company and Gene Lockhart in the Broadway production, proved a very effective alternative. The London *Times* review said that the production "really did the play proud," noting that *Salesman* "is an apt work for television. It bristles with rapidly changing scenes which are constantly trembling between immediate reality, literal memory, and tortured delusion."[37] The reviewer commended Narizzano for introducing the various levels of reality "with unerring smoothness" and distinguishing clearly among them without resorting to "visual trickery." Dekker's performance, modeled on the ponderously powerful Lee J. Cobb version of Willy rather than the "little man," came in for particularly high praise:

> Such was the force of Mr. Dekker's performance that all departures from reality seemed to burst irrepressibly from the potently disordered imagination of the central figure. Stumbling in speech and turning a massively brooding face towards the camera, he returned to scenes of crushing humiliation and desperate ambition with a haggard energy and retreated from them in abject exhaustion.[38]

So successful was the British version that Canadian Narizzano was invited to produce and direct a production of the adaptation by Canadian Stanley Mann the next year for CBC Television in Toronto, with Dekker repeating his role as Willy. The play was treated with unusual reverence by the CBC, which allowed Narizzano three weeks' rehearsal time before the production was filmed for broadcast on 9 December 1958. With some cuts from the script of the two-hour Granada version, it ran for 105 minutes, without commercial interruptions. Narizzano's goal was clearly to produce a filmed play rather than to adapt *Salesman* to the medium of television. As one reviewer put it:

> Using a minimum of distractions and a simple camera style he gave his cast the chance to develop, and consequently his scenes the opportunity to build to an emotional power and impact that were altogether splendid.
> Narizzano was not here concerned with making a television production out of "Death of a Salesman" but with bringing the play to television – which is not quite the same thing . . . Narizzano proved that a fine play can move from stage to TV screen not only without loss or distortion but with complete integrity.[39]

The production was an enormous critical success, with nearly every Canadian critic naming it the best television program of the year, and dozens of letters from viewers confirming their judgment. Dekker's performance was universally acclaimed. As one critic described it:

> Mr. Dekker was superbly real without loss of symbolic value. He started down but not out, depressed but genial as a salesman must be, and so he had plenty of strength to spare for Willy Loman's darkening last hours.[40]

The motive for Willy's suicide, this critic believed, had never been so clearly drawn, "a direct line established between recognition of his son's love for him and the get-rich-quick bait of the insurance." As is often the case, the role of Biff proved an opportunity for Leslie Nielsen, who had been acting in Hollywood films for a number of years, to show his talent as a serious actor. Most critics showed a just pride in this Canadian's powerful performance, although one critic thought he confused the emotions of frustration and anger, particularly in the Boston hotel scene.[41] The one performance that did not measure up to Dekker's was Amelia Hall's as Linda. As one critic put it: "She was not strong enough for the role. She was querulous when she should have been angry and merely pale when called upon to be bewildered."[42]

In 1962, the French Network of the CBC broadcast a version of *Salesman* that met with critical approval nearly as enthusiastic as the Narizzano production, although it reached a smaller French-speaking audience. The play, adapted for television by Marcel Dubé, was directed by Paul Blouin, and filmed live from beginning to end as a stage production. Jean Duceppe as Willy, Jacques Godin as Biff, and Janine Sutto as Linda were all praised for effective performances.

A 1966 television version by the BBC was not as successful as the CBC productions had been. Although Rod Steiger gave what one reviewer described as a "powerful, relentlessly explosive performance"[43] as Willy, and was provided with strong support by Betsy Blair, Tony Dill, and Brian Davis, the production did not make particularly good use of the television medium.

11. Albert Dekker and Leslie Nielsen in the CBC production, 1958

The first American television version of *Death of a Salesman* was a project of David Susskind, a respected producer who aimed to show that dramatic programs of high quality could still attract a large viewership on American commercial television. *Salesman* was the first of a series of programs he hoped to produce for CBS, including plays by Tennessee Williams and William Shakespeare as well as Miller.[44] With the support of CBS's top executives, William S. Paley and Frank Stanton, Susskind created a production that cost well over $400,000, a large amount for a single television program in the sixties. Although it was partially underwritten by Xerox, which paid

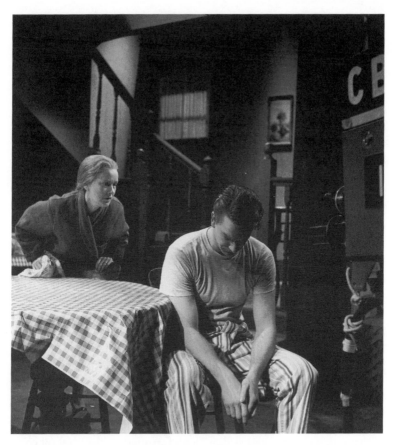

12. Amelia Hall and Leslie Nielsen in the CBC production, 1958

$200,000 for the air time while agreeing to keep its commercials to a minimum, the production represented a substantial commitment by the network to Susskind's experiment.[45]

Susskind and co-producer Daniel Melnick made brilliant choices in the production's director, Alex Segal, and its art director, Tom John. Segal, who was to win both an Emmy and a Directors Guild of America Award for his direction of *Salesman*, had been working in television since the early fifties on such dramatic series as *Pulitzer Prize Playhouse*, *Celanese Theater*, and the *US Steel Hour*. He had both an intelligent, creative understanding of the direction of dramatic literature and an imaginative assurance in his use of the camera. Tom John was to win a special Peabody Award and an Emmy nomination for his design for *Salesman*.

In choosing the writer and the actors, Susskind went to the source. Miller worked with Segal on the adaptation of the script, which amounted almost entirely to cutting about 18 percent of the dialogue, forty minutes running time, from the Broadway script. Although Miller was credited with the teleplay, he said in an interview that all he did "was approve the cuts made by Alex Segal." Miller had been hospitalized with hepatitis in London, and Segal had flown over to meet with him. As Miller described the collaboration:

> We laid out the play in one afternoon. I thought Segal did a great job of capitalizing on the strength of the play. Instead of changing it for TV, he made the medium fit the play . . . the force of the play was not weakened or compromised for a sponsor's approval.[46]

Although a few transitional lines were added, the script was essentially a leaner, more pointed version of the Broadway play. Susskind consciously built the production around the recreation of the roles of Willy and Linda by Lee J. Cobb and Mildred Dunnock.[47] Supporting them were George Segal as Biff, James Farentino as Hap, and Albert Dekker as Ben. A group of well known but underused television actors appeared in the smaller roles: Edward Andrews as Charlie, Marge Redmond as The Woman, Bernie Kopell as Howard, and Stanley Adams as Stanley. Gene Wilder made an early appearance as Bernard.

In approaching the script, Miller had seventeen years' experience with the play in various productions to guide him, as well as the input of a talented artistic collaborator. Many of the changes he and Segal made extended the lines of thought already evident in his revisions of the script in 1948. Most contributed to a general emphasis on Willy at the expense of developing the other characters and to a de-emphasis of the family theme in favor of the success myth. As was done in the 1951 film, Segal and Miller deleted all references to Willy's father in the teleplay, doing away entirely with Ben's function as father-surrogate and emphasizing his role as the embodiment of Willy's dreams of success.

Except for the "attention must be paid" scene, which was one of the few left completely intact, Linda's role was cut considerably, with some important thematic consequences. She was cut entirely from the first daydream sequence with Ben, where she blames him for deserting Willy and tries to stop Biff from boxing with him. In the Ebbets Field sequence, where she argues with Ben, reminding Willy of his dreams of success in order to keep him from going off to Alaska, Segal and Miller reduced Linda's part to two rather innocuous lines, "You're doing well enough, Willy!" and "Enough to be happy right here" (62). In Linda's phone call to Biff, they deleted her admonitions about how to make a good impression on Bill Oliver, and all references to Biff himself, emphasizing the fact that she is completely focused on Willy and de-emphasizing her involvement in the Loman success values. More than half of the discussion of the family finances during the first daydream scene was cut, emphasizing Linda's loyalty toward Willy and de-emphasizing the family's material demands on him. By reducing the evidence of Linda's complicity in Willy's values and focusing on her role as loyal housewife and victim, the writers reduced the complexity of Linda's character, and made her less of a force in the play.

Segal and Miller went through a similar process with the boys, particularly Hap. The scene where they made the heaviest cuts was the one in the boys' bedroom in which their characters are first revealed to the audience. The writers cut about half of Biff's speech in which he tries to explain why he is confused and dissatisfied with his life. They cut all of Hap's speech about his treatment of women, and about half of his description of his feelings about his job. Although part of the reason for this was clearly practical – these are awfully long speeches for television – the result was to place less emphasis on the effect that Willy has had on his family and its values, and to offer less explanation for Biff's behavior later on.

The writers also changed the character of Biff's conflict with Willy. When the Loman men are building their fantasy about Oliver toward the end of Act I, there are several instances in the play where Linda makes a remark and Willy shouts at her to stop interrupting. This undercurrent of tension builds until Biff tells Willy to "stop yelling at her" and Willy accuses Biff of trying to take over the house (47–48). Willy then snaps at Linda, which provokes Biff to an even greater outburst, completely deflating Willy and ending the scene. Willy's accusation that Biff is trying to take over the house was omitted from the teleplay, along with several of Willy's silencings of Linda. This made Willy a more sympathetic character and defused the generational challenge in Biff's opposition to Willy's values later on. Again, the effect was to de-emphasize the family conflict and focus on the social statement.

A number of sexual references were cut for the teleplay, although not nearly as many as had been cut for the film. As in the film, the major impact of these cuts was on Hap's character, making him appear much less sexually compulsive than he does in the play. Besides cutting Hap's own description of his activity, the writers cut Willy's line to Hap, "The world is an oyster, but you don't crack it open on a mattress!"(29), and Linda's lines, "Did you have to go to women tonight? You and your lousy rotten whores!" (90), removing the implication that his activity is habitual. Hap's showing off for the waiter and about half of his by-play with Miss Forsythe was cut from the restaurant scene, making his seductive behavior appear more abrupt, and less practiced and smooth. His claim to be disgusted by the ease with which he picks up the women reads more like straightforward truth in the television version than the obvious self-deception it is in the play.

A number of the cuts were made primarily to pick up the pace of the play. The writers cut thirty-two of the fifty-four lines in the card-playing scene between Willy and Charley, for example, without altering its thematic impact significantly, although they deleted several of the scene's memorable lines, such as Charley's,

"When a deposit bottle is broken you don't get your nickel back," and Willy's "A man who can't handle tools is not a man" (31). About half of the lines from the scene between Willy and Bernard in Charley's office were cut, deleting what little complexity Bernard's character has in the play. The reference to his fist fight with Biff and his advising Willy to "walk away" were both cut (69). The writers also made substantial cuts in the climactic scene in which Biff forces the family to see the truth, removing everything that was not related to Biff's confrontation with Willy, and deleting lines that interrupted the flow, such as Willy's objections that Biff's stealing was not his fault (96). The result was a more intense scene that built quickly to the confrontation between father and son and the display of love that ended it.

The remaining cuts mostly removed unnecessary exposition, and tended to make the play's themes more pointed. Willy's long speech while the boys are polishing the car, which had been expanded to allow for the actors to shift positions on stage, was cut back again. Miller and Segal also cut the conversation about the punching bag and about half of Willy's description of his selling trip. Besides cutting out Linda's dialogue and the references to Willy's father in the Ben sequences, they made further cuts that focused them more sharply on Ben as a representation of the success myth. The scene between Howard and Willy was cut considerably, particularly the conversation about the tape recorder, no longer a novelty in 1966. Even the small sparks of humanity Miller had originally allowed in Howard's character were cut – his promise, "when you feel better, come back, and we'll see if we can work something out" and his references to Willy's family (60). Bernard was also cut almost entirely from the scenes in the past, appearing only fleetingly to warn Willy about Biff's grades and to be abused by Hap.

In approaching the design for the production, art director Tom John retained Jo Mielziner's concept of the house dominating a basically single-set design, but he modified it slightly. While most of the scenes were played in the house and back yard, John constructed separate sets for Howard's office, Charley's office, the Boston hotel room, the restaurant, and the washroom. The Requiem was played on the back yard set, with a few tombstones set up to signify the location. This approach to the design allowed the production a degree of detail and solidity in the sets that had not been possible on stage, but retained the powerful visual statement of the house. It also encoded an epistemological statement through its juxtaposition of Willy's subjective world with the objectively real world he has to contend with.

The set for the house represented Willy's world through Willy's eyes. Like the house in Mielziner's design, John's was fragmentary, a roofless structure with open walls to the back yard in the kitchen and the living–dining room. The interior living-room wall was a transparent backdrop, which allowed for fluid scene changes from the present to daydream. Both the front and the back door were practical and realistic, making a clear delineation between the objective reality of the world outside the house and the subjective space of the Loman family. When a character came through the door, he clearly was entering Willy's subjective world. While Mielziner's set had represented a lower-middle-class milieu, however, with the family life centering around a bare and cheerless kitchen, John's set moved the Lomans up a notch in class. The kitchen in this production, with its pink and green color scheme, was clearly Linda's domain. Most of the family's life took place in the combination living and dining room, in which the Lomans' dreams of material success were clearly signified by heavy, dark Victorian furniture, mauve wallpaper and a glass cabinet displaying prized pieces of china. Unlike the family in the stage production, these people clearly had bourgeois pretensions.

In his design for Howard's office, John was able to juxtapose Willy's fantasy world with the cold, pragmatic world of business in a compelling visual statement. As Willy entered the office, a fragmented brick wall was seen to his left. Once he entered the office and met Howard, the camera showed only the fully realistic interior, with its drab green walls and office furniture, clearly the domain of Howard Wagner. Then, when Ben appeared in Willy's daydream, the scene was shot from a point behind him as he stood on the roof. The audience looked across Ben's shoulder and the open roof with a skylight and ventilation pipes coming out of it, through the fragmented wall of the office to see Willy standing in the middle of the room. The effect was a rather startling visual statement of the dreams of freedom and power Willy invested in Ben's version of success juxtaposed with the drab reality of the business world in which he was trapped.

For the Ebbets Field sequence, Segal cut from Willy in Howard's office to Linda in the back yard when Willy called her. Willy joined Linda in the back yard while Ben stayed in the office set, Segal cutting back and forth between them. Then Biff, Hap, Charley, and Bernard joined Willy and Linda in the back yard for the scene of their departure for the game. At the end of the scene, Willy went back to Ben in the office and the boys ran onto the office set, then Willy appeared in the dining room with Charley. When Charley exited, Segal cut to Bernard sitting in Charley's office, hearing Willy shouting about the game as he came down the hall. This almost seamless blending of time and environment made for a more effective representation of Willy's subjective experience than had been possible on the stage.

Like Howard's, Charley's office was represented with detailed realism. It made a clear visual statement that Charley's business was a step above the firm that Willy worked for. While Howard's office was a drab room furnished with simple, rather tacky office furniture, Charley's was an expensive paneled room furnished with leather chairs and fine furniture, fulfilling the Lomans' view of success and evoking Biff's description of Bill Oliver's office – "panelled wall, everything" (76). Coming on the heels of the daydream showing Willy's contempt for Charley and Bernard, this material representation of Charley's success emphasized the gap between Willy's failure and his dreams of success and gave concrete form to his jealousy of Charley and Bernard.

John's set for the restaurant scene was surprisingly bright and cheerful. Plants and wrought-iron furniture created a garden effect, and the tables were covered with bright red and white checkered cloths. The brightness of the set underlined the quick pace of the first part of the scene, helping to counter the rather dark, predatory sexual impulse that dominates the scene in the play. It also made for an effective contrast with Willy's guilt-ridden daydream in the dingy washroom. The cemetery scene was played effectively in the back yard. During the Requiem, the set was dark, with the characters placed in a spotlight as they were grouped around the wreath that signified Willy's grave. As Biff and Linda left the grave site, the lights came up on the rest of the set, revealing the house and placing Willy's grave in the center of what the audience had come to understand was his world.

John's set allowed for a simple and fluid handling of the daydream scenes. As in Mielziner's design, the shifts from present to past in the house were all done with light. Since there were no walls dividing the kitchen or the living room from the yard, Willy could simply walk from the present to the past as the back yard was flooded with sunshine. John added a few material touches to the scenes in the past, such as leaves on the trees in the back yard, green and white garden furniture, and of course the car for the boys to wax. The bright red Chevrolet of the past was contrasted with a dingy grey Studebaker that was visible in the back yard during the scenes in the present. The first daydream of The Woman, which comes to Willy when he is already in the past, was done through a close-up on Willy as Linda's laughter faded into The Woman's and then a shot of his face juxtaposed with the now transparent back fence, revealing The Woman. In the next shot, The Woman was framed between Linda sitting on a bench mending her stocking at stage right and Willy standing to the left, looking away from her. Willy simply walked away into the darkness for his scene with The Woman, which was filmed in a tight two-shot on the set for the hotel room, and then back into the brightly lit back yard with Linda.

When Ben made his first appearance during the card game, the light came up behind the transparent living room wall while Willy and Charley played cards at the table in the center of the room. As Ben walked through the door and crossed the room, the camera framed him in the foreground, with Willy and Charley spotlighted at the table behind him. Thus Ben became more real to the audience as Willy's memory of him grew more vivid, and the audience went through a version of Willy's conflict between trying to pay attention to the card game and attending to the much more vivid and interesting image of Ben that was forming in his mind. In the video, it seems quite natural that Ben would win in this struggle.

Segal and John used similar techniques to suggest the daydreams in the restaurant scene. The brief scene when Biff tells Linda and Bernard he has flunked math was projected onto the restaurant's brick wall next to a close-up of Willy. As Willy went deeper into his subjective world, the restaurant set became less and less visible to the audience. The Woman first appeared behind a transparent gauze door in the washroom set, but as the scene went on, it was transferred to the hotel room set. It ended with Willy pounding the floor of the hotel room, which became the floor of the washroom when the waiter came and interrupted his daydream. One of the most striking techniques was used to introduce Ben in the planting scene. Beginning with a dim spotlight on Willy as he was trying to make out the words on the seed packets with a flashlight, the set was suddenly flooded with the sunlight that always accompanied Ben in Willy's mind, and he appeared sitting on the back porch.

The costuming supported the shifts into subjectivity effectively, emphasizing the idea that the characters in the daydreams are as Willy sees them, not as they actually were in the past. Charley and Bernard, for example, wore better and more tasteful clothes than the Lomans did in the present, Charley a brown business suit and Bernard a navy blue blazer and slacks. In the daydreams, both were dressed in ridiculous-looking tweed knickerbockers and sweaters, with Gene Wilder's curly hair arranged to make him look like the classic "nerd". By contrast, Hap and Biff looked like typical high school sports heroes, with their initialed sweaters and their sporty clothing. Linda wore dark, rather shapeless clothes in the present, but in Willy's vision, she appeared in a hot pink linen sheath dress, wearing pearls and a frilly apron, and carrying the laundry basket, the image of the idealized wife and mother into which Willy's guilt transformed her.

The set and lighting design was clearly a result of successful artistic collaboration between Tom John and Alex Segal, who combined his use of the camera with the set's flexibility to create a fluidity between the objective and subjective worlds and to heighten John's juxtaposition of realism and expressionism. This was evident from the opening shot, played against Alex North's original flute theme, as the camera panned in over the darkened set of the house and yard, to the front door, moved slowly right to the back yard, and then through the open wall line into the living room. The camera then shot Willy from above, as he walked through the back yard carrying his heavy sample cases, opened the back door with his key, and walked through the kitchen into the living room, and back to the kitchen again. Segal cut back and forth between Willy in the kitchen and Linda in the bedroom until Willy walked into the bedroom from the kitchen, then the two of them went into the living room. This motion both established Willy's restlessness and defined the Lomans' environment, their home, which is also the substance of Willy's subjective life.

The boys were introduced through the first use of the transparent living room wall. As Willy talked to Linda, the light came up behind the wall, revealing the boys in their beds on the second floor. The camera angle then shifted to the foot of the boys' beds, framing Willy in the room below between the two boys. When Biff said, "I'm going to sleep" (13), Hap turned the light out and the living room below disappeared in the darkness, leaving a spotlight, representing the light from the window, on the boys as they talked. When Willy was heard shouting from below and the boys went back to bed, the scene shifted from the boys' room to Willy at the dining room table, then to the back yard flooded with sunlight to represent Willy's vision of the past. By this time, the production's idiom of juxtaposing realism and expressionism was familiar enough to the audience that it was ready to accept Willy's retreat into his subjective world. Segal also managed this deftly in the scenes with The Woman and with Ben.

Segal used some conventional film techniques as well, to indicate the relationships between characters and between the characters and the environment. In the scene where the Loman men discuss the Bill Oliver idea, the camera tracked Willy relentlessly pursuing Biff around the dining table as Biff tried to evade him both physically and emotionally. As Laslo Benedek had, Segal shot the "Attention" scene from the vantage point of Biff, crouched at the table, making Linda seem powerful and threatening as she stood above him. In the truth-telling scene, Segal also framed the four Lomans in a single shot, as Benedek had, except that he used a different pictorial composition. Willy sat at the table, with Linda behind him. Biff leaned across the table, a stance of power in relation to the seated Willy, and Hap stood behind Biff, staying out of things. Later, as Biff pleaded with Willy to see that he was only "a buck an hour" (97), Willy stood on the stairs above Biff, with the camera from Biff's point of view as he crouched below Willy, making Willy seem larger than life. This image of patriarchal power was replaced by one of filial rebellion when Biff ran up the stairs to grab Willy by the collar and shake him. As Biff broke into a sob and embraced his father, Segal placed them in a tight two-shot, at the same level, an image of familial love.

These scenes are good examples of the kinesic text through which Segal developed the relationships between the characters, particularly the members of the Loman family. In Segal's production, the Lomans habitually kept each other at arm's length, physically and emotionally. Willy's typical gesture of affection was to place his hands on a person's shoulders, keeping his arms straight, rather than to hug him. He did this with Linda in the present and with Biff in the past, although never with Hap. This physical distance made Biff's embracing Willy in the truth-telling scene a more significant gesture. Segal also foreshadowed this final embrace with the scene enacted by Willy and Biff in the hotel room. In that scene, Biff sat on his suitcase while Willy made up his story about The Woman being a buyer from down the hall, and then got up to leave. Willy tried to hold him there with an uncharacteristic embrace, to which Biff acquiesced momentarily, crying on Willy's shoulder. But then he pulled away. Biff's embrace of Willy in the truth-telling scene provided closure to this kinesic text, suggesting that the love between father and son had been restored.

In portraying Linda, Mildred Dunnock made use of the kinesic subtext involving Willy's coat that she had used in the Broadway production, cradling and stroking it during the "Attention" scene, although Segal did not use the Oedipal subtext that Kazan had developed by having Biff lean over and crush Willy's jacket in order to make direct contact with his mother. As in the Broadway production, Linda's movement and gestures around Willy indicated subservience and protectiveness. She knelt at his feet in the opening scene, and she hovered around him, although she did not behave quite as maternally as she had in the stage production. She did not, for example, check Willy's pockets for his glasses and handkerchief in the breakfast scene, although she said that she had put them and his saccharin in his pockets after she had mended the jacket. With the boys, Linda was much tougher. Segal saw that she offered no sign of physical affection to either of them, and he used the camera angles in the "Attention" scene and the scene in which Linda knocked Hap's flowers to the floor to indicate her strength and power over the boys. Like Kazan, Segal brought out the "tigress" in the gentle Dunnock, and the "cub" she was protecting was her husband, not her child.

With the boys, Segal created a physicality in their youthful scenes, which became an aimless restlessness in their thirties. In the daydream scenes, the boys did everything a measure too fast, polishing the car, passing the football, running off to steal the materials for the porch. Both flopped on their backs to get attention, Hap to pedal his feet and Biff to show off his sneakers with "University of Virginia" printed on them. In the bedroom scene, the pictorial image was of caged animals. The camera angles emphasized the closeness of the walls and the boys walked restlessly around the room as they talked. Biff looked yearningly out of the window as he said how foolish it was to work fifty-two weeks a year for the sake of a two-week vacation, "when all you really desire is to be outdoors, with your shirt off" (14). As Hap, James Farentino fidgeted about, using the business with the comb that Cameron Mitchell had used in the Broadway production and gazing narcissistically into the mirror. The boys briefly faced each other on the beds as they fantasized about going into business as "The Loman Brothers," but Segal emphasized their separation as Hap backed away from the idea because he had to "show some of those pompous, self-important executives over there that Hap Loman can make the grade" (16). During Hap's reiteration of the Loman dream, the camera showed him in the foreground, standing at the window, while Biff slouched on the bed, a figure of defeat. This perspective ironized Hap's gesture when he came over to Biff and hugged him immediately afterward, making it yet another empty statement by the narcissistic Hap.

Segal used objects in much the way Kazan had in the Broadway production. Each of the characters had a prop that made an important thematic statement. Linda's relationship to Willy was encoded in her gestures with the coat. Hap's character was summed up in his gestures with the comb and with the flowers, which he hid behind his back as he snuck into the house, hoping not to find his mother, but ready to try to charm her out of her anger if he did. Howard's childish love of gadgets and his attempt to evade his confrontation with Willy was evident in his nervous activity in the office scene, playing with a golf club and squirting some soda as well as fiddling with the tape recorder. Biff's relationship to the rubber tubing signified his acceptance of the role of truth-teller. He wrapped it around his hand after pulling it out from behind the furnace, and he pulled it out to confront Hap in the restaurant and Willy in the truth-telling scene. Willy's defeat and his bewildered desperation were evident in Cobb's use of the gold cigarette case that Bernard hands to Willy in Charley's office. One reviewer saw it as "the production's finest moment":

> Willy desperately tries to maintain the old razzle-dazzle about his own son Biff's "big deal." Bernard offers him a cigarette from a large, gold cigarette case. Willy stops talking, stares at the case, takes it, holds it, closes it, and passes it back – in a silent passage of torment, despair, and envy.
>
> The cigarette case is a symbol of everything Bernard has won in life – success, status, wealth – and a mocking sign of all that Willy and his two boys have failed to win. The pain on Mr. Cobb's face as his emotions overwhelmed him, the wordless eloquence of his baffled regard for that shining piece of rail that crushed his ego and pierced his boasting – were utterly communicated and shared.[48]

The response to the program was overwhelmingly positive. Its viewership was estimated at between 17 and 22.5 million, 28–30 percent of the television audience. Considering that it was shown on Mother's Day and opposite that year's most popular show, "Bonanza," the ratings were extraordinary. The program also won a number of awards. Besides the Directors Guild award given to Alex Segal and the Peabody given to Tom John, the program won Emmys for outstanding dramatic program and outstanding directorial achievement, and Miller was given a special Emmy for his adaptation. Cobb and Dunnock were also nominated for Emmys, losing out to Peter Ustinov and Geraldine Page. The art direction, the technical direction, the lighting, the editing, and the camera work were also recognized with nominations, a clear sign that those who worked in television understood that the program's quality was the result of a collaborative effort.

The critics were equally enthusiastic, with the *New York Times'* Jack Gould leading the chorus of raves. "An evening of exalted theater came to television last night in a revelation of Arthur Miller's 'Death of a Salesman' that will stand as the supreme understanding of the tragedy of Willy Loman," he wrote, calling the production "a veritable landmark in studio drama, an occasion of power so shattering and poignancy so delicate that there is no earlier parallel to cite."[49] *Time* summed up the response by commenting that "in the field of television, marked with the molehills of situation comedies and look-alike-sound-alike adventure shows, *Salesman* loomed as nothing less than Olympian."[50] Cobb and Dunnock were hailed as "the definitive Willy and Linda,"[51] and the critics had nothing but praise for the supporting cast.

The only disagreement among the critics centered on the social statement made by the play itself. One critic contended that the play appeared dated in 1966:

> Willy Loman in 1949, for audiences who remembered the great Depression, was an indictment of a social order that turned men into commodities. Willy Loman, the common man today, is still selling himself on the market of success, but he's no longer terror-ridden by the specter of material want. It's not the death of a salesman that needs to be written now but the death of a consumer.[52]

Another critic, however, noting that many viewers had probably turned on the program just because they were "curious to see whether the play had gone out of style since its première," asserted: "It hadn't. *Salesman* was never meant to be a documentary, and its X-ray examination of a man who is going under has kept it from becoming a period piece. Willy Loman, the salesman whose soul is as worn as his heels from his mindless pursuit of the American dream, is as pathetic today as he was seventeen years ago."[53] Regardless of its outcome, the debate showed that Miller and Segal had been success-ful at emphasizing the play's social statement and downplaying the more psychological family issues. Miller had once again succeeded in creating controversy about American society and its values.

CBS TELEVISION, 1985

The film of *Death of a Salesman* that was aired on CBS television on 15 September 1985 was part of the deal that was made to finance the 1984 Broadway revival. Under this agreement, CBS put up $600,000 of the $850,000 capitalization for the show in exchange for the television rights, and it received no share of the profits from the Broadway production. Dustin Hoffman and Arthur Miller, who received 90 percent of the profits from the Broadway production, agreed to serve as co-executive producers of the television production.[54] The "Roxbury and Punch" production was filmed in twenty-five days at the Kaufman Astoria Studios in New York, and was shown at film festivals in Toronto, Venice, and Deauville before it was aired on CBS.[55] After attracting a television audience of between 20 and 25 million viewers in the United States, it was released in movie theatres worldwide, except in the United States and Canada, where it was released on video by Lorimar.

Although Miller and Hoffman were restricted by CBS to a budget of $3 million and a shooting schedule of twenty-five days, they had full aesthetic control of the production.[56] As producers, their major aesthetic decision was the choice of German film director Volker Schlöndorff to direct the production. Miller said in an interview that Schlöndorff's work on *The Tin Drum* had impressed him as a good preparation for *Salesman*:

> There's an aspect of the surreal in "The Tin Drum" while still retaining a surface reality. That's one reason. Another is our talking together – it was a meeting of minds about what we wanted to do. This play, it has certain special problems. It's emotional, not analytical, as some good ones are. Emotional, but at the same time highly structured and it has certain distortions of reality. One has got to acknowledge this style.[57]

Specifically, Miller was impressed by Schlöndorff's familiarity with German expressionism. He was quoted as saying that Schlöndorff "understood that you could get to realism by a non-realistic technique . . . I broached this problem with several American directors, and there was an eagerness to deal with it, but I got the feeling we were in strange territory for them. Volker, being European, was used to this kind of talk."[58] In *Private Conversations on the Set of Death of a Salesman*, a video documentary that was made of the production's filming, Miller says that "it's a combination of the fantastic and a kind of super-reality. It's surreal, which is just what it should be."[59]

Schlöndorff prepared for the film by becoming a fixture at the theatre while the Broadway production was going on, observing and even taping parts of performances until he became thoroughly familiar with the production and its possibilities. He insisted on filming the production in a film studio, with a new set, and doing "it with a mixture of reality and dream, a mixture of cinema and theater." Above all, he was determined not to "treat it like a TV recording with three cameras criss-crossing, but do it properly, shot by shot."[60] Miller suggested that the production was not "a play in the real sense," nor was it "a movie in the real sense. It is a new beast and I don't know what its name is yet. Yet I think it's a genuine invention. There has been no adaptation . . . this has gone from the stage to the screen in its purest form."[61] "It was a weird way to do a film," said John Malkovich, who played Biff, "it was like doing a film we'd rehearsed a couple of hundred times."[62] And perfectionist Hoffman remarked that, for the first time, he had had enough rehearsal.[63]

In his conception of the production, Schlöndorff embraced Miller's and Hoffman's clear objective – realizing the stage production as closely as possible in the hybrid medium of film/television. Interestingly, the most extensive "opening out" he did was the introduction of a scene of Willy driving home over the opening credits, very similar to the opening of the 1951 film. While the camera angle in the 1951 version was mostly from behind Fredric March as he drove over the bridge, however, Schlöndorff's camera was focused on Hoffman's face, lit by the glare of oncoming headlights as he drove. The opening sequence ends with the near-accident that sends Willy home.

As Miller expected, Schlöndorff introduced a peculiarly German expressionist style to the production that was well suited to the conception of Willy as the "little man" that shaped Hoffman's performance. In this production, Willy does not enter the house through the kitchen on his return home, but through the front hall, a narrow, claustrophobic set with a black and white tiled floor and dark, tunnel-like walls that Schlöndorff used throughout the film to represent the oppression of the house and the way of life it represents. As Willy steps wearily into the hall, carrying the burden of his profession in two enormous sample cases, the walls appear to close in on him, and he becomes the image of the "little cashier" in Kaiser's classic German expressionist play, *From Morn to Midnight.*

Schlöndorff combined set and camera angles in a similar way several times throughout the production to provide enough of a visual subtext to keep the expressionist idea of the small man dwarfed by oppressive circumstances before the spectator, but not let it overwhelm the production. The image is repeated in Howard's office, when Willy comes in to ask for a New York job. After dragging a chair which seems much too big for him from the wall to the middle of the black and white tiled floor, directly in front of Howard's desk, Willy perches on it, pleading his case, while the camera reveals his subjective view of Howard, seemingly enormous as he stands before a glaringly yellow map of the New England territory and looks down at Willy. Then the camera moves behind Howard's shoulder, its gaze revealing Howard's view of Willy, tiny and negligible in the middle of the room, an embarrassing annoyance in the middle of his day.

When Willy complains to Linda about the apartment houses boxing them in, the camera gradually draws back to place Willy at the center of a visual image of the roofless set of the Lomans' bedroom against the wall of red brick apartment houses that closes it in. As he talks desperately for the last time about Biff's great future while planting his garden in the dimly lit back yard, Willy's small figure is again seen against the massive vault of apartment houses visible over the back fence – a concrete contradiction of his dreams.

Schlöndorff also used expressionist rhythms to convey Willy's increasing agitation and the disintegration of his mind as the play progresses. At the end of the first daydream sequence about The Woman, as Willy's memory of Linda's mending stockings triggers his guilt, and he starts remembering Bernard's and Linda's warnings that Biff wasn't studying and was stealing things, being "too rough with the girls," and driving the car without a license, Schlöndorff speeded up the pace with quick cuts from close-up to close-up of Bernard and Linda, creating a subjective feeling of disaster closing in on Willy as he shouts "shut up" and roars that he will whip Biff. The sequence ends with a camera angle from Hap's point of view at the top of the stairs down on Willy sitting at the table in the middle of the black and white tiled kitchen floor, again the image of the small man oppressed by his environment. Schlöndorff created a similar rhythm in the restaurant scene, as Biff tries to tell Willy about stealing Bill Oliver's pen while Willy is besieged by memories of Linda and Bernard talking about Biff's having flunked math. The overall effect is a more immediate participation in Willy's subjective experience by the audience at the same time that Willy's negligible importance to the outside world is kept constantly in view.

In conceiving the sets, Schlöndorff and designer Tony Walton kept the central visual statement of the Mielziner design. The house is clearly the central object in the production, although it is not a constant presence as it was in the stage production. Walton used the house as the main signifier for Willy's broken dreams as well as the key visual cue for the time shifts. His concept was fairly simple. In the play's present, the house is weather-beaten and badly in need of a paint job, a sad statement of its owner's failure to keep up appearances. In the past, the house fairly glows with a new coat of white paint. Combined with the generally dim lighting in the present and the bright lighting in the past, and the contrasting backgrounds of apartment buildings and a landscape dominated by two big elm trees for the back yard, this makes for an effective and meaningful representation of both periods. Schlöndorff shot enough of the opening scene in the Lomans' bedroom through the window, showing the peeling paint on the side of the house, to indicate an objective view of the Lomans' current condition and to contrast it with the shining dreams of the earlier years.

Walton made use of Mielziner's notion of abstract realism to help suggest the fluidity of experience with the other sets, but they are more solid and complete than the original stage sets. The boys' bedroom has a sharply angled dormer ceiling, an expressionistic suggestion of their oppression by the Loman way of life. Walton used separate sets for Howard's and Charley's offices, contrasting their approaches to business, as well as Charley's basic humanity with Howard's selfish pragmatism. Made of dark wood, frosted glass, and the pervasive black and white tiles, and dominated by Howard's desk with the map of New England behind it, Howard's office is a visual representation of the cold, impersonal business world that Willy has never been able to accept, and that is now killing him. Charley's office, on the other hand, is cluttered and homey, with warm light and a comfortable sofa where Willy has his talk with Bernard. Walton used the same bright red tin walls for the restaurant and the Boston hotel room, creating a sense of the salesman's relentlessly seedy life on the road in both.

Schlöndorff noted that the consciously "cinematic" devices for scene changes that had been developed for the play in 1949 would have seemed old-fashioned in 1985: "When Arthur wrote the play, he took cinema to enrich theater. We do the opposite. You don't need special effects or production values. With two people against a blank wall, you can create the most involving scene on film."[64] One major exception to this strategy was the Requiem scene, where Schlöndorff chose to segue from a shot of Willy's shadow moving away from the front door to the cemetery by means of a screen of white fog, which slowly clears until the characters are visible, grouped in a formal semicircle about the grave. Schlöndorff managed the segue from Howard's office to Charley's – the end of the Ebbets Field sequence, which took place on the subway in the 1951 film, and during which Lee Cobb had to run around the back of the set in the original stage production so that he could "appear" in Charley's office – by shooting a sequence of Willy walking down the street, yelling "Touchdown!" to himself. Schlöndorff then cut to Willy in the office talking to Jenny, eliminating the short scene between Jenny and Howard. Schlöndorff also included a shot through the window as Willy left the restaurant, muttering to passers-by on the street about planting his seeds.

Speaking of the television script in an interview, Arthur Miller remarked that "nothing was cut from the play this time. I think I added one line."[65] Although the spirit of the production was to remain faithful to the text of the play, this was not strictly true. Several cuts were made in the dialogue, most notably in the scene between Biff and Hap in the bedroom. Most of Biff's description of his work on the ranch and Hap's talk about the merchandise manager was cut, as was Hap's reference to taking bribes. The discussion of the Bill Oliver deal was also cut from this scene, presumably because it was thought an unnecessary foreshadowing of the discussion with Willy at the end of Act I. Linda's telephone call to Biff in Act II was cut, and was replaced by an extended kinesic sequence at the end of Act I, as Biff goes down to the cellar and finds the rubber tubing. As mentioned above, the segue into the scene in Charley's office was cut, as was the dialogue between Hap and Stanley at the beginning of the restaurant scene. The video *Private Conversations* records the process by which the opening of the restaurant scene was cut and two new lines added to make the scene work more effectively in the context of the whole production, a collaborative effort dominated by Dustin Hoffman.

The major change in the dialogue was the intercutting of scenes. Miller pointed out that the two ten-minute scenes that begin the play, one between Willy and Linda and one between Biff and Hap, were intercut "to accommodate television's brisker pace."[66] Each of the scenes was cut into three segments which were alternated, creating a sense of simultaneity in the opening scenes as well as picking up the pace. Schlöndorff also used a number of camera angles from inside and outside the house, creating a sense of nervous movement rather than the exhausted stasis which is often characteristic of the stage production.

The two scenes of Willy in the garden and of Linda's confrontation with the boys after they return from the restaurant were also intercut. Rather than beginning the sequence with Linda and the boys, and then shifting to Willy in the garden, Schlöndorff cut immediately from Willy muttering about seeds to passers-by in front of the restaurant to his planting the garden and talking to Ben about his suicide plan, then cut to the boys coming in the front door as Ben told Willy that Biff would hate him for killing himself. The scene then stays with Biff, moving out to the back yard when he goes looking for Willy. This change made the chronology of the scene clearer at the same time that it quickened the pace.

Schlöndorff's major contribution to quickening the play's pace was kinesic. Throughout the production, but particularly in the back-yard daydream scenes and the final confrontation between Willy and Biff, the Lomans seem to be in perpetual motion. Willy fidgets constantly, seeming to be in motion even while sitting down, as he adjusts his tie or cleans his glasses. In the daydream scenes, the boys toss the football, play at boxing, polish the car, do push-ups, or run here and there, all more or less aimlessly. The same patterns of aimless motion are there as Biff and Happy talk in their room, where they help to achieve a sense of undirected animal spirits confined in a small, constricted space. In both adolescence and young manhood, they cuff each other and catch each other in bear hugs that suggest friendly den mates. The movement supplies a sense of action to the production, but more importantly it provides an important kinesic subtext to the characterization of the Loman men. These are clearly men who should be outside with their shirts off rather than confined in an office and a three-piece suit.

In the confrontation scene, Schlöndorff made good use of John Malkovich's gift for explosive, physical acting to bring the scene to a compelling emotional climax. The scene builds from almost a whisper as the men talk in the back yard to a desperate fury as Biff and Willy argue about being "a dime a dozen," and reaches a climax when Biff says, "will you let me go, for Christ's sake? Will you take that phony dream and burn it before something happens?" (97). Kneeling before the seated Willy, Biff engulfs him in a powerful embrace, and the camera comes in for a tight close-up as he deliberately kisses Willy's cheek. The tension is immediately dispelled as Willy says in amazement that Biff likes him, and Linda says, "he loves you, Willy" (97). The katharsis is palpable as the scene shifts to a mood of exhausted, spent emotion.[67]

The production was a critical and popular success. Its estimated audience of between 20 and 25 million constituted a market share of 26 percent, compared with NBC's 18 percent and ABC's 27 percent.[68] The reviews were overwhelmingly positive. They tended to focus on Hoffman's performance, with some attention to John Malkovich, Stephen Lang, Kate Reid, and Charles Durning, who had replaced David Huddleston as Charley in the film, although a few recognized Schlöndorff's contribution. One reviewer called the production "a splendid marriage of theater and television."[69] Another said it was "somewhere between a Broadway play and a TV movie."[70] A number of reviewers noted the play's relevance to the social conditions of 1985.

There were some complaints, most having to do with the "scaling down" of the actors' performances from the theatre to television. As one reviewer put it,

Hoffman's performance is effective, gripping, spectacular at times. But it is not without flaws. He does look too young at times, especially in the TV-necessitated closeups. His scaling down of the role is a negative as well as a positive, mainly because he makes Willy almost thoroughly pathetic. Pathos is clearly in the guts of this play, but Cobb's more grandiose style definitely pushed Willy to a more traditionally heroic stature.[71]

While one critic said that "Hoffman's Willy Loman is probably easier to appreciate on the home screen, where its nuances and inward drive can be caught in closeup,"[72] another complained that "in general the close-ups, rather than bringing the viewer closer to the characters, kept reminding him that they were really actors."[73] The age question bothered several reviewers. One suggested that, while Hoffman's make-up was fully effective on the stage, when it came to the television close-up, "we were clearly watching an actor in his forties made up to look like a man in his sixties, and we didn't know what to do about the lie. It was a superb performance seen at the wrong distance."[74] The same critic summed up his objections in a critique of the production's general approach to the play:

> The approach was too literal to catch the whirl of Willy's imagination. Yet, in another sense, it wasn't literal enough. You found yourself asking such primitive questions as: Why doesn't Willy's house have any ceiling, if he just put one up? How come all the floors in the play have black-and-white tiles? Why does Willy's prosperous neighbor Charlie (Charles Durning) keep on living in such a run-down neighborhood?[75]

Critiques like this were very distinctly in the minority, however. The general response was much more like that of the amazed appreciation expressed by the Detroit *Free Press*:

> You know Uncle Art. He's the stuffy, pretentious relative who always talks about cosmic themes of life. The guy who insists on making grand and important aesthetic statements. Only watches

public television . . . Well, surprise, surprise. And take a hike, Uncle Art. You don't have to be a snooty culture vulture to be swept away by the genuine artistry of a dazzling new production of Arthur Miller's American classic, *Death of a Salesman.*[76]

PRODUCTION CHRONOLOGY

1949

10 February, Morosco Theatre, New York, 742 perf.
Dir. Elia Kazan, Des. Jo Mielziner, Prod. Kermit Bloomgarden
WILLY Lee J. Cobb   LINDA Mildred Dunnock
BIFF Arthur Kennedy   HAPPY Cameron Mitchell
CHARLEY Howard Smith   BEN Thomas Chalmers
Music Alex North, Costumes Julia Sze

28 July, Phoenix Theatre, London, 204 perf.
Dir. Elia Kazan, Des. Jo Mielziner, Prod. H. M. Tennents
WILLY Paul Muni   LINDA Katherine Alexander
BIFF Kevin McCarthy   HAPPY Frank Maxwell
CHARLEY Ralph Theodore   BEN Henry Oscar
Music Alex North, Costumes Julia Sze

20 September, Erlanger Theater, Chicago and Tour
Prod. Elia Kazan, Dir. Harold Clurman, Des. Jo Mielziner
WILLY Thomas Mitchell   LINDA June Walker
BIFF Paul Langton   HAPPY Darren McGavin
CHARLEY Paul Ford   BEN Royal Beal
Music Alex North, Costumes Julia Sze

1950

4 April, Theater in der Josephstadt, Vienna
Dir. Rudolph Steinboeck, Des. Otto Niedermoser
WILLY Anton Edthofer   LINDA Adrienne Gessner
BIFF Kurt Heintel   HAPPY Hans Holt
CHARLEY (KARL) Hermann Erhardt BEN Hans Jungbauer
Trans. Ferdinand Bruckner, Music Alex North

27 April, Düsseldorf
Dir. Ulrich Erfurth, Des. Herta Bohm
WILLY Rudolph Therkatz   LINDA Gerda Maurus
BIFF Wolfgang Wahl   HAPPY Peer Schmidt
CHARLEY (KARL) Wilhelm Wahl   BEN Gerhard Geisler

28 April, Munich
Dir. Hans Schweikart, Des. Wolfgang Znamenacek
WILLY Erich Ponto   LINDA Lotte Stein
BIFF Hans Christian Blech   HAPPY Hans Reiser
CHARLEY Walter Lantzsch   BEN Rudolf Vogel

1951
Rome
Dir. Luchino Visconti
WILLY Paolo Stoppa   LINDA Rina Morelli
BIFF Giorgio di Lullo   HAPPY Marcello Mastroiani

16 January, Brooklyn
Prod. Goldberg and Jacobs, Dir. Joseph Buloff,
Des. Saltzman Bros.
WILLY Joseph Buloff   LINDA Luba Kadison
BIFF (BILL) Lewis Norman   HAPPY (HARRY) Yokob
CHARLEY Sam Gertler   Gusonoff
Trans. into Yiddish, Joseph Buloff   BEN Nathan Goldberg

2 April, Gaiety Theatre, Dublin
Prod. Gate Theatre, Dir. Hilton Edwards, Des. Tony Inglis
WILLY Hilton Edwards   LINDA Coralie Carmichael
BIFF Michael Lawrence   HAPPY Michael Devine
Subject of demonstrations against Miller's politics

8 September 1951–5 January 1952, US Tour, Bridgeport–Richmond
Dir. Del Hughes, Des. Jo Mielziner, Prod. Kermit Bloomgarden
WILLY Duncan Baldwin   LINDA Sylvia Davis
BIFF Steven Ritch   HAPPY Ted Jordan
CHARLEY Arthur Tell   BEN Frederic Downs

20 November, Labia Theatre, Cape Town
Prod. Jacob Ben–Ami and Leon Gluckman, Dir. Jacob Ben–Ami,
Des. Joseph Cappon

WILLY Jacob Ben–Ami	LINDA Sarah Sylvia
BIFF Leon Gluckman	HAPPY David Barnett
CHARLEY George Cormack	BEN Robert Del–Kyrke

20 December, Columbia Pictures
Prod. Stanley Kramer, Dir. Laslo Benedek, Des. Rudolph
Sternad

WILLY Fredric March	LINDA Mildred Dunnock
BIFF Kevin McCarthy	HAPPY Cameron Mitchell
CHARLEY Howard Smith	BEN Royal Beal

Screenplay Stanley Roberts

1952

10 January, La Compañía Lope de Vega, Madrid
Dir. José Tamayo, Des. Sigfredo Burman

WILLY Carlos Lemos	LINDA Josefina Diaz
BIFF Francisco Rabal	HAPPY Angel de La Fuente
CHARLEY Alfonso Muñoz	BEN (TIO FRED) Ramón Elías

Trans. José Lopez Rubio

18 January, Reps Theatre, Johannesburg, 64 perf.
Dir. Jacob Ben–Ami, Des. Ellie Swersky and Harry Ligoff

WILLY Jacob Ben–Ami	LINDA Sarah Sylvia
BIFF Leon Gluckman	HAPPY Anthony Wright
CHARLEY George Cormack	BEN Robert Del–Kyrke

1953

18 April, Palacio de Bellas Artes, Mexico City
Prod. and Dir. Alfredo Gómez de la Vega, Des. Julio Prieto

WILLY Alfredo Gómez de la Vega	LINDA Virginia Manzano
BIFF Alberto Mariscal	HAPPY Antonio Carbajal
CHARLEY José Elías Moreno	BEN Alvaro Matute

Trans. Alfredo Gómez de la Vega

1954

26 February, The Actor's Workshop, San Francisco, 9 perf.
Dir. Jules Irving, Des. Ralph McCormic

WILLY Maurice Argent   LINDA Muriel Landers
BIFF Tom Rasqui   HAPPY Jules Irving
CHARLEY James Haran   BEN Richard Glyer

Production considered the "coming of age" of San Francisco
theatre.

11 April, NBC Star Playhouse, NBC Radio, New York
Adaptation Robert Cenedella
Taped 8 April 1954

9 December, The Glen Players, Glenwood Landing, Long Island, 3 perf.
WILLY Charles H. Gerald, Jr.   LINDA Charlotte Burnhans
Production attacked by American Legion for leftist leanings.

1957

January, Seoul, Korea
Dir. Kyu–dai Kim, Des. Sok–in Park

27 November, ITA Television, Great Britain
Dir. Silvio Narizzano

WILLY Albert Dekker   LINDA Vera Cook
BIFF George Baker   HAPPY John Stratton
CHARLEY George Woodbridge   BEN Henry Oscar
Adaptation Stanley Mann

1958

9 December, CBC Television, Toronto
Dir. Silvio Narizzano, Des. Rudi Dorn

WILLY Albert Dekker   LINDA Amelia Hall
BIFF Leslie Nielsen   HAPPY George Carron
CHARLEY Douglas Master   BEN Robert Christie
Adaptation Stanley Mann

1959

July, Pushkin Academic Theatre of Drama, Leningrad and Moscow
Dir. Rafail Suslovich, Des. Aleksandr Tyshler, Prod. Iurii Dubravin

WILLY Iu. V. Tolubeev　　　　　LINDA N. V. Mamaeva
BIFF V. I. Chestnokov　　　　　HAPPY V. A. Medvedev
CHARLEY V. I. Iantsat　　　　　BEN G. M. Michurin

1960

16 March, Boston
Prod. Frank Sugrue and R. J. Calvin, Dir. Michael Murray,
Des. Robert G. Skinner

WILLY Herbert Voland　　　　　LINDA Jean Arnold
BIFF Mitch Ryan　　　　　　　HAPPY Joseph Plummer
CHARLEY S. Harris Young　　　　BEN Lee Henry

20 June, Playhouse in the Park, Philadelphia
Dir. George Keathley, Des. Charles Evans

WILLY Luther Adler　　　　　　LINDA Mildred Dunnock
BIFF Alan Mixon　　　　　　　HAPPY Charles Robinson, Jr.
CHARLEY Hal Burdick　　　　　BEN Royal Beal

1961

1 February, Akademie Theater, Burgtheater, Vienna
Dir. Paul Hoffmann, Des. Lois Egg

WILLY Heinz Rühmann　　　　　LINDA Käthe Gold
BIFF Erich Auer　　　　　　　HAPPY Peter Weck
CHARLEY Manfred Inger　　　　　BEN Meinz Moog

1962

10 March, Theater Für Vorarlberg, Vienna
Prod. and Dir. Rudolf Kautek, Des. Karl Weingärtner

WILLY Richard Riess　　　　　　LINDA Erika Ziha
BIFF Hans Brenner　　　　　　HAPPY Gunther Fischeraurer
CHARLEY (KARL) Willy Dunkl　　　BEN Robert Marencke

16 April, Clark College Playhouse, Atlanta
Dir. Esther Merle Jackson, Des. Roger Furman

WILLY Frederick O'Neal   LINDA Georgia Allen
BIFF Floyd Gaffney   HAPPY Ted Price
CHARLEY Carl Wilen   BEN Lonnie Thomas

First African–American prod. with professional actors.

18 November, CBC Television, French Network, Montreal
Dir. Paul Blouin, Adaptation Marcel Dubé

WILLY Jean Duceppe   LINDA Janine Sutto
BIFF Jacques Godin   HAPPY Benoit Girard
CHARLEY Roland Chenail   BEN Gilles Pelletier

Production filmed live for television.

1963

16 July, The Guthrie Theater, Minneapolis
Prod. Tyrone Guthrie, Dir. Douglas Campbell, Des. Randy
Echols

WILLY Hume Cronyn   LINDA Jessica Tandy
BIFF Lee Richardson   HAPPY Nicolas Coster
CHARLEY Paul Ballantyne   BEN Ken Ruta

1965

1 May, Théâtre de la commune d'Aubervilliers, 32 perf.
Dir. Gabriel Garran, Des. André Acquart

WILLY Claude Dauphin   LINDA Héléna Bossis
BIFF Gérard Blain   HAPPY Pierre Santini
CHARLEY Marc Dudicourt   BEN Pierre Meyrand

Adaptation Eric Kahane

9 May, Städtische Bühne Augsburg
Dir. Helmut Gaick, Des. Hans–Ulrich Schmückle

WILLY Jörg Schleicher   LINDA Inge Conradie
BIFF Horst Reckers   HAPPY Sepp Strubel
CHARLEY Robert Dittmann   BEN Sepp Wäsche

1966

Caedmon Recording, New York
Dir. Ulu Grosbard
WILLY Lee J. Cobb   LINDA Mildred Dunnock
BIFF Michael Tolan   HAPPY Gene Williams
CHARLEY Ralph Bell   BEN Royal Beal
Music Alex North; Bernard played by Dustin Hoffman

8 May, CBS Television, New York
Prod. David Susskind, Dir. Alex Segal, Des. Tom John
WILLY Lee J. Cobb   LINDA Mildred Dunnock
BIFF George Segal   HAPPY James Farentino
CHARLEY Edward Andrews   BEN Albert Dekker
Music Robert Drasnin; Segal and Miller won Emmys

24 May, BBC Television, London
WILLY Rod Steiger   LINDA Betsy Blair
BIFF Tony Dill   HAPPY Brian Davies

1970

31 January, Old Tote Theatre Company, Sydney
Dir. Robin Lovejoy, Des. Kim Carpenter
WILLY Ben Gabriel   LINDA Betty Lucas
BIFF Ken Shorter   HAPPY John Wood
CHARLEY Barry Lovett   BEN Gordon McDougall
Music Roger Covell

April, Octagon Theatre, Bolton, England
Dir. Robin Pemberton–Billing
WILLY David Miller   LINDA Thomasine Heiner
BIFF Barry McGinn   HAPPY Adrian Shergold

1972
Mainzer Stadtheater, Mainz
Dir. Hans Schweikart
WILLY Horst Tappert   LINDA Marilene von
BIFF Jochen Busse   Bethmann
CHARLEY Walter Morbitzer HAPPY Harry Bong
           BEN Sigrid Lohde

8 April, Center Stage, Baltimore
Dir. Lee D. Sankowich
WILLY Richard Ward   LINDA Barbara Clark
BIFF Dennis Tate   HAPPY Terry Alexander
Stanley played by Howard Rollins

May, Arlington Park Theater, Arlington Park, Illinois
Dir. Harvey Medlinsky
WILLY Jack Warden   LINDA Jo Van Fleet
BIFF Scott Marlowe   HAPPY Ben Hayes

1974
26 February, Philadelphia Drama Guild
Prod. Sidney Bloom, Dir. George C. Scott, Des. Jo Mielziner
WILLY Martin Balsam   LINDA Teresa Wright
BIFF Scott Marlowe   HAPPY Rod Loomis
CHARLEY John Randolph   BEN Lawrence Tierney
Music Alex North

1975
2 July, Rome, Pompeii, Milan
Dir. Edmo Fenoglio, Des. Berto Gavidi
WILLY Tino Buazzelli   LINDA Gabriella Giacobbe
BIFF Massimo De Francovich HAPPY Berto Gavioli
CHARLEY Tino Bianchi   BEN Roberto Paoletti
Trans. Gerardo Guerrieri

26 July, Circle in the Square Theatre, New York
Dir. George C. Scott, Des. Marjorie Kellogg

WILLY George C. Scott		LINDA Teresa Wright
BIFF James Farentino		HAPPY Harvey Keitel
CHARLEY Dotts Johnson		BEN Roman Bieri

1979

20 September, Lyttelton Theatre, London
Prod. National Theatre, Dir. Michael Rudman, Des. John Gunter

WILLY Warren Mitchell		LINDA Doreen Mantle
BIFF Stephen Greif		HAPPY David Baxt
CHARLEY Harry Towb		BEN Harold Kasket

Music John White
Previews in Leeds, 4 September, Norwich, 10 September

1980

8 May, Steppenwolf Theater Co., Chicago
Dir. Sheldon Patinkin, Des. David Emmons

WILLY Mike Nussbaum		LINDA May Seibel
BIFF John Malkovich		HAPPY Terry Kinney
CHARLEY John Mahoney		

1982

11 July, York Theatre, Seymour Centre, Sydney
Dir. George Ogilvie, Des. Kristian Fredrikson

WILLY Warren Mitchell		LINDA Judi Farr
BIFF Mel Gibson		HAPPY Wayne Jarratt
CHARLEY Leslie Dayman		BEN Peter Gwynne

24 September, Amsterdam and tour, Netherlands, 73 perf.
Prod. Jochen Neuhaus, Dir. Josephine Soer, Des. Frank Raven

WILLY Bernhard Droog		LINDA Do van Stek
BIFF Guy Lavreysen		HAPPY Harry van Rijthoven
CHARLEY Jan Gorissen		BEN Hans Veerman

1983

7 May, Beijing People's Art Theatre
Dir. Arthur Miller

WILLY Ying Ruocheng   LINDA Zhu Lin
BIFF Li Shilong   CHARLEY Zhu Xu

1984

Institute of Dramatic Arts, Tokyo
Dir. John Dillon, Des. Laura Maurer and Tim Thomas

WILLY Akira Kume   LINDA Keiko Niimura
BIFF Kouki Kataoka   HAPPY Masahiko Tanaka

29 March, Broadhurst Theater, New York
Prod. Robert Whitehead, Dir. Michael Rudman, Des. Ben Edwards

WILLY Dustin Hoffman   LINDA Kate Reid
BIFF John Malkovich   HAPPY Stephen Lang
CHARLEY David Huddleston   BEN Louis Zorich
Music Alex North
Previews Chicago, 19 January, Washington

1985

15 September, CBS Television, New York
Prod. Arthur Miller and Dustin Hoffman, Dir. Volker
Schlöndorff, Des. Tony Walton

WILLY Dustin Hoffman   LINDA Kate Reid
BIFF John Malkovich   HAPPY Stephen Lang
CHARLEY Charles Durning   BEN Louis Zorich
Photography Michael Balhaus, Teleplay Arthur Miller

1986

February, Royal Exchange Theatre, Manchester, England
Dir. Gregory Hersov, Des. Laurie Dennett

WILLY Trevor Peacock   LINDA Avril Elgar
BIFF Rory Edwards   HAPPY Colum Convey
CHARLEY Arthur Whybrow   BEN Jack Carr

1987
2 January, Actors Theatre of Louisville, Kentucky
Dir. Tom Bullard, Des. James Joy

WILLY Eddie Jones
BIFF James Eckhouse
CHARLEY Bob Burrus

LINDA Lenka Peterson
HAPPY Steve Rankin

1988
April, Birmingham Repertory Theatre, England
Dir. Michael Meacham, Des. Douglas Heap

WILLY Bill Wallis
BIFF Ian Tyler
CHARLEY Paul Imbusch

LINDA Ann Firbank
HAPPY Terry John
BEN Brendan Barry

1989
28 October, Los Angeles Theatre Center
Dir. Bill Bushnell

WILLY Philip Baker Hall
BIFF Christopher McDonald

LINDA Edith Fields
HAPPY Gregory Wagrowski

1992
18–26 April, The Performance Workshop, National Theater
Taipei, Taiwan
Dir. Yang Shipeng

WILLY Li Lichun

LINDA Deng Chenghui

NOTES

THE BROADWAY PRODUCTION

1 Arthur Miller, *Timebends: A Life* (New York: Grove, 1987),
   130–31. Subsequently cited in the text as *T*.

2 Miller discusses his father's relation to Willy in Olga Carlisle and
   Rose Styron, "Arthur Miller: An Interview," *Paris Review* 10
   (Summer 1966). Reprinted in Robert A. Martin, ed., *The Theater
   Essays of Arthur Miller* (New York: Viking, 1978), 267–68
   (subsequently cited in the text as *TE*). The relationship is also
   discussed in an interview in Christopher Bigsby, ed., *Arthur Miller
   and Company* (London: Methuen, 1990), 15–16 (subsequently
   cited in the text as CB). Miller speaks of the other salesman in
   Timebends (126–27) and in the 1966 interview (268).

3 Miller's handwritten working notebook is in the HRHRC
   (unpaginated). Subsequently cited in the text as NB.

4 Arthur Miller, "Introduction," *Arthur Miller's Collected Plays* (New
   York: Viking, 1957). Reprinted in Martin, *The Theater Essays*, 135.

5 Carlisle and Styron, "Interview," 272.

6 *Elia Kazan: A Life* (New York: Knopf, 1988), 361. Subsequently
   cited in the text as *K*.

7 "Death of a Salesman," Final Script with revisions, HRHRC, 1:1.
   Written on the first page is "This is my final script but one; –
   includes some obvious work that did not survive rehearsal, and
   scenes which were later added and reshaped Arthur Miller."
   Subsequently cited in the text as R.

8 *Death of a Salesman*, Acting Edition (New York: Dramatists Play
   Service, 1952), 7. Because it contains a fuller description of the play
   as it was performed in the original production than the reading

version, subsequent references in the text will be to this, the acting version of the play, unless otherwise noted.

9   Matthew C. Roudané, "An Interview with Arthur Miller," *Michigan Quarterly Review* 24 (1985). Reprinted in Matthew C. Roudané, ed., *Conversations with Arthur Miller* (Jackson: University Press of Mississippi, 1987), 370.

10   Carlisle and Styron, "Interview," 272.

11   Roudané, "An Interview," 364.

12   V. Rajakrishnan, "After Commitment: An Interview with Arthur Miller," *Theatre Journal* 32 (1980); reprinted in Roudané, *Conversations*, 341.

13   *Designing for the Theatre: A Memoir and a Portfolio* (New York: Bramhall House, 1965) 24. Subsequently cited in the text as JM.

14   *One Naked Individual: My Fifty Years in the Theatre* (Indianapolis: Bobbs-Merrill, 1977), 213.

15   Clipping, New York *Sun*, 3 September 1948, Arthur Miller Scrapbook, HRHRC.

16   Robert Sylvester, "Brooklyn Boy Makes Good," *Saturday Evening Post* 222 (16 July 1949). Reprinted in Roudané, *Conversations*, 16.

17   Clipping from *Variety*, 29 December 1948, Arthur Miller Scrapbooks, HRHRC.

18   "The Original *Death of a Salesman* – Myths, Icons, and a Few Facts," MS, NYPL, 3.

19   Sylvester, "Brooklyn Boy," reprinted in Roudané, *Conversations*, 26. See also Murray Schumach, "Miller Still a 'Salesman' for a Changing Theater," *New York Times*, 26 June 1975: 32.

20   "Death of a Salesman," *Life* 26 (21 February 1949): 115. See also Mielziner, *Designing*, 62.

21   "Noted in Passing," *House and Garden* 95 (May 1949): 218.

22   Quoted in Michel Ciment, *Kazan on Kazan* (London: Secker & Warburg, 1974), 32.

23   Unidentified newspaper clipping dated 24 November 1947 and clipping from the *New York Tribune*, 29 May 1948, Scrapbook, HRHRC.

24 Ciment, *Kazan*, 41.

25 Arthur Miller, "The American Theater," *Holiday* 17 (January 1955). Reprinted in Martin, *The Theater Essays*, 46.

26 Mielziner's original script, with his sketches and notations, is in the HRHRC.

27 Miller believes that the leaf effect never quite worked: "We had never really succeeded with this in the original New York production, which was in every other respect a scenic triumph, because for some reason the leaves became a merely speckled light whose meaning was never quite clear" (*Salesman in Beijing*, New York: Viking, 1983, 211).

28 See Mielziner, *Designing*, 50–55, for a description of the lighting process. The lighting plots and light cues are in the HRHRC.

29 Howard Taubman, "Plays with Music Between the Lines," *New York Times*, 27 March 1949, section 2: 3.

30 The music and sound cues for the production are in the HRHRC. A summary of the leitmotifs can be found in Taubman, "Plays with Music," 3 and in Robert Bagar, "*Death of a Salesman* an Unsung Opera," *New York World-Telegram*, 26 March 1949: 5, NYPL. The music from the Alex North score is used on the Caedmon recording of *Death of a Salesman*, no. TRS-310-S (3), 1966.

31 The music cues are indicated in the "Death of a Salesman" script marked "final mimeo script used by actors, director, and stage manager," HRHRC.

32 Ciment, *Kazan*, 40.

33 See Ciment, *Kazan*, 21, 40–41; Kazan, *A Life*, 49, 90.

34 "The *Salesman* Has a Birthday," *New York Times*, 5 February 1950. Reprinted in Martin, *The Theater Essays*, 13.

35 "Arthur Miller Ad-Libs on Elia Kazan," *Show* (January 1964); reprinted in Roudané, *Conversations*, 70.

36 *Ibid.*, 71.

37 *Ibid.*

38 "Excerpts from the notebook kept by Elia Kazan in preparation for directing *Death of a Salesman* by Arthur Miller," reprinted in

Kenneth Thorpe Rowe, *A Theater in Your Head* (New York: Funk and Wagnalls, 1960), 44. Subsequently cited in the text as KN.

39 Miller has indicated that the piece of business was Lee J. Cobb's idea, referring to it as "Lee's masterstroke, a little thing that shone forth his greatness" in *Salesman in Beijing* (197), although it appears in Kazan's original annotation of the script (KN 52).

40 "Miller Ad-Libs," 74.

41 Russell Rhodes, "The Story of an Odd-Job Man Who Refused to Leave," *New York Herald Tribune*, 20 February 1949, section 5: 2.

42 The incident is based on a real camping trip during which Miller's cousins found "an old whore in a local tavern and spen[t] the night taking turns with her in the pup tent and in the morning cut her reward by half, figuring that as brothers they should only be charged one fee" (*T* 122–23).

43 The line was revised to read, "Where's that girl? I'm going in tonight," before it was finally cut altogether.

44 In *Timebends: A Life*, Miller offers an explanation for his revision of the restaurant scene: "My one scary hour came with the climactic restaurant fight between Willy and the boys, when it all threatened to come apart. I had written a scene in which Biff resolves to tell Willy that the former boss from whom Biff had planned to borrow money to start a business has refused to so much as see him and does not even remember his working for the firm years ago. But on meeting his brother and father in the restaurant, he realizes that Willy's psychological stress will not permit the whole catastrophic truth to be told and he begins to trim the bad news. From moment to moment the scene as originally written had so many shadings of veracity that Arthur Kennedy, a very intelligent citizen indeed, had trouble shifting from a truth to a half-truth to a fragment of truth and back to the whole truth, all of it expressed in quickly delivered, very short lines. The three actors, with Kazan standing beside them, must have repeated the scene through a whole working day, and it still wobbled. 'I don't see how we can make it happen,' Kazan said as we left the theatre that evening. 'Maybe you ought to try

simplifying it for them.' I went home and worked through the night and brought in a new scene, which played much better and became the scene as finally performed" (*T* 189).

45   Hewitt, "The Original," 2.

46   Quoted in James Poling, "Handy 'Gadget,'" *Collier's* 129 (31 May 1952): 58.

47   *Ibid.*

48   *Ibid.*

49   *Ibid.*

50   There has been some confusion about the premiere date in Philadelphia. Mielziner records it as 24 January in *Designing for the Theatre*, but the Philadelphia reviews clearly state that it was Saturday, 22 January. Hewitt remembered that, because the premiere was Saturday evening, the company had to wait until late Sunday afternoon for the first reviews (Hewitt, "The Original," 4).

51   "Living Theater," *Philadelphia Evening Bulletin*, 24 [?] January 1949: 22.

52   Edwin H. Schloss, "*Death of a Salesman* on Locust Stage," 24 January 1949, unidentified newspaper, clippings file, PFL.

53   Arthur Miller Scrapbook, HRHRC.

54   "The Theatre," *Town and Country* 17 (1949): 65.

55   Robert Coleman, "*Death of a Salesman* Is Emotional Dynamite," New York *Daily Mirror*, 11 February 1949. Reprinted in Rachel W. Coffin, ed., *NYTC*, 10 (1949): 360.

56   "*Death of a Salesman*, a New Drama by Arthur Miller, has Premiere at the Morosco," *New York Times*, 11 February 1949. Reprinted in Coffin, *NYTC*, 361.

57   "Triumph at the Morosco," New York *Sun*, 11 February 1949. Reprinted in Coffin, *NYTC*, 360.

58   "*Death of a Salesman* A Powerful Drama," *New York Post*, 11 February 1949. Reprinted in Coffin, *NYTC*, 359.

59   "Audience Spellbound by Prize Play of 1949," *New York Journal-American*, 11 February 1949. Reprinted in Coffin, *NYTC*, 358.

60   Louis A. Capaldo to Arthur Miller, 23 May 1949, HRHRC.

61 "A Salesman is Everybody," *Fortune* 39 (May 1949): 79.

62 Rust Hills, "Conversation: Arthur Miller and William Styron," *Audience* 1 (November–December 1971). Reprinted in Roudané, *Conversations*, 224–25.

63 "Old Glamour, New Gloom," *Partisan Review* 16 (1949): 633.

64 "Notes on the Theatre," *Hudson Review* 2 (1949): 272.

65 *Ibid.*

66 "New Plays in Manhattan," *Time* 53 (21 February 1949): 75.

67 "Drama," *The Nation* 168 (5 March 1949): 284.

68 Howard Barnes, "A Great Play Is Born," *New York Herald Tribune*, 11 February 1949: 14. Reprinted in Coffin, *NYTC*: 358.

69 Coleman, "Emotional Dynamite."

70 William Hawkins, "*Death of a Salesman* Powerful Tragedy," *New York World-Telegram*, 11 February 1949: 16. Reprinted in Coffin, *NYTC*, 359.

71 "Arthur Miller's New Play An Absorbing Experience," *Christian Science Monitor*, 19 February 1949: 12.

72 "Seeing Things: Even as You and I," *Saturday Review* 32 (26 February 1949): 31.

73 "Tragedy and the Common Man," *New York Times*, 27 February 1949. Reprinted in Martin, *The Theater Essays*, 3.

74 See Clark, "Old Glamour"; George Jean Nathan, "The Theatre," *American Mercury* 68 (June 1949): 679–80; Eric Bentley, "Back to Broadway," *Theatre Arts* 33 (November 1949): 13; and John Gassner, *The Theatre in Our Times* (New York: Crown, 1954), 65 and "Tragic Perspectives: A Sequence of Queries," *Tulane Drama Review* 2 (May 1958): 20–22. Even Eleanor Roosevelt had her say, making it clear that she had experienced no tragic katharsis from the production: "I remained untouched and somewhat critically aloof. One does not hear voices at one moment and talk sensibly to the son of one's old employer a little later on. Surely, there are dreamers and there are totally untruthful people in the world, people who are untruthful with themselves, with their families and with the world as a whole. They fail everyone, including

themselves, but I don't know whether one really needs a whole evening of gloom to impress that truth upon one ... If you go to see this play, be sure you don't happen to be in a gloomy mood. If you are you will come out even gloomier than when you went in" ("Gloomy Hit Show Fails to Depict Average Man," *New York World-Telegram,* 28 April 1949).

75   "Well Worth Waiting For," *New Yorker* 24 (19 February 1949): 58.

76   Clark, "Old Glamour," 633.

77   "The Success Dream on the American Stage," *Tomorrow* 8 (May 1949). Reprinted in *Lies Like Truth* (New York: Macmillan, 1958), 69.

78   Bentley, "Back to Broadway," 13.

79   Harvey Breit, "A Brief Visit – And Some Talk – With Thomas Mann," *New York Times,* 29 May 1949, section 7: 12.

80   Quoted by Thomas Mitchell in Philip K. Scheuer, "Mitchell Calls 'Salesman' Stage Portrait of Emotions," unidentified newspaper, clippings file, PFL.

81   "Powerful Drama."

82   "Powerful Tragedy," 359.

83   "Seeing Things," 32.

84   "Theatre: Attention!" *New Republic* 120 (28 February 1949): 27.

85   "Drama," 284.

86   "Playgoing ...," *Theatre Arts* 33 (April 1949): 16.

87   Leslie Midgley, "New *Salesman* – Gene Lockhart Returns to Broadway," *New York Herald Tribune,* 6 November 1949.

88   "Gene Lockhart Acting the Chief Part in Miller's *Death of a Salesman,*" *New York Times,* 4 March 1950, section 2: 1.

89   Quoted in Midgley, "New *Salesman.*"

90   "Thomas Mitchell Brings his Portrait of Willie Loman to the Morosco," *New York Times,* 21 September 1950: 20.

91   "Thomas Mitchell," 20.

92   Quoted in Ward Morehouse, "Keeping up with Kazan," *Theatre Arts* 41 (June 1957): 22.

93   Quoted in Scheuer, "Mitchell Calls."

94   "Thomas Mitchell," 20.

PRODUCTIONS IN ENGLISH

1   *New York Times,* 5 February 1950: 2.

2   Luke P. Carroll, "Birth of a Legend: First Year of *Salesman,"*
    New York Herald Tribune, 5 February 1950.

3   Unpublished letter from Paul Muni to Elia Kazan, 10 May
    1949, HRHRC.

4   *Ibid.*

5   Quoted in William Attwood, "Kazan Says London Will Like
    Death of a Salesman," *New York Herald Tribune,* 5 June 1949,
    section 5: 1.

6   W. A. Darlington, "London Sees Miller's *Death of a Salesman,"*
    New York Times, 7 August 1949, section 2: 1.

7   Quoted in Ward Morehouse, "Keeping up with Kazan," *Theatre
    Arts* 41 (June 1957): 22.

8   Quoted in Ronald Hayman, "Interview," *Arthur Miller* (London:
    Heinemann, 1970). Reprinted in Matthew C. Roudané, ed.,
    Conversations with Arthur Miller (Jackson: University Press
    of Mississippi, 1987), 187.

9   *Salesman in Beijing* (New York: Viking, 1983), 152–53.

10 Quoted in "Muni to Quit Salesman," *New York Times,*
    11 December 1949: 84.

11 Samuel G. Freedman, "*Salesman* Extended Run Imperiled,"
    New York Times, 20 April 1984: C3.

12 "*Death of a Salesman* Moves Londoners," *New York Times,* 29 July
    1949: 12.

13 "*Death of a Salesman* by Arthur Miller," *The Times* (London),
    29 July 1949: 9.

14 "Poetry Without Words," *New Statesman and Nation* 38
    (6 August 1949): 146.

15 *Ibid.* J. C. Trewin also objected, calling the play "needlessly
    portentous" ("The World of the Theatre," *Illustrated London
    News* 215 [1949]: 320).

16 "Poetry," 146. Although Alan Dent complained that the play
    was "rambling episodic . . . all over the place in time as well as

whereabouts" (*News Chronicle*, quoted in "*Death of a Salesman*
Moves Londoners"), Eric Keown wrote in *Punch* (217 [10 August
1949]: 163) that the play was "extremely interesting in construction, its frequent dips into the past are so smoothly managed that
the main flow of the story towards its tremendous climax is
never checked . . . Mr. Miller's sleight-of-hand is always strictly
relevant."

17 Peter Fleming, "The Theatre," *Spectator* 183 (5 August
1949): 173.

18 Ivor Brown, "As London Sees Willy Loman," *New York Times
Magazine*, 28 August 1949, section 6: 59.

19 E. B. Cronston, Letter to the Editor, "Bounder and Cad?" *New
York Times*, 11 September 1949, section 6: 6.

20 Quoted in "Grand Slam," *Time* 54 (8 August 1949): 59.

21 "Author Accused of Supporting Reds," *Irish Independent*,
3 April 1951.

22 Leaflet in the Arthur Miller Collection, HRHRC.

23 Unpublished letter from Max (Mordecai) Gorelik to Arthur Miller,
3 April 1951, HRHRC.

24 J. J. Hayes, "Willy Loman in Dublin," unidentified newspaper
clipping, HTC.

25 *Ibid.*

26 Gabriel Fallon, "*Death of a Salesman*," unidentified newspaper
clipping, HTC.

27 *Ibid.*

28 *Ibid.*

29 K. "*Death of a Salesman* at the Gaiety," *Irish Times*, 3 April 1951.

30 Maurice Kennedy, "Out of the New World," *Sunday Press*, 8 April
1951.

31 Gorelik to Miller, 3 April 1951.

32 See Martin Squire, "Johannesburg Bad Manners Marred Opening
Night," Johannesburg *Sunday Times*, 21 January 1952, and Morris
Edges, "A Spark of Revolt in the Theatre," Johannesburg *Herald*,
15 February 1952: 9.

33 "Ben-Ami's Triumph in a Drama of American Life," *The Cape Argus*, 21 November 1951.

34 I. J., "Theatrical Night to Remember," *Cape Times*, 21 November 1951.

35 "Talk of the Town: For Your Diary," *Cape Times*, 24 November 1951: 20.

36 Squire, "Johannesburg Bad Manners."

37 Edges, "A Spark of Revolt," 9.

38 "Thank You, Ben-Ami," Johannesburg *Sunday Times*, 27 March 1952.

39 Louis Calta, "News of the Stage," *New York Times*, 4 November 1973: 83.

40 Quoted in Bernard Carragher, "Their Fathers were Salesmen, so they Understand Willy Loman," Philadelphia *Evening Bulletin*, undated newspaper clipping, PFL.

41 Carragher, "Their Fathers were Salesmen."

42 See Bob Sokolsky, "Drama Guild Tests Miller's *Death of a Salesman*," Philadelphia *Evening Bulletin*, 1 March 1974 and Howard A. Coffin, "Balsam Powerful in *Death of a Salesman*," *Philadelphia Inquirer*, 2 March 1974: B2.

43 Sokolsky, "Drama Guild."

44 Coffin, "Balsam Powerful," B2.

45 *Ibid.*

46 Arthur Massolo, "SRO Sign Up for Play Hit by Legion," *New York Post*, 10 December 1954: 6.

47 *Ibid.* Actually, Miller was not called before the Committee until the passport investigations of 1956.

48 Quoted in "Play Group Ignores *Salesman* Protest," *New York Times*, 12 November 1954: 23.

49 "Protested Play Given," *New York Times*, 10 December 1954: 42.

50 George Ross, "*Death of a Salesman* in the Original," *Commentary* 11 (February 1951): 184.

51 *Ibid.*

52 *Ibid.*, 186.

53 Howard Taubman, "Theater: Willy Revisited," *New York Times*, 20 July 1963: 11.

54 Henry Hewes, "Opening Up the Open Stage," *Saturday Review* 46 (24 August 1963): 34 and John K. Sherman, "Decline, Fall of Willy Loman Shown with Impact, Pathos," *Minneapolis Star*, 17 July 1963.

55 Taubman, "Theater," 11.

56 John H. Harvey, "Guthrie *Salesman* Called Blockbuster," *St. Paul Pioneer Press*, 17 July 1963.

57 Hewes, "Opening Up," 34.

58 Dan Sullivan, "Guthrie Theater Debuts its Version of *Death of a Salesman*," *Minneapolis Morning Tribune*, 17 July 1963.

59 Unpublished letter from Hume Cronyn to Arthur Miller, 29 July 1963, HRHRC.

60 Sullivan, "Guthrie Theater."

61 Hewes, "Opening Up," 34.

62 Unpublished letter from Terry Carter to Kay Brown, January 1960, HRHRC.

63 Unpublished letter from Arthur Miller to George [C. Scott], 28 April 1975, HRHRC.

64 Quoted in Mel Gussow, "Stage: Black *Salesman*," *New York Times*, 9 April 1972: 69.

65 Quoted in Carl Schoettler, "Actor in *Death of a Salesman* Went on Stage at Age 13," Baltimore *Evening Sun,* 3 April 1972: C6. See also Larry Siddons, "A Black Willy Loman Talks of *Salesman*'s Soul," *New York Post*, 4 April 1972: 60.

66 Quoted in Siddons, "A Black Willy Loman."

67 *Ibid.*

68 Gussow, "Black *Salesman*."

69 *Ibid.*

70 Hollie I. West, "*Death of a Salesman*," *Washington Post*, 14 April 1972: D1.

71 *Ibid.*, D7.

72 *Ibid.*

73 Unpublished letter from Arthur Miller to George [C. Scott], 28 April 1975, HRHRC.

74 William A. Raidy, "Scott Towers in *Salesman*," *Long Island Press*, 27 June 1975.

75 Leonard Probst, NBC Radio, 26 June 1975. Reprinted in Joan Marlowe and Betty Blake, eds., *NYTC* 36 (1975): 225.

76 Martin Gottfried, "Rebirth of the *Salesman*," *New York Post*, 27 June 1975. Reprinted in Marlowe and Blake, *NYTC* 36, 222.

77 "The Salesman Dies Again," *New York Magazine* 8 (7 July 1975): 74. Willy, of course, does not say that Bernard is "looking anemic," but says to the boys, "What an anemic!" (23) in reference to his behavior. Christopher Sharp ("*Death of a Salesman*," *Women's Wear Daily*, 27 June 1975. Reprinted in Marlowe and Blake, *NYTC* 36, 221) remarked that, "with the introduction of black performers it makes no sense for Willy to call Bernard 'you anemic.'"

78 Douglas Watt, "Scott in Miller's *Salesman*," New York *Daily News*, 27 June 1975. Reprinted in Marlowe and Blake, *NYTC* 36, 221.

79 Stanley Kauffmann, "Death of a Salesman," *New Republic* 173 (19 July 1975): 33.

80 Gottfried, "Rebirth."

81 Watt, "Scott."

82 Walter Kerr, "This Salesman is More than Myth," *New York Times*, 29 June 1975, section 2: 5.

83 Unpublished letter from Arthur Miller to George C. Scott, 1 June 1975, HRHRC.

84 "Scott Puts Acting Magic in *Salesman*," *New York Times*, 27 June 1975. Reprinted in Marlowe and Blake, *NYTC* 36, 225.

85 Sharp, "*Death of a Salesman.*"

86 Gottfried, "Rebirth."

87 T. E. Kalem, "A Défi to Fate," *Time* 106 (7 July 1975): 43. Reprinted in Marlowe and Blake, *NYTC* 36, 222.

88 Gottfried, "Rebirth."

89   John Beaufort, "Visions of America's Past – Recent and Not," *Christian Science Monitor*, 27 June 1975: 23.

90   Watt, "Scott."

91   Jack Kroll, "Triumph," *Newsweek* 86 (7 July 1975). Reprinted in Marlowe and Blake, *NYTC* 36, 224.

92   Harold Clurman, "Theatre," *Nation* 221 (19 July 1975): 60.

93   Probst, NBC Radio.

94   Gottfried, "Rebirth."

95   Michael Billington, "The Not-So-Damn Yankees," *Guardian*, 5 September 1979.

96   Robert Cushman, "Triumph of a Salesman," *Observer*, 23 September 1979: 15.

97   Peter Jenkins, "The Ugly Spectacle of Failure," *The Spectator*, 29 September 1979: 25.

98   Clive Hirschhorn, "Arthur Miller's Death of a Salesman," *Sunday Express*, 23 September 1979.

99   Peter Hepple, "*Death of a Salesman* at the Lyttelton," *The Stage and Television Today* (London), 27 September 1979: 15.

100   Peter Lewis, "Willy May Be Dead, But His Story Won't Lie Down," *Daily Mail* (London), 21 September 1979: 3.

101   Kenneth Hurren, "Selling Handicap," *What's On In London*, 28 September 1979: 34.

102   Barry Took, "Hello, Willy," *Punch* 277 (3 October 1979): 581.

103   Quoted in Ian Lyness, "Miller on Monroe – and a Prophesy [*sic*] Come True," *Yorkshire Post*, 3 September 1979.

104   John Barber, "Guilt Edged Miller," *Daily Telegraph*, 10 September 1979.

105   Quoted in Christopher Bigsby, ed., *Arthur Miller and Company* (London: Methuen, 1990), 59.

106   Mitchell, quoted in Bigsby, *Arthur Miller*, 73.

107   *Ibid.*, 74.

108   *Ibid.*, 73.

109   Joseph H. Mazo, "*Death of a Salesman*," *Women's Wear Daily*, 26 December 1979: 10.

110 B. A. Young, "Death of a Salesman," *Financial Times*, 21 September 1979.

111 Rivers Scott, "Injecting Life and Laughter into Miller's *Salesman*," *Now!* 28 September–4 October 1979: 120.

112 Jenkins, "The Ugly Spectacle," 25.

113 Sheridan Morley, "Miller's *Salesman* in Strong Revival," *International Herald Tribune*, 26 September 1979.

114 Mazo, "*Death of a Salesman*," 10.

115 C. V. R., "Royal *Salesman* Doubly Compelling," *Eastern Daily Press*, 11 September 1979.

116 John Elsom, "Likely Lads," *Listener*, 27 September 1979: 431.

117 Ken Healey, "Nimrod: Unique, Trail-Blazing, But Can It Survive Financially?" *Canberra Times*, 25 July 1982: 8.

118 Brian Hoad, "A Salesman That Doesn't Quite Sell," *Bulletin*, 27 July 1982.

119 H. G. Kippax, "Drama of Shattering Power," *Sydney Morning Herald*, 12 July 1982.

120 *Ibid.*

121 John Moses, "Contemporary Warning in a 30-Year-Old Play," *Australian*, 12 July 1982.

122 "A Veritable Feast," *National Times*, 18–24 July 1982.

123 Healey, "Nimrod."

124 See Hoad, "A Salesman," and Kippax, "Drama."

125 Healey, "Nimrod."

126 Kippax, "Drama."

127 *Elia Kazan: A Life* (New York: Knopf, 1988), 338.

128 Stephen Schiff, "A Conversation," *Vanity Fair* (September 1985): 94.

129 Bigsby, *Arthur Miller*, 71.

130 Quoted in Richard Christiansen, "Dustin Hoffman and the Rebirth of a Classic *Salesman*," *Chicago Tribune*, 15 January 1984, section 13: 18.

131 Mel Gussow, "Dustin Hoffman's *Salesman*," *New York Times Magazine*, 18 March 1984: 40.

132 Samuel G. Freedman, "*Salesman* Collaborators Part Ways," *New York Times*, 15 August 1984: C17.

133 *Ibid.*

134 Gussow, "Dustin Hoffman," 48.

135 *Ibid.*, 46.

136 Quoted in Christiansen, "Classic *Salesman*," 18.

137 Quoted in Gussow, "Dustin Hoffman," 46.

138 Freedman, "*Salesman* Extended," C3.

139 Richard Christiansen, "Hoffman, *Salesman* Deliver a Powerful Product," *Chicago Tribune*, 20 January 1984, section 2: 8.

140 David Richards, "Rebirth of a *Salesman*," *Washington Post*, 27 February 1984: B6.

141 *Ibid.*

142 Holly Hill, "Why Tootsie Looks to be Heading for Tony," *The Times* (London), 3 April 1984: 13.

143 Jack Kroll, "Hoffman's Blazing Salesman," *Newsweek* 103 (9 April 1984): 107. Reprinted in Joan Marlowe and Betty Blake, eds., *NYTC* 45 (1984): 327.

144 "*Death of a Salesman*," *Women's Wear Daily*, 30 March 1984. Reprinted in Marlowe and Blake, *NYTC* 45, 329.

145 Kissel, "*Death of a Salesman*."

146 Robert Brustein, "Show and Tell," *New Republic* 190 (7 May 1984): 29.

147 John Simon, "Salesmen Go, Salesmen Come," *New York* 17 (9 April 1984): 72.

148 Richard Schickel, "Rebirth of an American Dream," *Time* 123 (9 April 1984). Reprinted in Marlowe and Blake, *NYTC* 45, 330.

149 Lloyd Rose, "Lost in America," *Atlantic* 253 (April 1984): 130.

150 Brendan Gill, "Tears for Willy Loman," *New Yorker* 60 (9 April 1984): 121; Clive Barnes, "*Death of a Salesman* Comes Alive," *New York Post*, 30 March 1984. Reprinted in Marlow and Blake, *NYTC* 45, 327.

151 See Lloyd Grove, "Hoffman's High Powered Salesman," *Washington Post*, 2 March 1984, Weekend: 9 and Hill, "Tootsie."

152 Kroll, "Blazing *Salesman.*"

153 Hill, "Tootsie."

154 Freedman, "*Salesman* Collaborators," C17. Freedman reported that the initial investment had been completely recouped during the Chicago preview.

155 Freedman, "*Salesman* Extended," C3.

156 Freedman, "*Salesman* Collaborators," C17.

157 *Ibid.*

PRODUCTIONS IN OTHER LANGUAGES

1 "*DEATH OF A SALESMAN*, Foreign Productions," mimeographed sheet in Arthur Miller Collection, HRHRC.

2 Paul Barnett, "22 Vienna Curtain Calls for *Death of a Salesman*," *New York Tribune*, 19 March 1950.

3 "*Death of a Salesman* Acclaimed in Vienna," *New York Times*, 4 March 1950: 10.

4 Barnett, "Vienna."

5 *Ibid.*

6 Harold Van Allen, "An Examination of the Reception and Critical Evaluation of the Plays of Arthur Miller in West Germany from 1950–1961," diss., University of Arkansas, 1964, 86, 94.

7 Quoted in "*Salesman* Opens in Two German Cities," *New York Times*, 28 April 1950: 25.

8 "die erbarmungslose Ausstoßung des alt und müde gewordenen Menschen durch die gewinnbesessene Welt," Claude Hill, "Könige, Helden und Handlungsreisende" (April 1950), unidentified newspaper clipping, Arthur Miller Collection, HRHRC.

9 "Der Phantast Loman ist nicht nur ein Opfer des kapitalistischen Milieus." Dr. Fred Hepp, "Arthur Miller: Der Tod des Handlungsreisenden," *Kultur und Leben* 106 (10 May 1965): 13.

10 "Obwohl kein soziales Drama mehr Diskussionen über das Glück des Menschen ausgelöst hat, ist es allgemeinmenschlich." Walter G.

Busse, "Subtiles Stück über Vater-Son," unidentified newspaper clipping, Arthur Miller Collection, HRHRC.

11 Hans Braun, quoted in "*Salesman* Opens," 25.

12 Quoted in Van Allen, "An Examination," 74.

13 "Die Szene, das transparente Haüschen Willy Lomans mit den New Yorker Wolkenkratzern im Hintergrund, bleibt in allen Akten dieselbe." Quoted in Van Allen, "An Examination," 78.

14 *Westfälische Zeitung*, 11 November 1951; quoted in Van Allen, "An Examination," 79.

15 Jacques Huisman, quoted in Christopher Bigsby, ed., *Arthur Miller and Company* (London: Methuen, 1990): 225.

16 *Ibid.*

17 *Ibid.*, 226.

18 *Ibid.*, 227.

19 Jean-Jacques Gautier, "La Mort d'un commis voyageur," *Le Figaro*, undated newspaper clipping, Arthur Miller Collection, HRHRC.

20 "commode, suggestif, et gris sombre, comme la pièce." Robert Kemp, "La Mort d'un commis voyageur." Unidentified newspaper clipping, Arthur Miller Collection, HRHRC.

21 Quoted in Robert A. Martin, ed., *The Theater Essays of Arthur Miller* (New York: Viking, 1978), 271.

22 "What Makes Plays Endure," *New York Times*, 15 August 1965, section 2: 3. Reprinted in Martin, *The Theater Essays*, 262.

23 "un art de nouveau tourné vers la vie." B. Poirot-Delpech, "*Mort d'un commis voyageur* d'Arthur Miller," *Le Monde*, 11 May 1965: 16.

24 Jean Paget, "*La Mort d'un commis voyageur* d'Arthur Miller," *Combat*, 10 May 1965: 35.

25 N. Z., "Le Théâtre de la commune d'Aubervilliers fait preuve d'une belle vitalité," *Le Monde*, 8 May 1965: 16.

26 "étonnant, impressionnant, remarquable, inimitable," Jean-Jacques Gautier, "*Mort d'un commis voyageur*," *Le Figaro*, undated clipping, Arthur Miller Collection, HRHRC.

27 "Quel acteur, certes, mais quel personnage aussi, ce Loman! C'est

M. Quelconque, M. N'Importe Qui, M. Personne, M. Tout
le Monde, dans un univers de vie à crédit, de mort à crédit, de
capitalisme, de traites, d'assurance-vie, et encore de traites, et
toujours de traites, aux Etats-Unis – plus encore qu'ici." Gautier,
"*Mort d'un commis voyageur.*"

28 "Elle s'incrit, avec une admirable tension tragique, dans le temps et
dans l'espace, épaulée par les tres beaux décors d'inspiration presque
futuriste d'André Acquart." Paget, "*La Mort,*" 35.

29 "Bref, toute l'horreur du monde américanisé, dominé par
l'abominable dieu de l'argent, est cernée." Paget, "*La Mort,*" 35.

30 Claude Baignères, "Au théâtre d'Aubervilliers *Mort d'un commis-
voyageur* d'Arthur Miller," *Le Figaro,* 10 May 1965: 25.

31 Thomas Quinn Curtiss, "Miller's *Death of a Salesman,*"
International Herald Tribune, undated newspaper clipping, Arthur
Miller Collection, HRHRC.

32 André Ransan, "*Mort d'un commis voyageur* d'Arthur Miller,"
L'Aurore, 2 December 1970: 12a.

33 Curtiss, "Miller's *Death of a Salesman.*"

34 "la avidez del espectador, lo gana y lo mantiene en un apasionado
interés," *Primer Plano* (Madrid), quoted in *Noticiario del la
Compañía Lope de Vega* 1 (February 1952): 8.

35 J. M. A., "Una leccion de buen teatro," *Madrid.* Reprinted in
Noticiario de la Compañía Lope de Vega 1 (February 1952): 3.

36 "El Exito fue rotundo y unanime," *La Hoja del Lunes* (Madrid).
Reprinted in *Noticiario de la Compañía Lope de Vega* 1 (February
1952): 2; and Alfonso Sastre, "De una carta abierta, en favor de *La
Muerte de un viajante,*" *Arriba* (Madrid). Reprinted in *Noticiario de
la Compañía Lope de Vega* 1 (February 1952): 6.

37 Vane C. Dalton, "*Death of a Salesman,*" *Mexican Life* 6 (June 1953).

38 *Ibid.*

39 *Ibid.*

40 Unpublished letter from Gala Ebin to Kermit Bloomgarden, 8
September 1959, Arthur Miller Collection, HRHRC.

41 *Ibid.*

42 G. Kapralov, "The Tragedy of Willy Loman," *Pravda*, 29 July 1959. Trans. Elaine Rusinko.

43 Inge Morath and Arthur Miller, *Chinese Encounters* (New York: Farrar, Straus, and Giroux, 1979), 19.

44 See, for example, Arthur Miller, *Salesman in Beijing* (New York: Viking, 1983), 101, 163. Subsequently cited in the text as *B*.

45 Quoted in Bigsby, *Arthur Miller and Company*, 205.

46 Henian Yuan, "*Death of a Salesman* in Beijing," *Chinese Literature* 10 (1983): 105.

47 *Ibid.*

48 Catherine Diamond, "*Death of a Salesman*," *Theatre Journal* 45 (1993): 108.

49 *Ibid.*, 109.

50 *Ibid.*, 110.

51 *Ibid.*, 109.

52 John Dillon, "*Salesman* No Shi," *American Theatre* 1 (November 1984): 14.

53 Quoted in Nancy Spiller, "The International *Salesman*," *Los Angeles Herald Examiner*, 15 September 1985.

54 Dillon, "*Salesman* No Shi," 14.

55 *Ibid.*

56 *Ibid.*

57 *Ibid.*, 13.

58 Quoted in Spiller, "International *Salesman*."

MEDIA PRODUCTIONS

1 Al Hine, "*Death of a Salesman*," *Holiday* 11 (March 1952): 16.

2 "Play Into Picture," *Sight and Sound* 22 (October–December 1952): 82. Subsequently cited in the text as *LB*.

3 Miller has written that "March had been our first choice for the stage role but had turned it down – although he persuaded himself in later years that he had not been offered it formally" (*Timebends: A Life* [New York: Grove, 1987], 315).

4   Hine, "*Death of a Salesman*," 18.

5   For an analysis of these scenes, see Edward Murray, "Arthur Miller," in *The Cinematic Imagination* (New York: Ungar, 1972): 72–73.

6   *Death of a Salesman*, Acting Edition (New York: Dramatists Play Service, 1952), 89. Subsequent references appear in the text.

7   *Timebends*, 315.

8   *Ibid.* This line appears in the film, but Kevin McCarthy's delivery of it is mild and resigned, rather than "furious," as Miller's script indicates.

9   "The Movie Camera and the American: Arthur Miller, Samuel Goldwyn, and the Material World," *Commentary* 13 (1952): 276. See also Murray, *The Cinematic Imagination*, 74.

10   Warshow, "The Movie Camera," 276.

11   Quoted in Ronald Hayman, "Interview," in *Arthur Miller* (London: Heinemann, 1970). Reprinted in Matthew C. Roudané, ed., *Conversations with Arthur Miller* (Jackson: University Press of Mississippi, 1987), 187.

12   *Timebends*, 315.

13   Quoted in Christopher Bigsby, ed., *Arthur Miller and Company* (London: Methuen, 1990), 57.

14   *Ibid.*, 135.

15   "Introduction," *Arthur Miller's Collected Plays* (New York: Viking, 1957). Reprinted in Robert A. Martin, ed., *The Theater Essays of Arthur Miller* (New York: Viking, 1978), 139.

16   "Introduction," 140.

17   *Timebends*, 315.

18   Miller has told the story a number of times. See, for example, *Timebends* 315–16; Miller, "Introduction" 140–41; Bigsby, 57–58; and Hayman, 187.

19   See Hine, "*Death of a Salesman*," 16 and Bosley Crowther, "*Death of a Salesman* with Fredric March and Mildred Dunnock, at Victoria," *New York Times*, 21 December 1951: 21.

20   John McCarten, "The Current Cinema," *New Yorker* 27 (22 December 1951): 62.

21 See, for example, Hollis Alpert, "Mr. Miller's Indignant Theme," *Saturday Review* 34 (22 December 1951): 34; "The New Pictures," *Time* 58 (31 December 1951): 60; and Warshow, "The Movie Camera," 275–76.

22 Hine, "*Death of a Salesman*," 18.

23 "The New Pictures," *Time*, 60.

24 McCarten, "Current Cinema," 62.

25 Hine, "*Death of a Salesman*," 16.

26 See McCarten, "Current Cinema," 62 and Alpert, "Indignant Theme," 34.

27 Alpert, "Indignant Theme," 34.

28 "The New Pictures," *Time*, 60.

29 *Ibid.*

30 Philip T. Hartung, "'It Comes with the Territory,'" *Commonweal* 55 (1951): 300.

31 *Ibid.*

32 Crowther, "*Death of a Salesman*," 21.

33 *Death of a Salesman*, adapted by Alan Savage, CBC Radio Script, HRHRC.

34 Act I ends with Biff, "horrified," saying to Happy: "Happy . . . Happy, wake up . . . It's true. I found the rubber tubing down the cellar just now. I took it away . . . but oh, my God, it's true!" (*Death of a Salesman*, adapted by Robert Cenedella, NBC Star Playhouse, episode no. 28, taped 8 April 1954, broadcast 11 April 1954. Script at HRHRC).

35 *Salesman*, NBC Playhouse Script, 1.

36 Unpublished letter from Peter Witt to Arthur Miller, 17 December 1957, Arthur Miller Collection, HRHRC.

37 "Independent Television," *The Times*, 28 November 1957: 3.

38 *Ibid.*

39 Pat Pearce, unidentified newspaper clipping, HRHRC.

40 "A Great *Salesman*," *Toronto Globe and Mail*, 11 December 1958.

41 Ron Poulton, "See – Hear," *Telegram* (Toronto), 11 December 1958.

42 *Ibid.*

43 "Attention to Willy Loman," *The Times* (London), 25 May 1966.

44 "Exalted Theater," *Newsweek* 67 (23 May 1966): 74.

45 See "Exalted Theater," 74 and Jack Gould, "TV: *Death of a Salesman*," *New York Times*, 9 May 1966: 79.

46 Quoted in Stanley Frank, "A Playwright Ponders a New Outline for TV," *TV Guide* 14 (8 October 1966): 8, 10.

47 Cobb received top billing in the credits, even above the title.

48 Robert Lewis Shayon, "*Death of a Salesman*," *Saturday Review* 49 (28 May 1966): 39.

49 Gould, "TV," 79.

50 "Fine Hours," *Time* 87 (20 May 1966): 85.

51 "Exalted Theater," 74.

52 Shayon, "*Salesman*," 39.

53 "Fine Hours," 82.

54 Samuel G. Freedman, "*Salesman* Collaborators Part Ways," *New York Times*, 15 August 1984: C17.

55 Don Shewey, "TV's Custom-Tailored *Salesman*," *New York Times*, 15 September 1985, section 2: 1, 23; Bill King, "From *Tootsie* to *Salesman*: Hoffman Takes to Television," *Atlanta Journal*, 15 September 1985; Jacqui Tully, "Hoffman's *Salesman* Implodes on TV," *Arizona Daily Star*, 15 September 1985; Nancy Spiller, "The International *Salesman*," *Los Angeles Herald Examiner*, 15 September 1985.

56 Shewey notes the amount of the budget, but erroneously gives the shooting schedule as twenty days. Dustin Hoffman said in "A Conversation" that the play was shot in twenty-five days (*Vanity Fair*, September 1985: 94).

57 Jacqui Tully, "*Death of a Salesman* Comes to the Tube," *Arizona Daily Star*, 15 September 1985.

58 Shewey, "Custom-Tailored," 23.

59 *Private Conversations on the Set of Death of a Salesman*, dir. Christian Blackwood, Punch Productions, Lorimar Video, 1986.

60 Shewey, "Custom-Tailored," 23.

61 Quoted in Tully, "*Death of a Salesman* Comes to the Tube."

62 Quoted in Steve Sonsky, "Production Proves Art has a Place on TV," Miami *Herald*, 15 September 1985.

63 Shewey, "Custom-Tailored," 23.

64 *Ibid.*

65 Dustin Hoffman and Arthur Miller, "A Conversation": 94.

66 Sonsky, "Art Has a Place."

67 The video *Private Conversations* records the evolution of this scene, from what is clearly a filmed stage scene to the intimate television sequence it became under Schlöndorff's direction.

68 "*Death of a Salesman* Doubles 1966 Audience," *New York Times*, 17 September 1985: C17.

69 Mark Dawidziak, "Hoffman and *Salesman* Shine in TV Staging," *Akron Beacon Journal*, 15 September 1985.

70 "A *Death of a Salesman* for Our Time," *Newsday* (Long Island, New York), 12 September 1985.

71 Bill Carter, "Hoffman and Co.'s *Salesman* Holds Undeniable Power," Baltimore *Sun*, 13 September 1985.

72 Michael Feingold, "An American Tragedy, Like it or Not," *Village Voice* 30 (24 September 1985): 41.

73 Dan Sullivan, "*Salesman* – Shrunk in the Big Eye's Glare," *Los Angeles Times*, 22 September 1985.

74 *Ibid.*

75 *Ibid.*

76 Mike Duffy, "This *Salesman* Gets the Pitch Just Right," Detroit *Free Press*, 15 September 1985.

DISCOGRAPHY

Miller, Arthur, "Arthur Miller Speaking and Reading from *The Crucible* and *Death of a Salesman*," Spoken Arts, SA 704. 1956.

Death of a Salesman. Dir. Ulu Grosbard. Read by Lee J. Cobb, Mildred Dunnock, Michael Tolan, Gene Williams, Dustin Hoffman, Camila Ashland, Ralph Bell, Royal Beal, George Coe, Francine Beers, Tom Pedi, Ann Wedgeworth, Joyce Aaron. Music by Alex North. Caedmon TRS-310-S, 3 33 1/3 rpm records. 1966. Also Caedmon A310, two cassettes.

Death of a Salesman. Read by Lee J. Cobb, Mildred Dunnock. Sound recording, two cassettes. Harper Collins CPN 310.

Death of a Salesman. Sound recording, two records. Decca DL 9007.

Death of a Salesman. Sound recording, two cassettes. Recorded Books 20124.

Death of a Salesman. Read by Paul Douglas. Sound recording, one cassette. Mind's Eye.

VIDEOGRAPHY

Death of a Salesman. Dir. Alex Segal. Prod. David Susskind. Actors Lee J. Cobb, Mildred Dunnock, George Segal, James Farentino, Edward Andrews, Albert Dekker. Music Robert Drasnin. CBS Television. 1966. Three video cassettes. Museum of Television and Radio, New York.

Death of a Salesman. Roxbury and Punch Production. Dir. Volker Schlöndorff. Prod. Robert F. Colesberry. Actors Dustin Hoffman, Kate Reid, John Malkovich, Stephen Lang, Charles Durning. Music Alex North. KLV-TV Karl-Lorimar Video. 1986. One video cassette.

Private Conversations on the Set of Death of a Salesman. Lorimar Home Video. 1985. One video cassette. PBS documentary of the making of the 1986 film, includes Arthur Miller, Dustin Hoffman, Volker Schlöndorff, Stephen Lang, and John Malkovich.

BIBLIOGRAPHY

The bibliography is arranged in three sections. Section 1 lists the major collections of archival material. Section 2 lists reviews and criticism of specific productions, arranged chronologically. Section 3 lists general literary criticism and articles related to *Death of a Salesman*.

PRIMARY MATERIALS

Billy Rose Theatre Collection, New York Public Library for the Performing Arts

Contains sketches and drawings by Jo Mielziner for the original production of *Death of a Salesman*, as well as scripts, letters, photographs, memoirs, and clippings files related to this and later productions.

Harry Ransom Humanities Research Center, University of Texas at Austin

Arthur Miller Collection

Contains Miller's early working notebook and preproduction drafts of *Death of a Salesman*, prop, costume and lighting charts, music and sound cues, and other material related to the original production, as well as letters, photographs, scrapbooks, clippings files, correspondence, and scripts related to the original and later productions.

Theatre Collection

Contains photographs, drawings, and other material related to the original and later productions of *Death of a Salesman*.

Harvard Theatre Collection, Harvard College Library

Contains clippings files and photographs related to the original and later productions of *Death of a Salesman*.

Lilly Library, Indiana University
Contains letters, documents, and other materials related to several productions of *Death of a Salesman.*

Theatre Collection, Philadelphia Free Library
Contains clippings files and photographs related to the original and later productions of *Death of a Salesman,* particularly those related to Philadelphia.

CRITICISM OF SPECIFIC PRODUCTIONS

Theatre USA

1949 January. Philadelphia premiere of February 1949 production
Sensenderfer, R. E. P., "Living Theater." *Evening Bulletin* [Philadelphia] 24 [?] January 1949: 22.

1949 10 February, New York, Morosco
Allison, Gordon, "Day After a Hit: Rush for Seats, Rest for Author." *New York Herald Tribune* 12 February 1949.
Arnold, Jerome, "Vetoes the *Salesman.*" *New York Herald Tribune* 22 May 1949.
Atkinson, Brooks, "At the Theatre." *New York Times* 11 February 1949: 27.
"*Death of a Salesman.*" *New York Times* 20 February 1949, section 2: 1.
"Much Prized Play." *New York Times* 15 May 1949, section 2: 1.
Avedon, Richard, *Theatre Arts* 33 (July 1949): Cover.
Bagar, Robert, "*Death of a Salesman* an Unsung Opera." *New York World-Telegram* 26 March 1949: 5.
Barnes, Howard, "A Great Play is Born." *New York Herald Tribune* 11 February 1949: 14.
"Broadway Borrows Some Tricks from Hollywood for the Theater." *New York Herald Tribune* 8 May 1949, section 5: 1+.
"*Death of a Salesman* Sets the Pace for Broadway." *New York Herald Tribune* 20 February 1949, section 5: 1–2.

Beaufort, John, "Arthur Miller's New Play an Absorbing Experience."
  Christian Science Monitor 19 February 1949: 12.

Bentley, Eric, "Back to Broadway." *Theatre Arts* 33 (November
  1949): 12–15.

Beyer, William, "The State of The Theatre: The Season Opens."
  School and Society 70 (1949): 363–64.

Blum, Daniel, "*Death of a Salesman,*" in *Theatre World 1948–49*,
  vol. V (New York: Greenberg, 1949): 91.
  "*Death of a Salesman,*" in *Theatre World 1949–50*, vol. VI
  (New York: Greenberg, 1950): 112.

Breit, Harvey, "A Brief Visit – and Some Talk – with Thomas
  Mann." *New York Times* 29 May 1949, section 7: 12.

Brown, John Mason, "Seeing Things: Even as You and I." *Saturday
  Review* 32 (26 February 1949): 30–32.

Calta, Louis, "*Salesman* Tops Theatrical Polls." *New York Times*
  12 July 1949: 31.

Carmody, Jay, "Drama Finds New Life in Play About Death."
  Washington Sunday Star 15 May 1949: C6.

Carroll, Luke P., "Birth of a Legend: First Year of *Salesman.*"
  New York Herald Tribune 5 February 1950, section 5: 1.

Chapman, John, "*Death of a Salesman* a Fine Play, Beautifully
  Produced and Acted." *New York Daily News* 11 February
  1949.

Clark, Eleanor, "Old Glamour, New Gloom." *Partisan Review*
  16 (1949): 631–36.

Clippings Files: HRHRC, NYPL, PFL.

Clune, Henry W., "Seen and Heard." *New York Democrat and
  Chronicle* [Rochester] 24 February 1949.

Clurman, Harold, "Theatre: Attention!" *New Republic* 120
  (28 February 1949): 26–28.

Coffin, Rachel W., ed., "*Death of a Salesman.*" *New York Theatre
  Critics' Reviews* 10 (1949): 358–61. (Reprints of Atkinson,
  Barnes, Chapman, Coleman, Garland, Hawkins,
  Morehouse, Watts)

Coleman, Robert, "*Death of a Salesman* is Emotional Dynamite."
  Daily Mirror 11 February 1949.

Dash, Thomas R., "'Life' of a Salesman." *Women's Wear Daily*
  24 February 1949: 51.

"*Death of a Salesman.*" *Life* 26 (1949): 115, 117–18, 121.

Gabriel, Gilbert W., "Playgoing …" *Theatre Arts* 33 (April
  1949): 15–17.

Garland, Robert, "Audience Spellbound by Prize Play of 1949."
  New York Journal-American 11 February 1949: 16.

Gassner, John, "The Theatre Arts." *Forum* 111 (1949): 219–21.

Gibbs, Wolcott, "The Theatre: Well Worth Waiting For."
  New Yorker 24 (19 February 1949): 58, 60.

Harper's Bazaar 83 (March 1949): 161.

Hawkins, William, "Death of a Salesman: Powerful Tragedy."
  New York World - Telegram 11 February 1949: 16.

"Higher Call." *New Yorker* 25 (26 March 1949): 21.

Hughes, Elinor, "*Death of a Salesman* Fulfills Promise of Author."
  Boston Herald 13 March 1949.

Kaye, Joseph, "*Death of a Salesman*, A Man's Failure in Life."
  Kansas City Star 17 April 1949: C18.

Krutch, Joseph Wood, "Drama." *Nation* 168 (5 March 1949):
  283–84.

"Magnificent Death." *Newsweek* 33 (21 February 1949): 78.

Miller, Arthur, "The *Salesman* Has a Birthday." *New York Times*
  5 February 1950, section 2: 1–3.

Morehouse, Ward, "Triumph at the Morosco." *New York Sun*
  11 February 1949.

Morgan, Frederick, "Notes on the Theatre." *Hudson Review* 2
  (1949): 272–73.

Nathan, George Jean, "The Theatre" *American Mercury* 68
  (June 1949).

"New Plays in Manhattan." *Time* 53 (21 February 1949):
  74–76.

"Noted in Passing." *House and Garden* 95 (May 1949): 218.

Phelan, Kappo, "*Death of a Salesman.*" *Commonweal* 49 (1949): 520–21.

"Pulitzer Prizes Announced by Columbia University." *Publishers Weekly* 155 (1949): 1877.

Rhodes, Russell, "The Story of an Odd-Job Man Who Refused to Leave." *New York Herald Tribune* 20 February 1949, section 5: 1–2.

Roosevelt, Eleanor, "Gloomy Hit Show Fails to Depict Average Man." *New York-World Telegram* 28 April 1949.

"*Salesman, Kate* Win Perry Awards." *New York Times* 25 April 1949: 19.

Shea, Albert, "*Death of a Salesman.*" *Canadian Forum* 29 (July 1949): 86–87.

Taubman, Howard, "Plays with Music Between the Lines." *New York Times* 27 March 1949, section 2: 3.

"The Theatre." *American Mercury* 68 (June 1949): 679–80.

Vogue 113 (1 March 1949): 157.

Watt, Douglas, "He Couldn't Have a Pleasanter Name; Some Inside Stuff." *New York Daily News* 21 July 1949: 63.

Watts, Richard, "*Death of a Salesman* a Powerful Drama." *New York Post* 11 February 1949.

  "Two on the Aisle." *New York Post Home Weekend Magazine* 13 March 1949: 13.

Wyatt, Euphemia Van Rensselaer, "The Drama." *Catholic World* 169 (April 1949): 62–63.

1949 November. Lee J. Cobb replaced by Gene Lockhart

Atkinson, Brooks, "Portrait of Willy." *New York Times* 12 March 1950, section 2: 1.

Calta, Louis, "A New Willy Loman." *New York Times* 10 November 1949: 40.

"Gene Lockhart Acting the Chief Part in Miller's *Death of a Salesman.*" *New York Times* 4 March 1950, section 2: 1.

Midgley, Leslie, "New *Salesman* – Gene Lockhart Returns to
 Broadway." *New York Herald Tribune* 6 November 1949.

1950 May. Gene Lockhart replaced by Albert Dekker
Dekker, Albert, "*Salesman*'s Travelling Understudy." *New York
 Times* 30 April 1950, section 2: 2.

*1950 September. Albert Dekker replaced by Thomas Mitchell, who had
taken* Death of a Salesman *on tour between February and September
1950.*
Atkinson, Brooks, "Thomas Mitchell Brings his Portrait of Willy
 Loman to the Morosco." *New York Times* 21 September 1950:
 20.

1949 20 September. Chicago and Tour, Erlanger Theater
Cassidy, Claudia, "*Death of a Salesman.*" *Chicago Daily Tribune*
 21 October 1949.
Clippings File: HRHRC.

1951 8 September. Touring Company
Blum, Daniel, "*Death of a Salesman,*" in *Theatre World 1951–52,*
 vol. VIII (New York: Greenberg, 1952).

1954 26 February. San Francisco, The Actor's Workshop
Nichols, Luther, "Proof that Local Theater can Outshine
 Broadway." *San Francisco Chronicle* 4 March 1954: 14.
Vickers, John, "Theatre." *The Argonaut* 12 March 1954.

1954 9 December. Glenwood Landing, Long Island, The Glen Players
Clippings Files: HRHRC, NYPL.
Massolo, Arthur, "SRO Sign Up for Play Hit by Legion." *New York
 Post* 10 December 1954: 6.
"Play Group Ignores *Salesman* Protest." *New York Times*
 12 November 1954: 23.
"Protested Play Given." *New York Times* 10 December 1954: 42.

1960 June. Philadelphia, Park Playhouse
Clippings File: PFL.
Gaghan, Jerry, "*Death of a Salesman* in Park." *Philadelphia Daily News* 21 June 1960.
Murdock, Henry T., "*Salesman* Still Magical." *Philadelphia Enquirer* 21 June 1960.

1963 16 July. Minneapolis, The Guthrie Theater.
Blum, Daniel, "*Death of a Salesman*," in *Theatre World 1963–64*, vol. xx (Philadelphia: Chilton, 1964).
Clippings Files: HRHRC, NYPL.
Harvey, John H., "Guthrie *Salesman* Called Blockbuster." *St. Paul Pioneer Press* 17 July 1963.
Hewes, Henry, "Opening Up the Open Stage." *Saturday Review* 46 (24 August 1963): 34.
Sherman, John K., "Decline, Fall of Willy Loman Shown with Impact, Pathos." *Minneapolis Star* 17 July 1963.
Sullivan, Dan, "Guthrie Theater Debuts its Version of *Death of a Salesman.*" *Minneapolis Morning Tribune* 17 July 1963.
Taubman, Howard, "Theater: Willy Revisited." *New York Times* 20 July 1963: 11.

1972 8 April. Baltimore, Center Stage
Gussow, Mel, "Stage: Black *Salesman.*" *New York Times* 9 April 1972: 69.
Schoettler, Carl, "Actor in *Death of a Salesman* Went on Stage at Age 13." *Evening Sun* (Baltimore) 3 April 1972: C6, 28.
Siddons, Larry, "A Black Willy Loman Talks of *Salesman*'s Soul." *New York Post* 4 April 1972: 60.
West, Hollie I., "*Death of a Salesman.*" *Washington Post* 14 April 1972: D1, 7.

1972 May. Arlington Park (Illinois), Arlington Park Theater
Leonard, Will, "*Death of a Salesman* Stirring." *Chicago Tribune* 26 May 1972, section 2: 7.

1974 26 February. Philadelphia, Philadelphia Drama Guild

Calta, Louis, "News of the Stage." *New York Times* 4 November 1973: 83.

Clippings File: PFL.

Coffin, Howard A., "Balsam Powerful in *Death of a Salesman.*" *Philadelphia Enquirer* 2 March 1974: B2.

Sokolsky, Bob, "Drama Guild Tests Miller's *Death of a Salesman.*" *Evening Bulletin* (Philadelphia) 1 March 1974.

Willis, John, "Philadelphia Drama Guild," in *Theatre World 1973–74*, vol. xxx (New York: Crown, 1974): 215.

1974 October. Washington DC, Arena

Coe, Rochard L., "Arena's *Death*: Alive and Well." *Washington Post* 24 (October 1974): B1, 11.

Richards, David, "*Salesman*: Masterpiece Masterfully Done." *Washington Star-News* 24 October 1974: C1, 3.

1975 26 July. New York, Circle in the Square

Barnes, Clive, "Scott Puts Acting Magic in *Salesman.*" *New York Times* 27 June 1975: 26.

Beaufort, John C., "Visions of America's Past – Recent and Not." *Christian Science Monitor* 27 June 1975: 23.

Clippings Files: HRHRC, NYPL.

Clurman, Harold, "Theatre." *Nation* 221 (19 July 1975): 59–60.

Gill, Brendan, "A Painful Case." *New Yorker* 51 (7 July 1975): 63.

Gottfried, Martin, "Rebirth of the *Salesman.*" *New York Post* 27 June 1975.

Hughes, Catherine, "Summer Session." *America* 133 (2 August 1975): 54.

Kalem, T. E., "A Défi to Fate." *Time* 106 (7 July 1975): 43.

Kauffmann, Stanley, "*Death of a Salesman.*" *New Republic* 173 (19 July 1975): 20, 33.

Kerr, Walter, "This *Salesman* is More than Myth." *New York Times* 29 June 1975, section 2: 1, 5.

Kroll, Jack, "Triumph." *Newsweek* 86 (7 July 1975): 61.

Marlowe, Joan and Betty Blake, eds., "*Death of a Salesman.*" *New York Theatre Critics' Reviews* 36 (1975): 221–25. (Reprints of Barnes, Beaufort, Gottfried, Kalem, Kroll, Sharp, Watt, Wilson.)

Probst, Leonard, "*Death of a Salesman.*" NBC Radio. 26 June 1975.

Raidy, William A., "Scott Towers in *Salesman.*" *Long Island Press* 27 June 1975.

Schumach, Murray, "Miller Still a *Salesman* for a Changing Theater." *New York Times* 26 June 1975: 32. Reprinted in *International Herald Tribune* 1 July 1975.

Sharp, Christopher, "*Death of a Salesman.*" *Women's Wear Daily* 27 June 1975.

Simon, John, "The Salesman Dies Again." *New York Magazine* 8 (7 July 1975): 74.

Watt, Douglas, "Scott in Miller's *Salesman.*" *New York Daily News* 27 June 1975.

Wilson, Edwin, "Contrasting Views of American Life." *Wall Street Journal* 27 June 1975.

1980 8 May. Chicago, Steppenwolf Theater Co.

Winer, Linda, "Miller Classic Still Powerful Theater." *Chicago Tribune* 9 May 1980, section 3: 3.

1984 19 January. Chicago preview, Blackstone Theater

Christiansen, Richard, "Arthur Miller's Verdict on Willy: He Has Elements of Nobility." *Chicago Tribune* 15 January 1984, section 13: 19.

  "Dustin Hoffman and the Rebirth of a Classic *Salesman.*" *Chicago Tribune* 15 January 1984, section 13: 18–19.

  "Hoffman, *Salesman* Deliver a Powerful Product." *Chicago Tribune* 20 January 1984, section 2: 8.

  "*Salesman* Hits Road with Better Wares." *Chicago Tribune* 17 February 1984, section 5: 2.

1984 February/March. Washington preview, Kennedy Center

Grove, Lloyd, "Hoffman's High Powered *Salesman.*" *Washington Post* 2 March 1984, Weekend: 9.

Richards, David, "Rebirth of a *Salesman.*" *Washington Post* 27 February 1984: B1, 6.

1984 29 March. New York, Broadhurst Theater

Barnes, Clive, "*Death of a Salesman* Comes Alive." *New York Post* 30 March 1984.

Beaufort, John, "Miller's *Death of a Salesman* is Reborn on Broadway." *Christian Science Monitor* 30 March 1984.

Brenner, Marie, "Rebirth of a *Salesman.*" *New York* 17 (26 March 1984): 32–38.

Brustein, Robert, "Show and Tell." *New Republic* 190 (7 May 1984): 27–29.

Clippings File: HRHRC.

Cunningham, Dennis, "*Death of a Salesman.*" WCBS TV 2 29 March 1984.

Franklin, Rebecca, "Hoffman Singular Willy in *Salesman.*" *Birmingham News* (Alabama) 22 April 1984.

Freedman, Samuel G., "*Salesman* Collaborators Part Ways." *New York Times* 15 August 1984: C17.

   "*Salesman* Extended Run Imperiled." *New York Times* 20 April 1984: C3.

Gill, Brendan, "Tears for Willy Loman." *New Yorker* 60 (9 April 1984): 121.

Gilman, R., *Harpers Bazaar* 117 (March 1984): 60.

Gussow, Mel, "Dustin Hoffman's *Salesman.*" *New York Times Magazine* 18 March 1984, section 6: 36–38, 40, 46, 48, 86.

Hill, Holly, "Why Tootsie Looks to be Heading for Tony: *Death of a Salesman.*" *The Times* (London) 3 April 1984: 13.

Hughes, Catharine, "Salesmen." *America* 150 (28 April 1984): 320.

Kissel, Howard, "*Death of a Salesman.*" *Women's Wear Daily* 30 March 1984.

Kroll, Jack, "Hoffman's Blazing *Salesman.*" *Newsweek* 103 (9 April 1984): 107.

Marlowe, Joan and Betty Blake, eds., *New York Theatre Critics' Reviews* 45 (19 March 1984): 324–32.

Mason, M. S., "*Death of a Salesman.*" *Christian Science Monitor* 83 (27 August 1991): 10.

Rich, Frank, "Theater: Hoffman *Death of a Salesman.*" *New York Times* 30 March 1984: C3.

Rose, Lloyd, "Lost in America." *Atlantic* 253 (April 1984): 130, 132.

Sauvage, Leo, "On Stage: Corrupted Salesmen." *New Leader* 67 (16 April 1984): 20–21.

Schickel, Richard, "Rebirth of an American Dream." *Time* 123 (9 April 1984): 104–105.

Schiff, Stephen, "A Conversation." *Vanity Fair* (September 1985): 91–95.

Siegel, Joel, "*Death of a Salesman.*" WABC-TV 29 March 1984.

Simon, John, "Salesmen Go, Salesmen Come." *New York* 17 (9 April 1984): 72–73.

Watt, Douglas, "*Death of a Salesman.*" *New York Daily News* 30 March 1984.

Weales, Gerald, "Rewarding Salesmen: New from Mamet, Old from Miller." *Commonweal* 111 (4 May 1984): 278–79.

Wilson, Edwin, "*Death of a Salesman.*" *Wall Street Journal* 4 April 1984.

1987 2 January. Kentucky, Actors Theater of Louisville.

Mootz, William, "*Death of a Salesman.*" *Courier Journal* (Louisville) 3 January 1987.

1989 October. Los Angeles, LA Theater Center

Miller, Daryl H., "Production Gives New Life to *Death of a Salesman.*" *Daily News* (Los Angeles) 30 October 1989.

1991 August. Minneapolis, Tyrone Guthrie Theater

Mason, M. S., "The Guthrie's Shows Tap Many Cultures."
Christian Science Monitor 83 (27 August 1991): 10.

"A Season of Fortitude, Farce, and Charm at the Theater."
Christian Science Monitor 83 (27 August 1991): 10.

Theatre: England

1949 28 July. London, Phoenix Theatre

Attwood, William, "Kazan Says London Will Like *Death of a
Salesman*." *New York Herald Tribune* 5 June 1949, section 5:
1–2.

Brown, Ivor, "As London Sees Willy Loman." *New York Times* 28
(August 1949), section 6: 11, 59.

"Loman Over Jordan." *Observer* 31 July 1949: 6.

Clippings File: HRHRC.

Cronston, E. B., Letter to the Editor, "Bounder and Cad?"
New York Times 11 September 1949, section 6: 6.

Darlington, W. A., "London Sees Miller's *Death of a Salesman*."
New York Times 7 August 1949, section 2: 1.

"*Death of a Salesman* at the Phoenix." *Theatre World* 45 (October
1949): 11–18.

"*Death of a Salesman* by Arthur Miller." *The Times* 29 July 1949: 9, 12.

"*Death of a Salesman* Moves Londoners." *New York Times* 29 July
1949: 12.

Fleming, Peter, "The Theatre." *Spectator* 183 (5 August 1949): 173.

"Grand Slam." *Time* 54 (8 August 1949): 59.

Henderson, James W., "Willy Loman." *New York Times* 11
September 1949, section 6: 6.

Hobson, Harold, "From America." *Sunday Times* 31 July 1949: 2.

Hope-Wallace, Philip, "*Death of a Salesman*." *Guardian*
(Manchester) 30 July 1949: 5.

Keown, Eric, "At the Play." *Punch* 217 (10 August 1949): 163.

"Muni to Quit Salesman." *New York Times* 11 December 1949: 84.

S., F., "*Death of a Salesman*." *Theatre World* (September 1949): 9, 29.

"The Return of Paul Muni." *Sphere* 198 (1949): 247.

Trewin, J. C., "Plays in Performance." *Drama* 15 (Winter 1949): 8.
"The World of the Theatre." *Illustrated London News* 215 (1949): 320.

Worsley, T. C., "Poetry Without Words." *New Statesman and Nation* 38 (6 August 1949): 146–47.

1965 2 November. Cambridge University Amateur Dramatic Club, ADC Theatre
"Outstanding *Salesman*." *The Times* 3 November 1965: 17.

1970 April. Bolton, Octagon Theatre
Bates, Merete, "*Death of a Salesman* in Bolton." *Guardian* (Manchester) 1 April 1970: 8.

1979 20 September. London, National Theatre, Lyttelton
"Acting Triumph for Alf." *Daily Express* 22 September 1979.

Barber, John, "*Death of a Salesman*." *The Times* 21 September 1979: 15.
"Guilt Edged Miller." *Daily Telegraph* 10 September 1979.

Barker, Felix, "Cheers, But No Tears for the Death of Willy." *Eastern News* 21 September 1979.

Billington, Michael, "The Hard Sell." *Guardian* 22 September 1979: 11.
"The Not-So-Damn Yankees." *Guardian* (Manchester) 5 September 1979.

Chambers, Colin, "Not Just What You Do But the Way You Do It." *Morning Star* 10 April 1979.

Clippings File: HRHRC.

Critics' Forum, with Paul Bailey, Hilary Spurling, John Carey, and John Weightman. BBC Radio 3. 29 September 1979.

Cushman, Robert, "Triumph of a *Salesman*." *Observer* 23 September 1979: 15.

"Death us do Part." *Gay News* 4 October 1979.

Elsom, John, "Likely Lads." *Listener* 27 September 1979: 431.

Grant, Steve, "*Death of a Salesman.*" *Time Out* 27 September 1979.

Hepple, Peter, "*Death of a Salesman* at the Lyttelton." *The Stage and Television Today* (London) 27 September 1979: 15.

Hirschhorn, Clive, "Arthur Miller's *Death of a Salesman.*" *Sunday Express* 23 September 1979.

Hurren, Kenneth, "Selling Handicap." *What's On In London* 28 September 1979: 34.

Jenkins, Peter, "The Ugly Spectacle of Failure." *Spectator* 29 September 1979: 25–26.

King, Francis, "End of Alf Garnett." *Sunday Times* 23 September 1979: 14.

Leech, Michael, "National Pride is Justified." *Where To Go* 10 November 1979.

Lewis, Peter, "Willy May Be Dead, But His Story Won't Lie Down." *Daily Mail* (London) 21 September 1979: 3.

Lyness, Ian, "Miller on Monroe – and a Prophesy [*sic*] Come True." *Yorkshire Post* 3 September 1979.

Mazo, Joseph H., "*Death of a Salesman.*" *Women's Wear Daily* 26 December 1979: 10.

Mitchell, Warren, "Garnett's Creator and Champion." *Sunday Times* 30 September 1979: 13.

Morley, Sheridan, "Miller's *Salesman* in Strong Revival." *International Herald Tribune* 26 September 1979.

Nathan, David, "The Sin of Success." *Jewish Chronicle* 28 September 1979.

Nightingale, Benedict, "Hard Slog." *New Statesman* 98 (28 September 1979): 478–79.

Nurse, Keith, "Arthur Miller to See Revival." *The Times* 26 July 1979: 15.

R., C. V., "Royal *Salesman* Doubly Compelling." *Eastern Daily Press* 11 September 1979.

Scott, Rivers, "Injecting Life and Laughter into Miller's *Salesman.*" *Now!* 28 September–4 October 1979: 120.

Shulman, Milton, "The Dreams Die, Too." *Evening Standard* 21 September 1979: 15.

Taylor, John Russell, *Drama* 135 (1980): 38–40.

Thickell, Arthur, "Proof of His Talent." *Daily Mirror* 22 September 1979.

Took, Barry, "Hello, Willy." *Punch* 277 (3 October 1979): 581.

Watters, Tamie, "*Death of a Salesman.*" *Christian Science Monitor* 5 December 1979: 23.

Young, B. A., "*Death of a Salesman.*" *Financial Times* 21 September 1979.

1986 February. Manchester, Royal Exchange Theatre

Wilcocks, Dick, "*Death of a Salesman.*" *Plays and Players* 389 (February 1986): 28.

1988 12 March. Birmingham, Birmingham Repertory Theatre

Allen, Paul, "Capitalism's Children." *New Statesman* 115 (8 April 1988): 31–32.

Eyres, Harry, "Failure in Focus." *The Times* 17 March 1988: 18.

Thornber, Robin, "*Death of a Salesman.*" *Guardian* (Manchester) 17 March 1988: 32.

Theatre: other English language productions

Australia

1982 11 July. Sydney, York Theatre

Clippings File: HRHRC.

Dance, Carol, "*Death of a Salesman* – Brilliant." *Wentworth Courier* 16 July 1982.

Davis, Taffy, "Mel's Towering Performance." *Sun* 7 July 1982.

Gerrett, Virginia, "*Salesman* ... Story of Willy Who Could Not Accept Reality." *Manly Daily* 16 July 1982.

Harris, Frank, "*Salesman* Gets Star Treatment." *Telegraph* 10 July 1982.

Healey, Ken, "Nimrod: Unique, Trail-Blazing, But Can it Survive Financially?" *Canberra Times* 25 July 1982: 8.

Hoad, Brian, "A *Salesman* that Doesn't Quite Sell." *Bulletin* 27 July 1982.

Hourihan, Michael, "*Death of a Salesman.*" *Education* (July 1983).

Kippax, H. G., "Drama of Shattering Power." *Sydney Morning Herald* 12 July 1982.

L., R. E., "*Death of a Salesman.*" *Maritime Worker* (August 1982): 31.

Lonoff, Judith, "Nimrod Shoots High with *Death of a Salesman.*" *City Express* 21 July 1982.

Menzies, Colin, "Mitchell's Superb in *Salesman.*" *Sun-Herald* 18 July 1982.

Moses, John, "Contemporary Warning in 30-Year-Old Play." *Australian* 12 July 1982.

Payne, Carol, "Strong Example of Materialism." *North Shore Times* 14 July 1982.

"A Veritable Feast," *National Times*, 18–24 July 1982.

Ireland

1951 2 April. Dublin, Gaiety Theatre

"Author Accused of Supporting Reds." *Irish Independent* 3 April 1951.

Clippings Files: HRHRC, HTC.

K., "*Death of a Salesman* at the Gaiety." *Irish Times* 3 April 1951.

Kennedy, Maurice, "Out of the New World." *Sunday Press* 8 April 1951.

South Africa

1951 20 November. Cape Town, Labia Theatre

"Ben-Ami's Triumph in a Drama of American Life." *The Cape Argus* 21 November 1951.

Clippings File: HRHRC.

J., I., "Theatrical Night to Remember." *Cape Times* 21 November 1951.

Sachs, Joseph, "Cape Town Theatre: *Death of a Salesman.*" *Trek* 15 (December 1951): 13–14.

"Talk of the Town: For Your Diary." *Cape Times* 24 November
1951: 20.

1952 18 January. Johannesburg, Reps Theatre
Clippings File: HRHRC.
"Decline and Fall of a Salesman Make Moving Drama."
unidentified newspaper, clippings file, HRHRC, 21 January
1952: 7.
Egdes, Morris, "A Spark of Revolt in the Theatre." *Herald*
15 February 1952: 9.
H., H., "Ben-Ami's Unforgettable Performance." *Jewish Herald*
25 January 1952.
"Jacob Ben Ami's Triumphant Night." *Sunday Express* 20 January
1952.
Squire, Martin, "Johannesburg Bad Manners Marred Opening
Night." *Sunday Times* (Johannesburg) January 1952.
"Thank You, Ben-Ami," *Sunday Times* (Johannesburg), 27 March
1952.

Theatre: productions in translation

Austria
1950 4 April. Vienna, Theater in der Josephstadt
Barnett, Paul, "22 Vienna Curtain Calls for *Death of a Salesman*."
New York Tribune 19 March 1950.
"*Death of a Salesman* Acclaimed in Vienna." *New York Times*
4 March 1950: 10.

China
1983 7 May. Beijing, Beijing People's Art Theatre
Adams, Phoebe-Lou, "*Salesman* in Beijing." *Atlantic* 253 (June
1984): 124.
Broder, Jonathan, "Arthur Miller and *Salesman* Hit the Road to
Peking." *Chicago Tribune* 20 April 1983: 1–2.
Lord, Bette Bao, "*Salesman* in Beijing." *New York* 17 (14 May
1984): 77–78.

Miller, Arthur, *Salesman in Beijing* (New York: Viking, 1984).

Rosinger, Lawrence, "*Salesman* in Beijing." *The Drama Review* 28 (Fall 1984): 106.

Wren, Christopher, "Willy Loman Gets China Territory." *New York Times* 7 May 1983.

Yuan, Henian, "*Death of a Salesman* in Beijing." *Chinese Literature*, 10 (1983): 103–109.

1992 18 April Taipei, Taiwan, National Theatre
Diamond, Catherine, "*Death of a Salesman*." *Theatre Journal* 45 (1993): 108.

Denmark
1950 21 October. Copenhagen, Odense Teater
"*Salesman* in Denmark." *New York Times* 16 March 1950: 41.

France
1952 January. Paris, Théâtre de Paris
Clippings File: HRHRC.

Joly, G., "Le Théâtre National de Belgique Nous a Présenté: *La mort d'un commis voyageur* Tragédie Moderne d'Arthur Miller." *L'Aurore* 9 January 1952.

1965 1 May. Aubervilliers, Théâtre de la commune d'Aubervilliers
Abirached, Robert, "Allez à Aubervilliers." *Le Nouvel Observateur* 27 (20 May 1965): 32–33.

Baignères, Claude, "Au Théâtre d'Aubervilliers *Mort d'un commis voyageur* d'Arthur Miller." *Le Figaro* 10 May 1965: 25.

Clippings File: HRHRC.

France Illustration 331 (16 February 1952): 163.

Gilles, Edmond, "Un Réquistitoire Contre Le 'Mode de Vie' Américain." *L'Humanité* 10 May 1965.

Paget, Jean, "*La mort d'un commis voyageur* d'Arthur Miller." *Combat* 10 May 1965: 35.

"Parisiens décentralisés pour *Le commis voyageur.* Claude Dauphin à
Aubervilliers." *France-Soir* 9 May 1965.

Poirot-Delpech, B., "*Mort d'un commis voyageur* d'Arthur Miller."
Le Monde 11 May 1965: 16.

Z., N., "Le théâtre de la commune d'Aubervilliers fait preuve d'une
belle vitalité." *Le Monde* 8 May 1965: 16.

1970 30 November Paris
Clippings File: HRHRC.
Ransan, André, "*Mort d'un commis voyageur* d'Arthur Miller."
L'Aurore 2 December 1970: 12a.

Germany
1950 Berlin
Clippings File: HRHRC.
"May Offer *Salesman* in Berlin." *New York Times* 9 June 1949: 35.

1950 27 April Düsseldorf, 28 April Munich
Clippings File: HRHRC.
Neue Literarische Welt 7 (1953): 4.
"*Salesman* Opens in Two German Cities." *New York Times* 28 April
1950: 25.

1965 9 May Augsburg Städtische Bühne
Clippings File: HRHRC.
Hepp, Dr. Fred., "Arthur Miller: *Der Tod des Handlungsreisenden.*"
Kultur und Lebeln 106 (10 May 1965): 13.

Hungary
1984 December Csokonai Theatre
Bognár, Lambert, "Arthur Miller: *Az Ügynök Halála.* A Debreceni
Csokonai Szinház Elöadása." *Vigilia* 50 (1985): 279–80.

Kiss, Eszter, "Arthur Miller: *Az Ügynök Halála* és Tennessee
Williams: *A Vágy Villamosa* Cimü Drámá já Nak
Magyarországi Bemutatóiról." *Szinháztudomanyi Szemle* 10
(1986): 21–42.

Somlyia, János, "Egy Föszerep Metamorfózisa. *Az Ügynök Halála Debrecenben.*" *Szinház* 18 (January 1985): 17–19.

Italy

1975 2 July Rome, Pompeii, Milan
Clippings File: HRHRC.
"*Il commesso* con Buazzelli per la riapertura di un teatro." *La Stampa* 25 September 1975.

Japan

1984 Tokyo, Institute of Dramatic Arts
Dillon, John, "*Salesman No Shi*: A Director Discovers the Japanese Essence." *American Theatre* 1 (7) (November 1984): 12–15.
Spiller, Nancy, "The International *Salesman.*" *Los Angeles Herald Examiner* 15 September 1985.

Mexico

1953 18 April. Mexico City, Palacio de Bellas Artes
Dalton, Vane C., "*Death of a Salesman.*" *Mexican Life* 6 (June 1953): 1, 29.

Spain

1952 10 January. Madrid, La Compañía Lope de Vega
Clippings File: HRHRC.
"La Critica, Ante el Estreno en Madrid *La Meurte de un Viajante.*" *Noticiario de la Compañía Lope de Vega* 1 (February 1952): 1–9.

Soviet Union (Russia)

1959 July. Leningrad and Moscow, Pushkin Academic Theatre of Drama
Kapralov, G., "The Tragedy of Willy Loman."
Trans Elaine Rusinko. *Pravda* 29 July 1959.
Miller, Arthur, "In Russia." *Harper's* 239 (September 1969): 37–78.

United States

1951 16 January. Brooklyn, NY, Parkway Theater, Yiddish production: Toyt Fun a Salesman

Ross, George, "*Death of a Salesman* in the Original." *Commentary* 11 (1951): 184–86.

Television/Film

1951 United States, Columbia Pictures.

Alpert, Hollis, "Mr. Miller's Indignant Theme." *Saturday Review* 34 (22 December 1951): 34.

Benedek, Laslo, "Play Into Picture." *Sight and Sound* 22 (October–December 1952): 82–84, 96.

Crowther, Bosley, "*Death of a Salesman* with Fredric March and Mildred Dunnock, at Victoria." *New York Times* 21 December 1951: 21.

"Current Feature Films." *Christian Century* 69 (20 February 1952): 231.

"*Death of a Salesman.*" *Newsweek* 38 (31 December 1951): 56–57.

"*Death of a Salesman.*" *Life* 32 (14 January 1952): 63–64, 66.

Hartung, Philip T., "'It Comes with the Territory'." *Commonweal* 55 (1951): 300–301.

Hatch, Robert, "Movies." *New Republic* 125 (31 December 1951): 22.

Hine, Al, "*Death of a Salesman.*" *Holiday* 11 (March 1952): 14, 16, 18.

Houston, Penelope, "Kramer and Company." *Sight and Sound* 22 (July–September 1952): 20–23, 48.

Kass, Robert, "Film and TV." *Catholic World* 174 (1952): 386.

McCarten, John, "The Current Cinema." *New Yorker* 27 (22 December 1951): 62.

McDonald, Gerald D., "*Death of a Salesman.*" *Library Journal* 77 (1952): 140.

"The New Pictures." *Time* 58 (31 December 1951): 60.

Reisz, Karel, "Hollywood's Anti-Red Boomerang." *Sight and Sound* 22 (January–March 1953): 132–37, 148.

Warshow, Robert, "The Movie Camera and the American: Arthur Miller, Samuel Goldwyn, and the Material World." *Commentary* 13 (1952): 275–81.

Zunser, Jesse, "*Death of a Salesman*." *Cue* 22 December 1951: 16.

1958 9 December. Toronto, CBC Television
Clippings File: HRHRC.

"A Great *Salesman*" *Globe and Mail* 11 December 1958.

Poulton, Ron, "See–Hear." *Telegram* (Toronto) 11 December 1958.

Wedman, Les, "CBC's Best Drama Show." *The Province* 11 December 1958: 35.

1961 March. Russia, LenFilm, The Bridge Cannot Be Crossed
Archer, Eugene, "Pirated US Play Filmed in Soviet." *New York Times* 10 March 1961: 24.

1962 18 November. Montreal, CBC Television, French Network
Clippings File: HRHRC.

Keable, Jacques, "Radio Télévision." *La Press* (Montreal) 19 November 1962: 24.

1966 5 May. New York, CBS Television
Adams, Val, "Willy Loman Irks Fellow Salesman." *New York Times* 27 March 1966, section 2: 25.

Cuno, John M., "TV: *Death of a Salesman*." *Christian Science Monitor* 11 May 1966: 8.

Dallos, Robert E., "*Death of a Salesman* Wins Emmy as Best Drama." *New York Times* 5 June 1967: 87.

"Exalted Theater: *Death of a Salesman*." *Newsweek* 67 (23 May 1966): 74.

"Fine Hours: *Death of a Salesman*." *Time* 87 (20 May 1966): 82, 85.

Frank, Stanley, "A Playwright Ponders a New Outline for TV." *TV Guide* 14 (8 October 1966): 7–8, 10–11.

Gent, George, "CBS Seeks Out Original Dramas." *New York Times* 22 June 1966: 95.

Gould, Jack, "Good, Bad, And In Between." *New York Times* 11 June 1967: D17.

"New Life of a *Salesman*." *New York Times* 15 May 1966, section 2: 15.

"TV: *Death of a Salesman*." *New York Times* 9 May 1966: 79.

"Looking Backward." *Newsweek* 67 (6 June 1966): 84–85.

Meehan, Thomas, "Life of a Salesman: A Television Epilogue." *Saturday Evening Post* 239 (18 June 1966): 20.

Shayon, Robert Lewis, "TV and Radio: *Death of a Salesman*." *Saturday Review* 49 (28 May 1966): 39.

"TV and Radio: The Stampede for Excellence." *Saturday Review* 49 (23 July 1966): 66.

"The 'Two-Season' Season." *Newsweek* 68 (22 August 1966): 99–100.

1985 15 September New York, CBS Roxbury and Punch Production

"A *Death of a Salesman* For Our Time." *Newsday* 12 September 1985.

Arnold, Christine, "The Theater Critic: Can Hoffman Match his Stage Brilliance?" *Miami Herald* 15 September 1985.

Canby, Vincent, "*Private Conversations* on Filming of *Salesman*." *New York Times* 7 October 1985: C16.

Carman, John, "Dustin Hoffman Splendid as Salesman." *Atlanta Journal* 13 September 1985.

Carter, Bill, "Hoffman and Co.'s *Salesman* Holds Undeniable Power." *Sun* (Baltimore) 13 September 1985.

Champlin, Charles, "Dustin Brings *Death* to Life on Film." *San Francisco Examiner* 15 September 1985.

Dawidziak, Mark, "Hoffman and *Salesman* Shine in TV Staging." *Akron Beacon Journal* (Ohio) 15 September 1985.

"*Death of a Salesman* a Hit for Living Rooms." *St. Petersburg Times* (Florida) 13 September 1985.

Dhont, F. and J. MacTrevor, "*La mort d'un commis-voyageur*." *CineRevue* 65 (19 September 1985): 20–23.

Duffy, Mike, "This *Salesman* Gets the Pitch Just Right." *Detroit Free Press* 15 September 1985.

"Dustin Hoffman *Death of a Salesman.*" *Viewers' Guide* CBS TV. 1985.

Feingold, M., "An American Tragedy, Like it or Not." *Village Voice* 30 (24 September 1985): 41.

Garron, Barry, "Reviving *Salesman.*" *Kansas City Morning Star* 15 September 1985.

Glackin, William, "TV Revives Miller Classic: *Death of a Salesman.*" *Sacramento Bee* 12 September 1985.

Hart, Jonathan, "The Promised End: The Conclusion of Hoffman's *Death of a Salesman.*" *Literature/Film Quarterly* 19 (1991): 60–65.

Holsopple, Barbara, "CBS Updates *Death of a Salesman* for '85." *Pittsburgh Press* 10 September 1985.

Humm (R. Hummler), "*Death of a Salesman.*" *Variety* 320 (18 September 1985): 54.

Johnson, B., "*Death of a Salesman.*" *On Location* 9 (September 1985): 44+.

Jones, David, "Hoffman Improves with Age as Willy Loman." *Columbus Dispatch* (Ohio) 15 September 1985.

King, Bill, "From *Tootsie* to *Salesman*: Hoffman Takes to Television." *Atlanta Journal* 15 September 1985.

McCreadie, Marsha, "*Death of a Salesman.*" *Arizona Republic* 15 September 1985.

McNeil, Helen, "American Distress: *Death of a Salesman.*" *Times Literary Supplement* 26 August 1988: 932.

Mitchell, Elvis, "TV's *Death of a Salesman* is a Refresher Course in Great American Literature." *Los Angeles Herald Examiner* 15 September 1985.

Newman, Mark, "*Death of a Salesman* is a Gem on the Tube." *Grand Rapids Press* (Michigan) 15 September 1985.

O'Connor, John J., "TV Weekend: Hoffman in *Death of a Salesman.*" *New York Times* 13 September 1985: C26.

"*Death of a Salesman* Doubles 1966 Audience." *New York Times* 17 September 1985: C17.

Ostrow, Joanne, "*Salesman* Packs Power in TelevisionTreatment." *Denver Post* 14 September 1985.

Rhein, Dave, "Hoffman's *Death of a Salesman* One of Television's Finest Moments." *Des Moines Register* 15 September 1985.

Rozmiarek, Joseph T., "*Death of a Salesman* on TV" *Honolulu Advertiser* 13 September 1985.

Shewey, D., "TV's Custom-Tailored *Salesman*." *New York Times* 15 September 1985, section 2: 1, 23.

Siegel, Ed, "CBS to Film *Death of a Salesman*." *Boston Globe* 13 October 1984: 57.

Snook, Debbie, "Hoffman Triumphs as Willy Loman in TV's *Salesman*." *Times Union* (Albany) 15 September 1985.

Sonsky, Steve, "Production Proves Art Has a Place on TV." *Miami Herald* 15 September 1985.

Sullivan, Dan, "*Salesman* – Shrunk in the Big Eye's Glare." *Los Angeles Times* 22 September 1985.

Tully, Jacqui, "*Death of a Salesman* Comes to the Tube." *Arizona Daily Star* 15 September 1985.

"Hoffman's *Salesman* Implodes on TV." *Arizona Daily Star* 15 September 1985.

Watson, Keith, "Small Screen Adds Flaws to *Salesman*." *Houston Post* 12 September 1985.

LITERARY CRITICISM

Aarnes, William, "Tragic Form and the Possibility of Meaning in *Death of a Salesman*." *Furman Studies* 29 (1983): 57–80.

Adler, Henry, "To Hell with Society." *Tulane Drama Review* 4 (May 1959): 53–76.

August, Eugene R., "*Death of a Salesman*: A Men's Studies Approach." *Western Ohio Journal* 7 (Spring 1986): 53–71.

Aylen, Leo, *Greek Tragedy and the Modern World*. London: Methuen, 1964.

Bateman, Mary B., "*Death of a Salesman*: A Clinical Look at the Willy Loman Family." *International Journal of Family Therapy* 7 (Summer 1985): 116–21.

Bates, Barclay W., "The Lost Past in *Death of a Salesman*." *Modern Drama* 11 (September 1968): 164–72.

Becker, Benjamin J., "*Death of a Salesman*: Arthur Miller's Play in the Light of Psychoanalysis." *American Journal of Psychoanalysis* 47 (Fall 1987): 195–209.

Bettina, Sister M., "Willy Loman's Brother Ben." *Modern Drama* 4 (February 1962): 409–12.

Bigsby, C. W. E., *A Critical Introduction to Twentieth-Century American Drama*, vol. II Tennessee Williams, Arthur Miller, Edward Albee. Cambridge University Press, 1984.

Bigsby, Christopher, ed., *Arthur Miller and Company*. London: Methuen, 1990.

Bliquez, Guerin, "Linda's Role in *Death of a Salesman*." *Modern Drama* 10 (February 1968): 383–86.

Blumberg, Paul, "Sociology and Social Literature: Work Alienation in the Plays of Arthur Miller." *American Quarterly* 21 (1969): 291–310.

Bock, Hedwig, "Die Rolle der Frau in Arthur Miller's frühen Dramen: Untersuchung zu seinem Konzept gesellshaftlicher Wirklichkeit." *Literarische Ansichten der Wirklichkeit: Studien zur Wirklichkeitskonstitution in Englishsprachiger Literatur*. Frankfurt: Lang, 1980: 307–22.

Brucher, Richard T., "Willy Loman and *The Soul of a New Machine*: Technology and the Common Man." *Journal of American Studies* 17 (1983): 325–36.

Brusteni, Robert, "The Memory of Heroism." *Drama Review* 4 (March 1960): 5–7.

Carson, Neil, *Arthur Miller*. New York: Grove, 1982.

Ciment, Michel, *Kazan on Kazan*. London: Secker & Warburg, 1974.

Corrigan, Robert W., ed., *Arthur Miller: A Collection of Critical Essays*. Englewood Cliffs: Prentice-Hall, 1969.

Clurman, Harold, *Lies Like Truth*. New York: Macmillan, 1958.
   "The Success Dream on the American Stage." *Tomorrow* 8 (May
   1949) 48–51.
Crawford, Cheryl, *One Naked Individual: My Fifty Years in the
   Theatre*. Indianapolis: Bobbs-Merrill, 1977.
Epstein, Charlotte, "Was Linda Loman Willy's Downfall?"
   New York Times 20 July 1975, section 2: 5.
Falb, Lewis W., *American Drama in Paris 1945–1970*. Chapel Hill:
   North Carolina University Press, 1973.
Gardner, R. H., *The Splintered Stage*. New York: Macmillan, 1965.
Gassner, John, *The Theatre in Our Times*. New York: Crown, 1954.
   "Tragic Perspectives: A Sequence of Queries." *Tulane Drama
   Review* 2 (May 1958): 20–22.
Graybill, Robert V., "Why Does Biff Boff Bimbos? Innocence as
   Evil in *Death of a Salesman*." *Publications of the Arkansas
   Philological Association* 13 (Fall 1987): 46–53.
Gross, Barry, "Peddler and Pioneer in *Death of a Salesman*." *Modern
   Drama* 7 (February 1965): 405–10.
Hadomi, Leah, "Fantasy and Reality: Dramatic Rhythm in *Death
   of a Salesman*." *Modern Drama* 31 (1988): 157–74.
Hagopian, John V., "Arthur Miller: The Salesman's Two Cases."
   Modern Drama 6 (1963): 117–25.
Hark, Ina Rae, "A Frontier Closes in Brooklyn: *Death of a Salesman*
   and the Turner Thesis." *Postscript* 3 (1986): 1–6.
Hayashi, Tetsumaro, *Arthur Miller Criticism 1930–1967*.
   Metuchen: Scarecrow, 1969.
Hayman, Ronald, *Arthur Miller*. London: Heinemann, 1970.
Heaton, C. P., "Arthur Miller on *Death of a Salesman*." *Notes on
   Contemporary Literature* 1 (January 1971): 5.
Hirschhorn, Clive, "Memoirs of a Salesman." *Plays and Players*
   394 (1986): 7–10.
Hobson, Harold, *The Theatre Now*. London: Longmans Green, 1953.
Hoevler, Diane Long, "*Death of a Salesman* as Psychomachia."
   Journal of American Culture 1 (1978): 632–37.

Hogan, Robert, *Arthur Miller.* Minneapolis: University Press of Minnesota, 1964.

Huftel, Sheila, *The Burning Glass.* New York: Citadel, 1965.

Hume, Beverly, "Linda Loman as 'The Woman' in Miller's *Death of a Salesman.*" *Notes on Modern American Literature* 9 (Winter 1985): Item 14.

Hurrell, John D., *Two American Tragedies: Reviews and Criticism of* Death of a Salesman *and* A Streetcar Named Desire. New York: Scribner, 1961.

Hynes, Joseph A., "Attention Must Be Paid ..." *College English* 23 (April 1962): 574–78.

Jackson, Esther Merle, "*Death of a Salesman*: Tragic Myth in the Modern Theatre." *CLA Journal* 7 (September 1963): 63–76.

Jacobson, Irving, "Family Dreams in *Death of a Salesman.*" *American Literature* 48 (May 1975): 247–58.

Jacquot, Jean and Catherine Mounier, "*Mort d'un Commis Voyageur* d'Arthur Miller et ses Realisations à Broadway et au Théâtre de la Commune d'Aubervilliers." In Denis Bablet and Jean Jacquot, eds., *Les Voies de la Creation Théâtrale, IV.* Paris: CNRS, 1975: 11–62.

James, Stuart B., "Pastoral Dreamer in an Urban World." *Denver Quarterly* 1 (Autumn 1966): 45–57.

Kazan, Elia, *Elia Kazan: A Life.* New York: Knopf, 1988.

Kim, Yun-Cheol, "Degradation of the American Success Ethic: *Death of a Salesman, That Championship Season,* and *Glengarry Glen Ross.*" *The Journal of English Language and Literature* 37 (Spring 1991): 233–48.

Knauf, David M., ed., *Papers in Dramatic Theory and Criticism.* Iowa City: University of Iowa Press, 1967.

Koon, Hélène Wickam, ed., *Twentieth Century Interpretations of* Death of a Salesman. Englewood Cliffs: Prentice-Hall, 1983.

Krohn, Alan, "The Source of Manhood in *Death of a Salesman.*" *International Review of Psycho-Analysis* 15 (1988): 455–63.

Luft, Friedrich, "Arthur Miller's *Death of a Salesman*: Hebbel-

Theatre (Berlin)," in *Stimme der Kritik-Berliner Theater seit 1945.* Velber bei Hannover: Friedrich Verlag, 1965: 82–85.

Mander, John, *The Writer and Commitment.* London: Secker & Warburg, 1961.

Martin, Robert A., ed., *Arthur Miller: New Perspectives.* Englewood Cliffs: Prentice-Hall, 1982.

"Arthur Miller: Tragedy and Commitment." *Michigan Quarterly Review* 8 (Summer 1969): 176–78.

Martine, James J., ed., *Critical Essays on Arthur Miller.* Boston: G. K. Hall, 1979.

McAnany, Emile G., S. J. "The Tragic Commitment: Some Notes on Arthur Miller." *Modern Drama* 55 (May 1962): 11–20.

McCarthy, Mary, "American Realists, Playwrights." *Encounter* 17 (July 1961): 24–31.

McMahon, Helen, "Arthur Miller's Common Man: The Problem of the Realistic and the Mythic." *Drama and Theatre* 10 (1972): 128–33.

Meserve, Walter J., ed., *The Merril Studies in Death of a Salesman.* Columbus, OH: Merrill, 1972.

Mielziner, Jo, *Designing for the Theatre: A Memoir and a Portfolio.* New York: Bramhall House, 1965.

Miller, Arthur, *Death of a Salesman.* New York: Viking, 1949; New York: Dramatists Play Service, 1952; *Theatre Arts* 35 (October 1953): 49–91; *Collected Plays.* New York: Viking, 1957; Harmondsworth: Penguin, 1961.

Interview. *Let's Meet the Theatre.* By Dorothy and Joseph Samachson. New York: Abelard-Schuman, 1954: 15–20.

Salesman in Beijing. New York: Viking, 1983.

The Theater Essays of Arthur Miller, ed. Robert A. Martin. New York: Viking, 1978.

Timebends: A Life. New York: Grove, 1987.

"Tragedy and the Common Man." *New York Times* 27 February 1949, section 2: 1, 3.

"What Makes Plays Endure." *New York Times* 15 August 1965: 16.

Miller, Jordan Y., "Myth and the American Dream: O'Neill to Albee." *Modern Drama* 7 (1964): 190–98.

Mitchell, Giles, "Living and Dying for the Ideal: A Study of Willy Loman's Narcissism." *Psychoanalytic Review* 77 (Fall 1990): 391–407.

Morath, Inge and Arthur Miller, *Chinese Encounters*. New York: Farrar, Straus, and Giroux, 1979.

Morehouse, Ward, "Keeping up with Kazan." *Theatre Arts* 41 (June 1957): 20–22, 90–91.

Moss, Leonard, *Arthur Miller*, rev. ed. Boston: Twayne, 1980.
  "Arthur Miller and the Common Man's Language." *Modern Drama* 7 (May 1964): 52–59.

Murray, Edward, *Arthur Miller, Dramatist*. New York: Ungar, 1967.
  The Cinematic Imagination. New York: Ungar, 1972.

Nathan, George Jean, *The Theatre of the Fifties*. New York: Knopf, 1960.

Nelson, Benjamin, *Arthur Miller: Portrait of a Playwright*. New York: McKay, 1970.

Oberg, Arthur, "*Death of a Salesman* and Arthur Miller's Search for Style." *Criticism* 9 (Fall 1967): 303–11.

Överland, Orm, "The Action and Its Significance: Arthur Miller's Struggle with Dramatic Form." *Modern Drama* 18 (1975): 1–14.

Parker, Brian, "Point of View in Arthur Miller's *Death of a Salesman*." *University of Toronto Quarterly* 35 (1966): 144–57.

Parker, Dorothy, ed., *Essays on Modern American Drama: Williams, Miller, Albee, Shepard*. Toronto University Press, 1987.

Poling, James, "Handy 'Gadget.'" *Collier's* 129 (31 May 1952): 56–61.

Porter, Thomas E., *Myth and Modern Drama*. Detroit: Wayne State University Press, 1969.

Prudhoe, John, "Arthur Miller and the Tradition of Tragedy." *English Studies* 43 (1962): 430–39.

Ranald, Margaret Loftus, "*Death of a Salesman*: Fifteen Years After." *Comment* 6 (August 1965): 28–35.

Roudané, Matthew C., ed., *Conversations with Arthur Miller.*
Jackson: University Press of Mississippi, 1987.

Rowe, Kenneth Thorpe, *A Theater in Your Head.* New York: Funk
and Wagnalls, 1960.

Rusch, Frederick L., "Approaching Literature Through the Social
Psychology of Erich Fromm," in *Psychological Perspectives
on Literature: Freudian Dissidents and Non-Freudians: A
Casebook*, ed. Joseph Natoli. Hamden, CT: Archon, 1984:
79–99.

Schleuter, June, ed., *Feminist Rereadings of Modern American Drama.*
Rutherford: Fairleigh Dickinson University Press, 1989.

and James K. Flanagan. *Arthur Miller.* New York: Ungar, 1987.

Schneider, Daniel E., "Play of Dreams." *Theatre Arts* 33 (October
1949): 18–21.

Shaw, Patrick W., "The Ironic Characterization of Bernard in
Death of a Salesman." Notes on Contemporary Literature
11 (May 1981): 12.

Stambusky, Alan A., "Arthur Miller: Aristotelian Canons in the
Twentieth Century Drama," in *Modern American Drama,*
ed. William E. Taylor. Deland, FL: Everett/Edwards,
1968: 91–115.

Steene, Birgitta, "The Critical Reception of American Drama in
Sweden." *Modern Drama* 5 (May 1962): 71–82.

Steinberg, M. W., "Arthur Miller and the Idea of Modern Tragedy."
Dalhousie Review 40 (1961): 329–40.

Sylvester, Robert, "Brooklyn Boy Makes Good." *Saturday Evening
Post* 222 (16 July 1949): 26–27.

Trowbridge, Clinton W., "Arthur Miller: Between Pathos and
Tragedy." *Modern Drama* 9 (December 1967): 221–32.

Van Allen, Harold, "An Examination of the Reception and Critical
Evaluation of the Plays of Arthur Miller in West Germany
from 1950–1961." Diss., University of Arkansas, 1964.

Voegel, Dan, "From Milkman to Salesman: Glimpses of the Galut."
Studies in American Jewish Literature 10 (Fall 1991): 172–78.

Wattenberg, Richard, "Staging William James' *World of Pure Experience*: Arthur Miller's *Death of a Salesman*." *Theatre Annual* 38 (1983): 49–64.

Weales, Gerald, *American Drama Since World War II*. New York: Harcourt Brace, 1962.

"Arthur Miller," in *The American Theater Today*, ed. Alan S. Downer. New York: Basic Books, 1967: 85–98.

ed., *The Viking Critical* Death of a Salesman. New York: Viking, 1967.

Welland, Dennis, *Arthur Miller*. New York: Grove, 1961.

Miller the Playwright, rev. ed. London: Methuen, 1983.

Williams, Raymond, *Drama from Ibsen to Brecht*. London: Chatto and Windus, 1968.

"The Realism of Arthur Miller." *Critical Quarterly* 1 (1959): 140–49.

Zorn, Theodore E., "Willy Loman's Lesson: Teaching Identity Management with *Death of a Salesman*." *Communication Education* 40 (1991): 219–24.

INDEX